Half A Childhood

Quality Programs for Out-of-School Hours

2nd Edition, Completely Revised

by

Judith Bender
Charles H. Flatter
Jeanette M. Sorrentino

FREE After School Resource Catalog
School-Age NOTES
P.O. Box 40205
Nashville, TN 37204
1-800-410-8780
www.AfterSchoolCatalog.com

School-Age NOTES
Nashville, Tennessee

Half A Childhood
Quality Programs for Out-of-School Hours
by Judith Bender, Charles H. Flatter, and Jeanette M. Sorrentino

Published by: School-Age NOTES
P.O. Box 40205
Nashville TN 37204-0205
Toll Free: 1-800-410-8780
http://www.schoolagenotes.com
email: office@schoolagenotes.com

Credits:

Front and back cover photos courtesy of Judith Bender, and The Open Door of Maryland, Towson, MD.

Photo on page xii courtesy of Sally Wideroff, Boca Raton, FL

Photos on pages 1, 3, 35, 56, 61, 76, 139, 149, 163, 171, and 215 by Nancy Alexander

Photos on pages 2, 7, 9, 14, 15, 19, 47, 105, 134, 142, 154, 183, 201, 207, 217, and 236 by Janet Brown McCracken

Photos on pages 4, 70, 179, and 193 courtesy of the City of Tucson Arizona Parks and Recreation

Photos on pages 12, 42, 79, 189, and 230 courtesy of Judith Bender, author

Photos on pages 91, 107, 221, and 243 courtesy of The Children's Guild, Baltimore, MD

Photos on pages 96, 122, and 128 courtesy of the Latchkey Program, Egg Harbor Township Intermediate School, New Jersey

Photo on page 146 courtesy of The Open Door of Maryland, Towson, MD

Excerpt on page xiv reprinted with permission by Child Care Information Exchange (Sept. 1998), P.O. Box 3249, Redmond, WA 98073-3249, 800-221-2864, www.ccie.com

Library of Congress Catalog Card Number: 97-065339
ISBN: 0-917505-10-7
Printings: 10 9 8 7 6 5 4 3 2 1
Book Design: JM Press, Nashville, TN (http://www.jmpress.com)

CONTENTS

Chapter Seven
What Do The Children Do? Scheduling, Grouping, and
1,000 Things To Do! 221

Supplements

ABOUT THE AUTHORS

Judith Bender, M.Ed. served for 27 years as Child Development Specialist with the Maryland State Department of Health and Mental Hygiene's child care licensing program. She has taught school-age children in public and private programs, including children with special needs. She has instructed teachers and caregivers in both higher education and staff development settings, and served for many years as a member of the Maryland State Advisory Committee for the Office of Children and Youth.

Bender has authored many professional publications related to child development, curriculum and program planning. She co-authored *Half A Childhood: Time for School-age Child Care* (School-Age Notes, 1984).

Bender and her husband are the grandparents of five delightful school-agers.

Dr. Charles H. Flatter, a child development specialist and drug prevention consultant, is an Associate Professor of Human Development at the University of Maryland. He also serves as the Associate Director of the Institute for Child Study at the University.

Flatter is the author of several books on the development of children and youth as well as the developer of numerous substance abuse prevention materials for use in schools and the workplace. Flatter was principal author of the United States Department of Education's *Growing Up Drug Free: A Parent's Guide to Prevention*. He co-authored *Half A Childhood: Time for School-age Child Care* (School-Age Notes, 1984). Flatter writes a continuing child development column for *Sesame Street Parents* magazine and serves on the Board of Advisors of the Children's Television Workshop.

Flatter and his wife, Janice, have three children and two grandchildren.

Jeanette M. Sorrentino, M.Ed., served as accreditation specialist for 22 years at the Maryland State Department of Education, evaluating private nursery schools, kindergartens, and elementary schools. Sorrentino has an Advanced Graduate Specialist's Degree in Human Development from the University of Maryland. A former classroom teacher in public and private schools and Adjunct Professor of Early Childhood Education for Antioch University at the Columbia, Maryland campus, she also served as director of early childhood education in Columbia, Maryland, where she supervised nursery school and day care programs.

Sorrentino co-authored *Children: Their Growth and Development* with Charles H. Flatter and Sheila G. Terry and is currently providing consultant services to Head Start, federally sponsored day care centers, professional organizations, child development centers and county school systems.

Jean and her husband, Bill are the parents of three children.

ACKNOWLEDGEMENTS

We wish to acknowledge the many contributions of **Barbara Schuyler-Haas Elder**, who co-authored the first edition of *Half a Childhood: Time for School-Age Child Care* and who continued to offer her wisdom and encouragement as we completed this revised edition. We also thank Marlene Welsh for ideas and support as we ventured into this current text.

We are grateful for the thoughtful comments and suggestions of the following people who reviewed early drafts of this revision and whose insight helped guide the direction of the book: Laura Colker, Alan Malnak, Jeanne Page, Janice Silver, and Jennifer Walker.

We thank our spouses, Mel, Janice, and Bill, whose patience and good humor sustained us in this venture.

In conclusion, we honor the many enthusiastic and knowledgeable persons who continue to dedicate themselves to the care and nurture of school-agers.

DEDICATION

This book is dedicated to our children and grandchildren
from whom we have learned so much

WARNING — DISCLAIMER

This book is designed to provide information in regard to the subject matter covered and is based on information from sources believed to be reliable. Every effort has been made to make the book as complete and accurate as possible based on information available as of the printing date, but its accuracy and completeness cannot be guaranteed. Despite the best efforts of the authors and publisher, the book **may contain mistakes**, both typographical and in content, and the reader should use the book only as a general guide and not as the ultimate source of information about the subject of this book.

The book is not intended to reprint all of the information available to the author or publisher on the subject, but rather to simplify, complement and supplement other available sources. The reader is encouraged to read all available material and to learn as much as possible about the subject. Some of these materials are listed under **RECOMMENDED READINGS** at the end of chapters throughout the book.

This book does not take the place of the supervision and training necessary to work safely with children and youth or to work in their settings.

This book is sold without warranties of any kind, express or implied, and the publisher and authors disclaim any liability, loss or damage caused by the contents of this book.

If you do not wish to be bound by the above, you may return this book to the publisher for a full refund.

Found an error or have a suggestion?
See page ii for contact information.

To The Reader

HALF A CHILDHOOD: Quality Programs for Out-of-School Hours is the revised edition of our previous publication, *HALF A CHILDHOOD: Time for School-Age Child Care.* This second edition reflects our conviction that quality out-of-school experiences are essential for healthy human development as well as for the welfare of families and communities. It also responds to the heightened awareness of the dangers in the lives of many children and youth when they are unsupervised during their out-of-school hours, alone at home or in confusing or frightening communities. Unless we stay close to what is happening in children's lives and take action to support and enrich their lives, many school-agers simply will not do well now or later in life.

We know the impact of both appropriate and inappropriate out-of-school experiences. We know the lasting impression of these hours on the quality of the lives of school-agers — their future thinking, behavior, skills and interests. We now must make certain that all children who need out-of-school supervision not only receive it, but also receive the kind of care which respects the relationship of a healthy, happy childhood to a healthy, happy future.

Since the first publication, which cited the need for school-age services, there has been increased activity in the development of out-of-school programs for children and youth. There have been conferences, literature, media coverage, and legislation. We see many wonderful examples of out-of-school experiences and many programs still reaching for their sense of purpose and direction. Our focus is now on excellence of program: quality supervised experiences for children and youth who are otherwise unattended or inadequately supervised when school is not in session. Even by the roughest of calculations, *children are out of school more than half of their waking hours* when families are at work or otherwise unavailable. Many hours... *half a childhood.*

This text focuses on the five- to fourteen-year-olds who are cared for in both home and center programs. The content of the book is applicable to school-age care and also to the continuum of out-of-school programs not usually called "school-age care" but which serve the developmental needs of the many children and youth who are in formal or informal settings — youth groups and clubs, camps, group homes or community centers.

The focus is the quality of the experience for children. And this focus must not be lost in a community's well-intentioned scurry to string together a multitude of programs to fill up the hours. Children and youth have the same human needs regardless of the type of program in which they participate and every program should meet those needs.

This revised edition is addressed to the persons who work directly with the children, those persons in school-age programs who have by far the greatest effect on the lives of school-age children during their out-of-school hours. This includes in-home, family child care, and center staff. It includes group leaders and assistants, youth development workers and counselors. In addition, it is for course instructors and directors who have responsibility for staff development. The text should be useful as all of these professionals increase their competence to relate child and youth development to program practices. The presentation of materials recognizes both newcomers to the field and experienced staff. We have used a text-book format with ideas for discussion, suggestions for assignments, check lists, and resources for further information.

Although we address the child between five and fourteen, we recognize that a few school systems include four-year-olds who need extended care. We refer readers to resources on program planning for the four-year-old with the recognition that their out-of-school care must have all the components of a good preschool setting.

We discuss the special considerations when five-year-old children are in school-age programs and when school-agers are mixed with preschoolers. In addition, we incorporate planning for older children from age 10 to 14 as a response to the *National Study of Before- and After-School Programs, 1993,* which cites that only half the programs enrolling children in grades four and higher make special provisions for them. Even though programs for older children may depart in terms of context, sponsorship, and scheduling, we believe that discussion of out-of-school programming would be incomplete without considering the older child's continuing need for competent adult supervision and guidance.

More than ever there is a need for knowledgeable, caring, and dedicated people to assist children and their families during the vulnerable and valuable school-age years. You, the reader, can help provide essential quality experiences when school is not in session. You will be in touch with the worlds of the children. You will share in their enthusiasm and vitality and be there to encourage them through their troubled times. You are there for the children and youth who have everything going for them and for those who need a lot of help. You can make the growing up process a good one. This book is for everyone interested enough to make that happen.

Judith Bender
Charles H. Flatter
Jeanette M. Sorrentino

A Historical Overview of School-Age Care: What Has Happened in the Past and Where We Are Now

In the first edition of *Half A Childhood: Time for School-Age Child Care*, the publisher, Rich Scofield of School-Age NOTES, Inc., added a historical time line to the appendix. The following is Scofield's time line with his revisions and updating to the present. Also included are his additions and comments on the state of school-age care and after school programs today.

The History of School-Age Care: A Timeline

1894 - The Buffalo Charity Organization Society allowed school-age children to attend the Children's Home after school. The children helped wash younger children's clothing, wipe dishes, and peel potatoes.

1900s - By the early 1900s, many settlement houses, Y's, and day nurseries for "underprivileged" children were serving school-age children after school and in the summer.

1919 - The Summer Play Schools Committee of the Child Study Association of America established summer "play schools" in the public schools in New York City to help children who might be socially isolated during the summer months.

1930s - The Play Schools Association became an independent group establishing both Summer and Winter (after school) play schools in public school buildings. The philosophy of these programs, based on the concepts of John Dewey and others, emphasized "knowing the children and their individual differences, age-level interests, and potentialities for 'learning by doing.' " Play programs during this period focused on the contemporary scene and current events as well as the children's personal experiences.

1935 - Charles Stewart Mott, who established a foundation that bears his name, was concerned about the growing numbers of "latchkey children" who were left to fend for themselves while their parents worked - and the ensuing problem of "juvenile vagrancy and crime." He heard Frank J. Manley of the Flint, Michigan schools speak about "the value of keeping youngsters meaningfully occupied after school." Manley suggested using school buildings and keeping the "lights on in every school in the city all day, every day." Mott liked the idea and thus began the concept of community schools and community education. Manley established after school and weekend supervised recreation and later added classes for adults and ideas on community organizing, all of which was to become known as the Mott Program, a model copied all over the country by school systems and communities.

1940s - During World War II the Community Facilities Act (Lanham Act) created nearly 3,000 extended school programs, most of them set in school facilities. Training for school-age providers also flourished during this period. Federal funding stopped with the end of the war. In a few areas, California being one of them, state and local funds were used to continue these programs.

1950s - Many women continued working in unexpected numbers after the war years. Some state and local funding remained available, and considerable interest developed in establishing neighborhood-based programs which included school-age children. The emphasis, however, was mainly on the preschool child. Services for the older child were minimal, with most children on their own and others in scattered recreational and church settings or assimilated by the preschool day care programs.

Greenwich House was one of the first programs in New York City to serve school-agers whose mothers went to work during World War II.

1960s - Federal funding for child care expanded but most of it was directed to preschool.

1970s - Women's participation in the workforce continued to increase markedly. Renewed interest in school-age child care began to appear. In 1972 a governmental interagency School-Age Day Care Task Force was formed. Its report, which was never officially published, noted that there was a lack of programs and research. In 1978, the School-Age Child Care Project at the Wellesley College Center for Research on Women was established to serve as a national information and technical assistance resource.

Early 1980s - In 1982, the School-Age Child Care Project funded eight affiliate technical assistance sites for a two-year period. School-age child care began to be addressed in federal grant proposal requests. One funded project looked at care for older children and set up a Family Day Home Check-In System for 9-14-year-olds. The term "latchkey" (see 1935 above) became a household word prompted by articles and TV talk shows on the topic; creation of after school programs called "latchkey programs;" and the faddish development of variations such as "latchkey husbands" and "latchkey pets." This culminated with the Home Alone movies. By the early 1990s programs that called themselves "latchkey" were changing their names as they realized that "latchkey" referred to the problem, not the solution, which was after school programs.

1985 - The first federal funds under the Dependent Care Block Grant (DCBG) were distributed to states, 60% of which was to expand the availability and quality of school-age care. Initially $5 million and never topping $20 million, this grant program (and the later similar set aside in the Child Care Development Block Grant) was given to states to develop, implement and distribute to programs. The DCBG was probably the single most important stimulant to school-age program development for almost 15 years until the 21st Century Community Learning Centers (21st CCLC) initiative in the late 1990s. Successful states used small amounts - $2,000-$10,000 - as seed money to develop interest in starting or expanding school-age programs or develop programs for older kids. It also provided the seed money for many states to develop networks and alliances to produce state conferences and trainings. Today these grants seem meager as literally millions of dollars go to the schools to completely fund programs under the 21st CCLC initiative.

1990s - This was the decade of school-age care; one which even saw the change of terms from "school-age child care" to "school-age care" to recognize the needs of older children (9-14 years old) for programs that don't appear to be child care. As the field became more of a profession, a national program accreditation system was established; colleges and universities developed courses and school-age certificates, even a bachelors and masters degree in school-age care; research increased; and evaluation tools were developed. On the international front, Canadian provinces developed conferences and associations; Australia developed national "out-of-school hours" standards; and the European Network on School-Age Care which was established in 1988 continued to hold its conferences. There was tremendous growth in the profession throughout the decade. In 1994 alone, the U.S. Army launched the first school-age credential for school-age staff; the National School-Age Child Care Alliance was awarded an AmeriCorps grant for volunteers to help improve school-age care; the Carnegie Council on Adolescent Development focused on "How Youth Spend Their Out-of-School Time" and the "Core Elements of Effective After School Programs for Youth;" and the first (what became national) older kids conference was held.

1999 - The $40 million in 1998 and $200 million in 1999 in 21st CCLC grants produced an almost "gold rush" atmosphere in the after school field. There was a perceptible shift from school-age care to after school programs as professional surveys in 1998 and 1999 showed that the public understood the need for "after school programs" and was willing to be taxed to pay for them.

2000 - In the January State of the Union Address, President Clinton called for $1 billion for after school and summer programs which would more than double the $453 million enacted in late 1999 for the 21st Century Community Learning Centers program.

Advocates, Leaders, and Advocacy

Child Care Information Exchange, a national magazine for child care directors, characterized the history of the current school-age care movement and its advocates in its September 1998 issue as follows:

> The emergence of school-age care as a significant movement can be traced back to the tireless efforts of many individuals and organizations including the following:
>
> **National Institute on Out-of-School Time**. In 1978, responding to a deluge of inquiries from a Good Housekeeping article about her Brookline school-age program, Mickey Seligson organized the School-Age Child Care Project. In the intervening two decades, Seligson's organization, now titled the National Institute on Out-of-School Time, has been on the cutting edge of developments in the field. Its extensive research and technical assistance efforts continually propel the professionalism of the field.
>
> **School-Age NOTES**. Eighteen years ago [1980], Richard Scofield launched School-Age NOTES, a newsletter for school-age providers. Not only has the newsletter become the mainstay of the field with 5,700 subscribers, but Scofield has been an active advocate in nearly every key development in the school-age arena.
>
> **National School-Age Care Alliance**. In 1980, Mickey Seligson, Richard Scofield, and other key advocates had a discussion at the NAEYC [National Association for the Education of Young Children] convention that eventually led to establishing a professional organization for school-age professionals.
>
> Founded in 1987, the National School-Age Care Alliance (NSACA) now boasts 6,000 members and a host of high-impact projects. NSACA sees itself as a home for all types of school-age providers. Rather than advocating for one form of delivery, it advocates for all school-age care that is accountable to families and provides developmentally appropriate activities for children.
>
> In recent years [relative to 1998], NSACA has achieved major milestones: it hired Linda Sisson as its first executive director; in collaboration with the National Institute on Out-of-School Time, it published standards for school-age programs; it has sponsored increasingly successful national conferences; and it has launched a school-age accreditation project.

Today NSACA has over 35 state affiliates. Most are volunteer organizations but some have successfully gained federal dollars given to the states for development of after school programs and quality improvement and have hired staff to implement training programs and conferences. At the national level, besides its headquarters in Boston, it has a paid advocate in Washington DC; attracts 2000 professionals to its annual conference; launched in March 2000 a journal called *School-Age Review*; and is implementing various projects such as improving staff stability through mentoring and investigating the feasibility of a school-age care credential for individuals that would be accepted across the country.

The impact of the National Institute on Out-of-School Time (NIOST) on the professional field of school-age care continues. One of its on-going projects is M.O.S.T. (Making the Most of Out of School Time) which was started in 1993 and continues today through funding by the Dewitt Wallace-Reader's Digest Fund which has invested over $9 million dollars in the project. M.O.S.T. took a unique approach to increasing the supply and quality of after school programs in low-income communities, specifically Boston, Chicago and Seattle, by focusing on strengthening school-age care as a system. It linked community-based programs to external resources and institutions such as community colleges to help develop technical assistance and training. In 1999 the Executive Director of NIOST, Michelle Seligson, left that position to direct a three-year, million dollar project called "Building Relational Practices in Out-of-School Environments." The project is based on the belief that the after school program provides an opportune time to facilitate the social and emotional development of children and that the most significant ingredient in a program is the quality of the staff-child relationships. The project will create a new training practice curriculum that will focus on the development of relational skills for after school program staff, and in turn, their children.

21st Century To Be the Age of After School

The 21st Century Community Learning Centers (21st CCLC) initiative was established by Congress to award grants to rural and inner-city public schools in collaboration with community-based organizations to provide after school and summer projects that benefit "the education, health, social services, cultural and recreation needs of the community." Starting with just $750,000 in fiscal year 1995 to $40 million is fiscal year 1998 to $200 million in 1999 to $453 million for 2000, the 21st CCLC has become one of the U.S. Department of Education's most popular programs. One of the reasons for its incredible expansion is its bipartisan support among Democrats and Republicans. This support is driven by both ideological issues - Democrats want the social service aspect of the programs for the benefit of the children and Republicans want the improved grades, test scores, and reduced crime aspects - and polling results which show how popular the concept is with registered voters. Phenomenally, in national polls taken in 1998 and 1999, Americans were overwhelmingly in support of after school programs, including 94% who said they favored making daily programs available to all children. Amazingly, 80% of those surveyed would even be willing to raise taxes to provide after school opportunities.

In addition to funding the national polls, the Charles Stewart Mott Foundation in 1998 pledged $55 million in support of the $1 billion committed for five years ($200 million per year later to be more than doubled in 1999) for the 21st CCLC program. Mott's commitment toward development of after school programs within the context of community schools now approaches $100 million. In the professional field we now can see a shift in focus from talking about school-age child care spread across diverse providers in the community to a focus on the school providing after school programs that will provide extended learning opportunities and thus the 21st century will be "the age of after school."

The authors of this book send a clear message that we must put children's needs above the desires of school systems to improve test scores. The authors discuss children's developmental needs beyond intellectual development, i.e. social, self (emotional), and physical development and emphasize the importance of choice after school. Out-of-school time should be a time for fun and growth and learning beyond the school walls.

Where Are We Now?: Demographics, Need, and Programs

In 1984 the authors of the first edition of Half A Childhood wrote the following about the need for after school care:

> How many children need school-age services? Accurate figures on the number of 5-to-14-year-old children, nationwide, who may need school-age child care are impossible to obtain for several reasons. Relevant census statistics have limited value because of the categories used...Statistics are available for use, but consideration must be given to certain factors when determining need: child care services already in place, the number of children in informal care arrangements, social trends, and specific community circumstances. The following are a few statistics which may be used in estimating need.
>
> *How many children are home alone during out-of-school hours?*
>
> • Some estimates show that as many as 6 million children in America may be characterized as 'latchkey.'
>
> • The Children's Defense Fund estimates that of the 13 million children aged 13 and under with full-time employed mothers, almost half may be caring for themselves while mothers work.

Also in the early 1980s there were estimates reported of up to 15 million "latchkey children." Unfortunately in the ensuing two decades there has not been much better or more accurate reporting as noted by a 1999 U.S. Department of Education publication which stated, "At least 5 million children—possibly as many as 15 million—are left alone at home each week," basically the same estimates as 15 years earlier. The publication *Bringing Education into the Afterschool Hours*, also gives the following information:

- Over 28 million school-age children have both parents or their only parent in the workforce.

- Many children, especially low-income children, lose ground in reading if they are not engaged in organized learning over the summer.

- Experts agree that school-age children who are unsupervised during the hours after school are more likely to receive poor grades and drop out of school than those who are involved in supervised, constructive activities.

- Statistics show that most juvenile crime takes place between the hours of 2:00 and 8:00 p.m. and that children are also at much greater risk of being the victims of crime during the hours after school.

NATIONAL STUDY FINALLY ARRIVES!
The Where, What, Why & How Many of Before & After School Programs

by Richard Scofield

(*School-Age NOTES*, April, 1993, Reprinted with permission)

- Almost 50,000 programs
- 46% are in the South
- 1.7 million kids
- 83-90% are K-3rd grade

The long awaited study that looked at 1300 school-age care programs from a representative sampling of 144 counties across the country is now available.

Why is this study so important?

The huge scope of this study and the combination of forming a comprehensive statistical picture of SAC in the U.S. as well as painting a life picture of what goes on in SAC programs makes this the first and last such study for many years. This study will itself be studied and referenced for years to come. Congratulations to Michelle Seligson and the Wellesley SACC Project as well as RMC Research Corp., Mathematica Policy Research, Inc., and the U.S. Dept. of Education.

How Many Programs?

An estimated 49,500 programs provided before- and/or after-school services. Of these 71% provided both before and after school programs. These are only centers and does not include family day care or group homes in the number of programs or the number of children and youth served. Programs had to operate 4 days a week for at least 2 hours a day and not be exclusively drop-in. The age range was 5-13 (K-8th grade)

Where Are They?

Of the four areas of the country the South had 46% of all programs, followed by the West 21%, the Midwest 19%, and the Northeast 14%. Urban and suburban areas accounted for 87% of the programs with the rest categorized as rural.

Program Site: The three most common program locations were child care centers at 35%; public schools at 28% although they represented 35% of enrollment because public school sites had larger programs; and religious institutions at 14%. The other 23% were in six different types of locations: community centers, work sites, nonreligious private schools, universities, colleges, and municipal buildings.

Space: One of the most disturbing but not unexpected findings is that about half the programs are in shared space. Not surprising is that 67% of public school sites and 60% of religious institutions use shared space with 31% of SAC programs in child care centers sharing space. Disturbing because we know space and the environment is one of the key factors in quality care.

Operating in cafeterias, gyms, and banquet halls is an almost impossible situation if trying to provide a home-like environment. Certainly one goal for the future of school-age care should be to increase the number of programs that have dedicated space.

How Many Kids?

In 1991 an estimated 1,714,000 children and youth in kindergarten through eighth grade were enrolled on a regular basis in formal before- and/or after-school programs in the U.S.

What Ages?

Not surprising is that SAC in the U.S. is mostly made up of children in K-3rd grade. In fact 90% of before school enrollments are prekindergarten through grade 3 and 83% of after school enrollments are in this age range. A surprising statistic was the percentage of prekindergarten in SAC programs. They figured into the statistics at 24% of A.M. programs and 14% of P.M. programs.

Older Kids: Only 17% of after school enrollments were 4th grade and above. While K was 22%; 1st was 18%; 2nd was 16% and 3rd 14%, after school enrollment shows it dropped off with only 9% in 4th; 6% in 5th and 2% in 6th with less than 1% in grades 7 and higher.

Half A Childhood

Wisely Used or Wasted Hours?

An Introduction

"I am in the house alone at times.
Sometimes I feel like crying because
if something happens there is no one
to turn to. Sit and watch T.V. with
the phone next to me. Yes, I am afraid.
Just being there alone. Sit there and
don't say a word."

> Sequoia
> age 11

"To herd children for mere safekeeping without concern
for their emotional and intellectual needs makes them dull
in thought and feeling."

Albert Einstein
1879-1955

1

HALF A CHILDHOOD: WISELY USED OR WASTED HOURS?

"Half a childhood..."
the hours when school
is not in session and
parents are unavailable
to their children.
Half a childhood...

Many hours.

Many days.

Many children.

The Hours Between

Where are the children when school is closed?

What are they doing and who is responsible for them?

Are they assured of their basic rights to a safe and nurturing environment, to wise supervision and to healthy, satisfying companionship?

Is childhood strengthened or weakened during the hours between school and home?

School is out. What now?...

The fourth and fifth grade rooms have let out and Juan and his sister, Carla, hurry down the hall to the play center. They check in with Marti, their group leader, then Juan is off with a soccer ball to practice for the game. Carla tells Marti about the story she is writing until Rebecca, her very best friend, appears. A few minutes later they giggle from the sofa in the corner as they share the day's happenings. Juan and Carla and Rebecca, enjoying a school-age program. Daily after school. School holidays. Summer days. *Half a childhood.*

In school, after school

Three o'clock. The cafeteria is set up with its huge tables and chairs. "We sit, just waiting to go home... looking around for something good to do... but there's really nothing there... and it's so hard to be still and be quiet..." Wasted time. *Half a childhood.*

Ann, age 9

School will be out all week and it's only Tuesday! Ann's father is due home at six and Ann has spent the whole day alone, locked in the house to be safe. She played with her cat, did her homework, washed the dishes and made her bed... all before eating her lunch. Since then she's been watching TV. It's after six o'clock. Ann is bored and lonely and now worried about her father. Did something happen to him? She worries about herself. Who will take care of her if he doesn't come home? Who is taking care of her now? *Half a childhood.*

Darnell, age 6

Darnell has been at Mrs. Benson's home since seven this morning. His mother left him there on the way to her job in the city. Darnell's friend, Michael, is there too. They had breakfast with Mr. and Mrs. Benson and their baby. Mrs. Benson heard their spelling words, and now it's time for the school bus. After school Darnell and Michael return. Mr. Benson promised to help them use his woodworking tools. Many hours with loving care. An important part of Darnell's life. *Half a childhood.*

Mitch, age 7

Mitch comes home after school to be with his 15-year-old sister, Eileen. Every day the same thing happens. Eileen finds them a quick snack and then she turns on her favorite television show. After that Mitch never sees her. She is either on the telephone or she leaves to be with her friends. If she leaves, she always makes Mitch promise not to tell their mom. Many, many hours wondering who really cares and should he tell their mom about Eileen. *Half a childhood.*

Rosa, at home

No school today. Rosa, 11, is still asleep when her parents leave for work. Lisa Edwards, a college student who lives nearby, is waiting for her to wake up for breakfast. They've planned a busy day of swimming, a piano lesson, and a bath for Rosa's dog. Some days they go shopping or visiting friends, both Rosa's and Lisa's. On other days friends come in to play games or to do homework together or just to chat. Days at home with a caring someone. *Half a childhood.*

Larry, on the streets

Five o'clock on a winter afternoon, already quite dark. Larry, 12-years-old, strolls down the sidewalk hoping to find some cans to turn in for cash. His apartment is still locked and no one is at home. He'll go down to the corner to see if anyone's around. He hopes his grandmother gets home soon so he can fix something to eat. Long and lonely hours on the street. *Half a childhood.*

Jenny, age 14

Behind the apartment building the gang has gathered, shared smokes, and made plans for tomorrow's confrontation with the kids on the next street. Jenny is afraid of what might happen; she knows some kids have weapons. Her friend, Tess, went inside with her boyfriend. Jenny worries about going upstairs because her mother might be there with "company." Jenny spends many unsafe hours as she grows up too fast. *Half a childhood.*

Paul, Ryan, Jesse

Long days of summer... happy days, exciting and interesting. These children feel the specialness of summertime, playing with friends and close to caring adults. There is time to do the things there never seemed enough time for when school was open — play and play production, sports and shopping, carpentry and conversation —children participating as they are able and as they wish. Good times. Good days. *Half a childhood.*

The Hours Between

Paul, Ryan, and Jesse are children who are thriving, well cared for at home or in wisely planned family or center settings. With nurturing adults and the freedom to choose from interesting things to do, their development is wholesome; their growth is sound. Childhood hours are not wasted.

Children and youth experience the hours when school is closed in many ways: some are in supervised home or group settings, some are uncared for and alone; others are with brothers and sisters, parents or family members. Wherever the hours are spent and whatever the quality of these hours, the child's experience is significant, memorable, and lasting. The hours are many and represent a huge part of a child's life. It is essential time for healthy, happy growing up, and it must not be treated lightly. It is critical time and must not be taken away from a child.

The "hours between" are half a childhood.

Many hours.

Many days.

Many children.

Chapter One
School-Age Care: A Family Resource

"Children are people. They grow into tomorrow only as they live today."

"What the best and wisest parent wants for his own child, that must the community want for all its children."

John Dewey
1859-1952

"I was very nervous and happy that my mom was getting a new job. She was working at the mall. But then I was not very happy; it was that mother said, 'You will have to go to day care.' I was nervous about that, too. I tried to hide my red face, but I couldn't. So the next day I went to day care. The teacher looked nice. She knew I was new, so she told me her name. Her name, it was Mrs. Green. I said, 'Hello, Mrs. Green.' I really got used to her. The children were nice. My friend is Barbara."

Tami
age 9

"Let us not be blind to our differences, but let us also direct our attention to our common interests....In the final analysis, our most basic common link is that we all inhabit the same planet, we all breathe the same air, we all cherish our children's future."

John F. Kennedy, U.S. President
1917-1963

In this chapter...

- ➢ What is Happening?
- ➢ Who are the Families?
- ➢ Where are the Children?
- ➢ What is Needed?
- ➢ School-Age Care: A Family Resource
- ➢ School-Age Care: When Is It Needed and Where Is It Found?
- ➢ Quality Control

What Is Happening?

All children have the right to a combination of care and opportunities which promotes healthy growth and development. When there are dramatic changes in society, children, youth, and their families are deeply affected. The way a society cares about its children, youth, and families is an important measure of its value as a nation. When the well-being of children is threatened, a nation is endangered because each child is a contributing factor to the quality of life.

Traditionally, the family has provided healthy experiences and safe environments for children; however, the traditional family of wage-earner father, mother at home, and extended family is no longer available to many children. The societal changes that affect families are vast. Variations in family structures and relationships, changes in the economy, and advancements in technology have redefined how families are shaped and how they function.

Both parents in a family may work outside the home; a family may be a single working parent and children; families may move from community to community. They are in rural, suburban, and urban settings with a wide range of family income. As they attempt to meet the challenges of their daily lives, in whatever ways and with whatever means available, many families are successful in providing a healthy and safe life for their children. Others are not always available to provide the guidance, supervision, and nurturing their children need. It is no longer true that children and youth can depend on their families alone to nurture and protect them. Even the most capable families often must look outside of their own resources in caring for not only their preschoolers, but their school-agers as well.

What is happening to families as a result of societal changes directly affects children and youth. Now there is a need for programs of excellent quality that provide care for children when families are unavailable and school is closed.

School-age care, a basic definition:

School-age care is a service that provides programs for school-age children and youth and also support to the families who are unavailable to give care when school is not in session — year-round, before and after school, on school holidays and special closings, perhaps on weekends, and during school vacations — the out-of-school hours.

Who Are The Families?

Families come in all sizes, conditions, races, and religions, and reflect the diversity of cultures in a society. Family structures range from the two-parent working family to the unemployed, single parent. They range from the wealthy to the homeless, from the drug-addicted to the well-adjusted. To one extent or another, they need help raising their children, and their children deserve safe, nurturing, and interesting experiences.

While the most frequent users of school-age programs are the two-parent working family and the single working parent, the wide variety of settings also provides support for parents in school or training, the abusing or neglectful family, the adolescent parent, the family at risk, and the incapacitated family.

Families come in all sizes, conditions, races, and religions, and reflect the diversity of cultures in a society.

THE TWO-PARENT WORKING FAMILY

A reality of today's society is that it may take both parents employed to maintain the family. Consequently, with both parents out of the home for a significant number of hours, there is an increase in the number of children who need care.

Many children of two-parent working families already have made the adjustment to out-of-home care; for others, school and school-age care will be their first experience. It may be difficult for them to comfortably accept non-parental guidance. The parent-child separation and the caregiving arrangement may affect parent-child relationships; children may become uncooperative, withdrawn, or aggressive both at home and with program staff. Children may return to an earlier stage of development, when less was expected of them.

THE SINGLE-PARENT FAMILY

Single parents may have no option about working; they may need to work in order to survive. The demands on time are tremendous; the balance between home and workplace can be overwhelming, and children's behaviors may reflect their reactions to the limited time they have with their parent.

The financial and emotional strains on the single parent often affect both children and youth. They may worry about fitting into a parent's changing lifestyle or may miss an absent parent. All of this

9

may result in an inability to concentrate or take an active and enjoyable part in activities. These youngsters may make excessive demands on the staff members and may require much approval and affection.

PARENTS IN SCHOOL OR TRAINING

The days and hours when care is needed change frequently with this population, especially if the parent is working as well. Flexible scheduling, an important part of any child care service, is a special need of these parents.

Because of their parents' shifting schedules, some children may find it difficult to fit in and develop a sense of belonging to the group. They may withdraw and not participate or may attempt to disrupt activities until they believe that they are accepted and are an important part of the program.

FAMILIES AT RISK

Families with multiple problems

It is not unusual today for children to come from a family with multiple problems. Because of these problems, the home situation may deteriorate at any time. These problems might include poverty, marital discord, the birth of children in quick succession, unfamiliarity with the country's language, the prevalence of violence in some communities, and the high mobility of families in today's society. These families are better able to cope with their stresses if the demands of child care are lessened. Parenting support and guidance and education from program staff may avoid further family disintegration.

Children from a multi-problem family can thrive in an out-of-school program with its flexible yet reliable schedule and with consistent, dependable adults. Though perhaps distrustful initially, they soon benefit from the activities and experiences.

The abusing or neglectful family

Parents who themselves have been abused as children, those who are dealing unsuccessfully with stress, or those with unrealistic expectations for child behavior, may resort to undue physical discipline. The child becomes an easy target for their anger. In neglectful families, the parents cannot or do not provide for their child's basic needs. A safe and stimulating out-of-school program with caring adults to whom the child relates can meet these needs. This may prevent the deep scarring associated with abuse and neglect and may provide time for the families' counseling and treatment.

Fear and distrust of adults, worry about what is happening at home, feelings of worthlessness, and a poor self-image are all reflected in these children's behavior in school-age programs. They may withdraw. They may cling. They may be excessively aggressive — hitting and fighting, treating others as they are treated at home.

The incapacitated family

Chronically ill, emotionally unstable, or intellectually limited parents may be unable to provide their children with the guidance and stimulation they require. A school-age program during the many hours and days when school is not in session can make a significant difference in the quality of life for children in families where so little is available.

Without normal care and stimulation at home, children benefit from all the childhood activities they find in the school-age program. Behavior, however, may reflect the depth of the family's incapacity, ranging from withdrawal, worry, and depression, to physically aggressive acts. On the other hand, when family care, despite certain incapacities, has been nurturing, school-agers may fare very well.

Adolescent parents

It is possible today for a young school-age child to have a parent under the age of twenty. As adolescent parents are seeking their own identity, it is difficult for them to assume responsibility for another human being. Few adolescents are successful parents without extensive help.

A child may lack a sense of security without mature guidance. Since many teenage parents assume a sibling relationship with their child, the provider may become the one stable adult in the child's life.

Where Are The Children?

Many children are alone and lonely when families are unable to locate the resources they need. Children are often left to care for themselves in empty homes, and they spend their time watching television, well aware of neighborhood dangers. Parents instruct them to be careful of who calls or knocks at the door. They become fearful and wonder whom they can trust. Some are on the streets, exposed to violence, or in the houses of others, having inappropriate experiences and finding questionable role models. Some are cared for by older siblings who are still children themselves and are ill-prepared to give guidance to younger children.

Certainly many children and youth are in well-supervised settings that respond to the individual needs of children and their families. Nevertheless, many more are unsupervised, in poorly planned settings, and they need our nation's attention.[1,2,3]

THE RISKS OF SELF- AND SIBLING-CARE

There is a lingering assumption that when a child enters kindergarten, the need for a child care plan disappears as the school becomes accountable; that the hours between school and parent supervision can be filled with an array of activities; and that the child can be left alone or with siblings. The issue of children alone at home has become highly controversial and emotional. It must be examined carefully because there are many risks:

◇ physical risk of fire, accident, injury to self and others

◇ emotional risks of fear, distrust, loneliness, rejection, alienation

◇ developmental risks related to age-inappropriate responsibilities, lack of social and intellectual experiences, and damage to self-esteem

◇ sexual victimization

◇ substance abuse

◇ affiliation with street gangs and manipulating adults

◇ risks to communities in the form of delinquency and vandalism.

Self and sibling care plans are unwise, often illegal, unsafe, and unfair to children. Parents worry; they like to believe their kids are up to the task as they teach "survival skills" and hope for the best. Children are expected to deal with situations that are difficult for adults: obscene phone calls, strangers at the door, blown fuses, cut fingers, fires, dog bites. They are taught to lie to the telephone callers, hide their "latchkeys", stay inside, and keep the doors locked. Their parents want them to be safe, so they remain virtual prisoners in their own homes for hours on end.

Self-care for school-agers is not an acceptable substitute for responsible, nurturing, consistent adults.

Yet how safe are children who are home alone? Physically safe? Maybe and maybe not. Psychologically safe? Probably not. Self-care for school-agers is not an acceptable substitute for responsible, nurturing, consistent adults.

Scofield (1984) emphatically states, "From a developmental point of view children under the age of 12 are not ready to be left home alone. We know that the elementary-aged child has not reached the stage of abstract thinking. This means that they are not yet developmentally equipped to make all the appropriate judgments and decisions needed in common self-care predicaments or emergency situations."

Self-Care: A Dangerous Trend

Children without supervision are in danger. It is not fair to children for us to say, "Children are home alone, and we must teach them to cope." If we continue to promote programs to teach survival skills to young children who are left alone, we simply will come to believe that self-care is an acceptable child care option. It is not.

It is misleading to tell parents that survival skills will protect their children.

Of course there are emergency situations when children may be home alone, but not every day.

Children can learn survival skills for when they are home alone, but every day should not be viewed as a fight for survival.

What Is Needed?

Communities vary in terms of safety, family resources that reflect commitment to stable family life, and resources for children and youth that reflect a commitment to healthy growth and development. Families differ in terms of the amount and type of support services they want or need, but all seek assurance their children are not in jeopardy when family guidance and supervision are not possible. All school-agers in all communities deserve adult protection, supervision, guidance, and nurturing during these important years.

Child and youth services must continue to be developed in response to the particular needs of children, youth, and their families. To be useful and effective the services must be:

◆ **appropriate** — children's developmental needs are met and families receive support as appropriate.

◆ **available** — adequate number of services meet community needs when school is not in session.

◆ **accessible** — facilities are easily reached and transportation is minimal.

◆ **affordable** — cost is within family means.

School-Age Care: A Family Resource

Communities are responding to the needs of families when school is not in session. There is a proliferation of resources in many models that meet the needs of a variety of ages and interests of children and youth — recreation programs, drop-in centers, clubs, camps, *and* school-age child care programs.

This text examines the major approaches to school-age care for five- to fourteen-year-olds, emphasizing that the general principles and philosophy can also apply to other program models.

BACK TO OUR BASIC DEFINITION:

> **School-age care** is a service that provides programs for school-age children and youth and also support to the families who are unavailable to give care when school is not in session — year-round, before and after school, on school holidays and special closings, perhaps on weekends, and during school vacations — the out-of-school hours.

School-age care may be in a child's own home, in the home of a child care provider, or in a group center. **The program is designed to meet each child's developmental needs.** It is not designed as a program into which all children are automatically expected to fit.

School-age care is:

- **a program that meets the individual child's needs**. The program fits the child; it begins with where each child is developmentally and nurtures sound growth.

School-age care is support for parents whose needs for care fluctuate.

- **a service for parents who are working, training for jobs, or in school.** Parents need good care for their children while they work or obtain employment skills to support their family.

- **a supplement to the child's home**. The family is the strongest influence on the child, and there are frequent contacts between parents and staff; values and goals for the child are shared.

- **a supplement to the child's school.** Since attending school is an important part of a child's life, maintaining a close working relationship with the school provides a developing picture of the whole child and gives direction to appropriate guidance.

- **a place to develop skills, form relationships, discover interests, and mature as a healthy person**. It is a place to acquire healthy attitudes toward self, peers, adults, and the ever-expanding community.

- **a place to be with a caring adult**. Through companionship and understanding, guidance and nurturing, caregivers also help children to become caring persons.

- **a place to experience accomplishment and success, to flourish, to develop a sense of self-worth.** Skillful adults provide the opportunities for this growth.

- **an opportunity for the child to become comfortable in the broader community.** The care site is the base from which the child moves out to take advantage of all the good things a community offers.

- **a time for relaxing, for having fun, enjoying friends, doing what you want to for a while.** It is a time without bother, without bossiness, a time to acquire leisure-time skills.

- **a source of parent information.** Parents welcome meaningful, knowledgeable help with parenting responsibilities. This is true of all parents, those who appear to be stable as well as those with limited parenting skills. Staff may identify health, academic, or social problems and make appropriate resource suggestions.

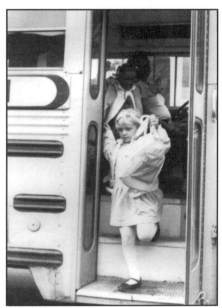

Often school systems will pick up and drop off children directly at family child care homes or centers.

- **a support for parents whose needs for care fluctuate** due to work-related travel, changing work hours, times of crisis or emergency.

- **a support for parents who are physically or mentally limited.** Limitations of families must not deny children the valuable experiences and growth opportunities which they need during these formative years.

- **a family service with equal concern for the needs and well-being of the child and the family.**

ADVOCATING (FIGHTING) FOR CHILDREN

The Need for Positive Protection

(*School-Age NOTES*, May/June, 1984, reprinted with permission)

"Suburban middle-class 'latchkey' children are happy and comfortable with their arrangements, a new national survey show." (from UPI National News Service)

"Latchkey kids come home to fear, isolation, boredom." (Gannett News Service)

School-age children, home alone: lonely and frightened? happy and comfortable? The really important question is: *Is it good for them?*

Sometimes children need to fight their own battles—to learn to assert themselves—to learn and perfect their conflict-solving skills. Sometimes, children need adults to fight battles in their behalf.

The place most of us find ourselves advocating for children is within the walls of the child care program. We try to protect children from injustices and from harm. Therefore, we intervene if two children are physically hurting each other or if one child never seems to get an opportunity to play with the basketball. We try to promote optimal experiences. We provide nutritious food. We strongly urge, promote, and plan a gymnastics class within the program. or we talk with parents and teachers about a child's difficulty with math. Most of the time, we do a good job advocating within our walls.

But children also need us to ADVOCATE for them outside the program in regard to their health, safety, education, community, and family as well as in regard to advertising and media (TV, radio, film). This advocating can occur at parent meetings, school board meetings, advertiser's offices, government proceedings and in legislative councils.

One area that concerns all of us in the school-age child care field is the need to advocate persistently, firmly, and even loudly that school-age children *need* supervised care. They need positive, nurturing protection. Many are already speaking out:

Dr. Virginia E. Pomeranz in the April 1984 issue of *Parents Magazine* wrote: "I make very few categorical statements, but this is one of them: no child of this age (5-6 years)—no matter how intelligent, resourceful, and reliable—is mature enough to be left home alone at home, *ever*."

The Child Care Action Campaign is alerting the public and government to a present crisis in child care. Their main objective is a national plan for affordable, accessible quality child care for children birth to 16-years-old.

From David Elkind as cited in *School-Age Child Care: A Policy Report* (Dec. 1983, p. 18): "Growing up too quickly—being given responsibility prematurely—can produce undue stress. The child's characteristic response to this stress is anxiety that is not attached to any specific fear."

From a developmental point of view children under the age of 12 are not ready to be left home alone. We know that the elementary aged child has not reached the stage of abstract thinking. This means that they are not yet developmentally equipped to make all the appropriate judgments and decisions needed in common self-care predicaments or emergency situations.

Yet...

Working Mother (Feb. 1984) published an analysis of results of a self-reporting survey of 709 six to fourteen-year-old latchkey children. These results were then picked up by the UPI News Service and printed nationally. Although it refers to the question of "whether this kind of unstructured, unsupervised afternoon is good for kids or not..." the seven-page article goes on to make the case that school-age children not only don't mind being home alone, but they actually enjoy it and may have opportunities for positive growth.

This recent trend of articles portraying children home alone as happy and comfortable is disturbing. In a sense it legitimizes the "latchkey situation" as an alternative to adult supervised care. This "latchkey alternative" is further validated in the eyes of the public by recent media attention to "latchkey phone hot-lines" and survival training.

Therefore, parents can feel that it is all right to leave their children home alone. This is especially true since most parents with school-age children are faced with little time, limited finances, and too few community child care resources. As much as parents may save in money and energy by leaving their children home alone, they worry about their safety, behavior, and possible negative effects. All of which adds to "working parent guilt."

Parents (as well as communities and governments) need to hear from us and reminded of the risks of "latchkey" care and the benefits of supervised care. As James Garbarino has stated: "risks associated with latchkey children are of four types: that they will feel badly (e.g., rejected and alienated); that they act badly (e.g., delinquency and vandalism); that they will develop badly (e.g., academic failure); and that they will be treated badly (e.g., accidents and sexual victimization). All four are quite real."

Positive protection is needed. Hot-lines and survival training are not a substitute for adult supervision, protections, and guidance. They are a last resort and should not usurp community resources that may be used for providing programs.

Quality adult supervised care promotes:

— successes and a sense of self-worth
— opportunities to take risks and responsibility within a secure setting
— a caring environment
— fun experiences with peers

This is **Positive Protection**.

Many misunderstandings continue to surround school-age care.

School-age care is not:

- **an assumption of the parent's role,** although it does assume some important nurturing responsibilities when the child is in care.

- **a babysitting service,** although it does assure parents that their children are well cared for and safe.

- **an extension of the academic school day,** although it does incorporate school achievements into leisure activities, providing learning opportunities, skill building, and intellectual motivation. While school projects and themes can be enhanced and reinforced in a child's school-age program, the staff does not attempt to take the place of the child's teacher.

- **a tutorial service,** although the staff may help with homework, encourage interests, and meet special academic needs. Staff may work closely with teachers to monitor the child's progress.

- **a recreation program,** although it does provide many of the activities found in recreation programs to enrich leisure time.

School-Age Care: When Is It Needed and Where Is It Found?

WHEN IS SCHOOL-AGE CARE NEEDED?

When do families use school-age programs? The hours and days when care is needed vary from family to family. Care may be needed:

- ✧ **before school** as early as 6 a.m. It may include breakfast and transportation to school.

- ✧ **after school** until parents are available. Depending on work schedules, school hours, or other circumstances, this period may be from one to six hours.

- ✧ **when school closes early.** Many schools have early closings for teachers' meetings, conferences, snow days, and other emergencies when parents are unable to plan in advance.

- ✧ **before or after half-day kindergarten sessions**.

- ✧ **half day for the first part of the school year.** First graders attend only half-day in some school systems.

- ✧ **full day on most school holidays and during school vacations.** In order to meet working parents' child care needs, it should be available on all but the primary legal holidays (in the U.S., Labor Day, Thanksgiving, Christmas, New Year's, Memorial Day, Fourth of July). Many programs operating in schools provide "extended-day" care only on those days when school is open. While this is adequate for some, most parents must seek other resources for the days when school is closed, but it is not a business holiday.

✧ **full day for a part of the school population, for a part of the school year.** This is necessary in year-round schools, which operate twelve months a year.

✧ **in emergency situations** when children cannot be in school because of illness or injury.

✧ **in any combination of hours and days when schedules are altered as family circumstances change.** This may include care on an occasional basis on certain days of the week, summer mornings, etc.

WHERE IS SCHOOL-AGE CARE FOUND?

In response to the rising demand, several types of programs have evolved, each with its own advantages, each raising certain concerns. The models are the result of the interests, capabilities, resources, and facilities of the providers or the sponsoring group. **Supervision by an adult** is basic to all of the approaches. There are three major models:

    1.) care in the **child's own home**

    2.) care in a **family child care home**

    3.) care in a **group center**

The potential advantages and concerns are based on the developmental needs of children and youth.

Regardless of where care is given, developmental needs must be met.

In-home programs

Care is provided in the child's own home by someone other than the child's parents. It is planned through personal communication between the parents and the program provider. In choosing in-home care, parents consider the unique characteristics, interests, and special developmental needs of their children and relate these to the personality and skills of the caregiver. They also consider their needs in terms of days and hours care is needed, other children to be cared for, other tasks to be done in the household, neighborhood safety, available playmates, and opportunities for play activities.

Possible advantages:

- The environment is comfortable in its familiarity.

- Normal social interactions with neighborhood friends continue and home interests are pursued.

- Children are free to choose how to spend their time— to rest, to read, to be active, to be with friends.

- Home is a great setting for ongoing interests and development of skills — caring for pets, practicing a musical instrument, cooking, working with a stamp collection, riding a bike.

- The situation is natural, relaxed, spontaneous, taken at one's own pace after a structured day at school.

- Transportation problems are minimal as a child walks to and from school or joins friends on the bus or in a carpool.

- When children are sick, injured, or disabled, they can receive individual attention, can stay inside, and can avoid exposure to other children. No transportation is needed, and the environment may be restful.

- In-home care may be the only option for care of the chronically ill child or the profoundly disabled.

- Siblings can remain together.

- Home is a comfortable place to be if the child is not feeling well or wants to be alone after a busy school day.

- The parents are directly involved on a day-to-day basis.

- Parents' nontraditional work hours and days can be accommodated.

Potential concerns:

- The child may be lonely if there are no play companions in the home or neighborhood.

- The parent is the sole monitor of care. If the parent is limited in understanding the child's needs or what constitutes appropriate guidance, there is no other source for supervision of the caregiver.

- The home may be limited in the amount of interesting and challenging materials through which a child may learn.

- The program provider may be untrained and lack knowledge of activities and experiences that are meaningful and interesting to the child.

- The caregiver may be limited in terms of language, interests, ability to relate to the child, or expectations for the child's behaviors.

- There can be many wasted hours if the caregiver is uninterested in the child.

- The caregiver may be preoccupied with housekeeping chores or the care of younger children.

- The care could be physically dangerous or psychologically damaging if the caregiver is immature or irresponsible.

Family child care programs

Care is provided for small groups of children and youth ranging in age from infancy through early adolescence. The setting is usually the program provider's own home. In most states a license or registration is required.

Possible advantages:

- Regulations usually limit the number of children in care, so individual attention is possible.

- The small group benefits the child who does not fare well in a large group.

- The setting may be close to the child's own home and allow continuation of neighborhood friendships and activities.

- The provider already may be known to the child and the family.

- The culture in the caregiver's home may be similar to that of the child's own family.

- Transportation arrangements can be eliminated if the program is in the vicinity of either the school or the child's own home.

- There is a home-like environment with a consistent, single adult.

- The possible wide age span allows siblings to be together.

- School-age children can benefit from associating with children of mixed ages.

- Time schedules for activities can be flexible and geared to the individual needs and interests of the child.

- The caregiver may be able to provide emergency care or extended hours on weekends, holidays, or evening hours.

- Providers may be able to accommodate unusual work schedules.

- The home may be well suited to the child with special medical, nutritional, or intellectual needs.

- The home may be used as a home base for the young adolescent.

- The home may be quiet and restful for children who are ill.

Potential concerns:

- The lone caregiver is the strength or weakness of the plan.

- With one adult in attendance there may be considerable risk in an emergency situation.

- Training, support, and consultation services may be unavailable or inaccessible to the caregiver.

- The wide age span may create difficulty in planning appropriate materials and activities.

- Both indoor and outdoor activities may be over- or under-supervised as the adult attempts to meet the varied developmental levels.

- Participation in community activities may be limited if the adult is occupied with infants and toddlers and unable to accompany the school-age child.

- The needs of the provider's family may take precedence over the needs of the children in care.

- The provider's awareness of the wear-and-tear on the house and property may result in curtailment of school-agers' activities.

- Both indoor and outdoor play space may be inadequate for active school-age children.

- Activities may be restricted because of a lack of materials, equipment, community experiences, and funds.

- In case of the caregiver's illness or an emergency, there may not be a backup arrangement.

Group programs

Care is provided in a program outside of the child's home at a facility for groups of children. The setting may be a home, school, work site, preschool center, religious-education site, community or recreation center, or a specially designed building. It may serve children of all ages or a particular age group. Licensing requirements are usually mandatory. There are several models.

Home-based group care

Located and operated in the home of the provider, these programs are licensed to serve larger numbers than the family child care home because a second adult works in the program. Adult-child ratios are mandated. The advantages and concerns are much the same as in family child care homes.

Possible advantages:

- The group may be smaller here than in other group settings and thus more appropriate for the young school-age child, the child with special needs, or the child who cannot cope well in large groups.

- Staff is usually required to have training.

- If school-age children are enrolled, the program can be geared more closely to that age group so that close friendships may develop.

Potential concerns:

- The basic equipment and supplies may be limited.

- Space, both indoor and outdoor, may be limited.

- Field trips and other special opportunities may not be as available as in larger centers with greater resources.

Combined preschool/school-age centers

While some centers plan for both age groups at the time they are established, most have expanded from preschool services to include the older child. Some include school-age children in a preschool group; others have special groups for them.

Possible advantages:

- The program may have a focus on play, still a necessary part of a child's life.

- Many preschool materials continue to be appropriate for school-agers, who use them in a more mature way.

- The training of preschool staff, with its emphasis on the individual child, is a strong basis for working with the school-age child.

- Contact with younger siblings is possible.

- Continuity is maintained for children who attended as preschoolers.

- If the age groups are separated, there are opportunities for rich, age-appropriate programming and community experiences.

- Staff training is required by most center licensing agencies.

Potential concerns:

- Equipment, materials, and activities may not be age-appropriate in variety, size, or quantity if the age groups are not separated.

- Space, both indoor and outdoor, may not accommodate the needs of the older, larger, active children.

- The staff, who have worked with younger children most of the day, may not be able to contend with active school-agers.

- The demands of younger children may prevent adequate attention to or close relationships with the school-agers.

- Older children may resent being part of a preschool center; they may be teased by schoolmates.

School-age centers

School-age centers have space and programs developed especially for the care of groups of school-age children and youth. They may function as accountable child care or as drop-in recreation programs. They are located in a variety of facilities, are under the administration of public or private groups or individuals, and usually require licensing by the local regulatory agency.

Possible advantages:

- Programs and physical sites are designed for the developmental needs of the age group.

- Equipment and materials are chosen specifically for the age group.

- Staff are likely to have training and experience related to school-age.

- Staff are able to focus on the particular needs of school-agers.

- Children have opportunities for same-age friendships.

- Less stigma is attached to a center which is only for school-age children than to a preschool "nursery."

Potential concerns:

- The center may become institutional and impersonal.

- There may be a lack of consistent caregiving due to split shifts in staffing, rotating volunteer help, or drop-in attendance.

- Some children may have difficulty continuing in yet another group setting after the group situation in school.

- Transportation may be complicated if the center is not within busing or walking distance of the school attended.

- There is no contact with preschool siblings.

School-based centers.

Centers located in school buildings are operated under either the school system or a private group or an individual who has contracted to operate the program. They often require licensing by the local regulatory agency. They are sometimes called "extended-day" programs. [4]

Possible advantages (with school or nonschool sponsorship):

• There are no transportation complications.

• The space is likely to have a variety of available facilities, both indoors and outdoors, such as playgrounds, libraries, or gyms.

• School and neighborhood friendships can continue.

• Good caregiver-teacher relations on behalf of the children are easily developed.

• The school-age center and special school activities are easily coordinated.

• There is easy access to after school clubs and sports activities sponsored by the school.

• The activity needs of older youth may be easily met.

Potential concerns: (with school or nonschool sponsorship):

• The program may be limited if the space must be shared.

• The designated space may be inappropriate or may need major changes — too small or too large a space, no storage areas, etc.

• Schools may be unwilling or unable to make space available before school and on nonschool days.

• The group sizes and staff-child ratios may be too large if not regulated.

• In shared space, storage may be limited, so there may be less equipment.

• If parents are dissatisfied with the service, it may be difficult to transfer to another center or plan.

Possible advantages (with school sponsorship):

• The cost of care may be lower because of the free use of space, shared custodial staff, shared equipment.

• Other school areas such as gymnasium, library, kitchen, etc., may be available.

• A combined staff of caregivers and teachers may make for better communication.

• Coordination of school projects is more likely to occur.

Potential concerns (with school sponsorship):

- An impersonal or highly-structured school may provide the same kind of out-of-school program.

- Activities may be simply more of the school's regular program, utilizing the same equipment, activities, and materials.

- The focus may be on tutorial and academic activities rather than on leisure-time skills and social and emotional growth.

- Children labeled as poor academic achievers may not be given opportunities to excel in other areas; labeled as disruptive or problematic in school, they may not be given opportunities to show other behaviors.

- School administrators may restrict access to some school facilities and resources.

Possible advantages (with nonschool sponsorship):

- The program is more likely to be fresh and different from the regular school day.

- Children and parents with poor school ties have an opportunity for something different.

- Community involvement in the schools is expanded.

Potential concerns (with nonschool sponsorship):

- Operating may be difficult unless there is adequate support and cooperation from the school with carefully delineated responsibilities for both the school and the provider.

- If the program is of inferior quality, it may reflect on the school.

Quality Control

Regardless of where care is given, developmental needs must be met, so factors such as group size, staff, activities, experiences, and environment all foster healthy growth. If these factors are maintained at a level of quality, school-agers have a good chance of developing well.

When children are cared for in their own homes, there are no licensing requirements and no monitoring other than by the family. Here the family must decide whether or not the child is receiving the attention, guidance, and nurturing that are conducive to sound growth.

In family child care homes and group centers, quality control is shared with a regulatory agency, and licensing and registration or certification requirements must be met. Supervision and monitoring help assure adherence to the standards. Technical assistance and consultation make upgrading possible. Sponsors and direct caregivers can identify weaknesses during periods of self-assessment and take steps to improve the program. Parents, too, can perform a monitoring function. They should be alert to the regulations and policies in force. By visiting and observing the school-age programs and by listening to their children, parents can help ensure that the programs are acceptable. The regulations should be evaluated from time to time and reviewed for possible upgrading, and effective enforcement procedures put into place.

Beyond the basic requirements of licensing, some communities include systems by a state or national accrediting organization to exceed minimal regulations in attaining quality. There continues to be resistance to licensing, accreditation, and monitoring among some providers. Caregivers may not understand that quality control is not only consumer and child protection but also *provider* protection. It addresses factors such as safe environment, group size, adult-child ratios, and age-appropriate equipment. Quality control helps caregivers function effectively in an environment that nurtures sound child and youth development. It helps adults identify program components that are already strong as well as those in need of strengthening.

Regulation of a school-age facility, however, does not guarantee excellence. Standards set by regulatory agencies are minimal, with an expectation that they are the foundation on which to build quality programs.

The availability and the range in training and technical assistance for school-age care vary widely. Therefore, we find a wide span of quality in programs. Regardless of the setting, there are basically four levels of service in school-age programs. Only level four meets all the needs of the child and the family.

Level 1: The child is safe. Under the supervision of an adult, the child is protected from harm. When interaction with the adult in charge is thus limited to physical well-being, the child initiates any activities, experiences, and friendships. This lowest level of care is frequently found in in-home care where a housekeeper has other responsibilities or when a neighbor periodically looks after a child.

Level 2: The child is safe and occupied. The child may be safe and activities are provided but without concern for the child's age, stage of development, or interests. This often occurs where the provider's orientation is to the preschool child in preschool centers or in family child care homes when the other children are infants or preschoolers. Yes, the child is safe and busy, but boredom soon sets in when there are no growth opportunities.

Level 3: The child is safe and occupied with activities geared to school-age children. The adult in charge has knowledge of age-appropriate activities and makes them available, but the program does not consider the individual child's interests or special needs. This is likely to be true where there is a group orientation with structured programming and few opportunities for personal choice of activities. There are limited benefits for many of the children.

Level 4: The child is safe, engaged in activities which foster individuality and healthy growth and development, and cared for by knowledgeable staff who relate to children within the context of each family situation.

Level 4 offers the best opportunity for children to reach their potential. Small group size and a limit to the number of children in the care of one adult allow the staff to know each school-ager, the family circumstances, and the other influences in each child's life. In such a program, there is a greater probability that all the child's needs will be met.

Many attitudes and behaviors of children are formed by their experiences in out-of-school settings. As more programs achieve the kind of school-age care environment described in Level 4, the more chances there will be for giving children the best care possible during these formative years.[5,6]

Things To Think About

I. STRETCH YOUR MIND ON NEW DESIGNS

Are before-and-after-school programs, camps, and recreation programs the only way to envision care for out-of-school hours? Think about new spaces, new hours, new styles.

As you expand your ideas, keep in mind that *any* program certainly must be developmentally appropriate for the children and must connect with the needs of the families and the resources of the community. Children and youth must be safe, genuinely cared about, accounted for, nourished, and adequately supervised. Programs must be accountable to appropriate regulations and must be operated by skilled, trained adults.

Here are a few samples of variations of school-age programs.

The Integrated School Day

Scandinavian countries incorporate this idea. Instead of before and after school experiences, activities are interspersed throughout a longer school day. For instance, a school day, instead of looking like this:

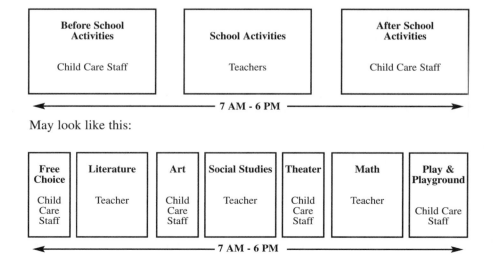

May look like this:

- How could schools, whether public or private, arrange staff and schedules to achieve this kind of a day?

- What are the advantages? Disadvantages?

- How will you convince school staff of the value and the importance of the child care curriculum?

- What are the implications for training of caregivers in an integrated-day program?

Neighborhood Clubs

The concept is like that of a family home. The hours may extend into the evening. These clubs may be in neighborhood buildings or houses with indoor and outdoor space and skilled supervision. Registered children and youth can congregate before and after school. They may stay and cook dinner, and on scheduled evenings parents may join them. They may come and go if safety permits and if their families want them to check in at their own homes, feed a pet, tend to a chore, or get their bikes. Areas are designated for recreational as well as skill-building activities — music room, game room, dining room and kitchen, woodwork and mechanical workshops, reading and homework areas, art studio, photography darkroom, theater space. Staff trained in special skills may circulate among the clubs, helping children with playing musical instruments, bike repair, sewing, dance, art, and drama.

- How do you feel about neighborhood clubs for neighborhood care?

- In what kind of communities might this work best?

- What might be the special problems to be solved?

- What are the advantages?

Playground Programs

Many countries have always been especially proud of their year-round outdoor programs, sometimes called adventure playgrounds. Indoor space is available for inclement weather, and trained staff supervise a variety of ages. Playgrounds are fenced, safe, and accessible to home and school. A great variety of outdoor-oriented materials (geared to both young and older children) might include:

lean-tos for shelter

playhouses, sheds, and tents

tables and benches

blacktop for skating and bikes

blacktop with rims to flood for ice skating

areas for puddles and pools for model boat sailing and water play

repair sheds for bikes and cycles

carpentry areas with wood and tools

artificial hills for rope climbing

large blocks, crates, and lumber for construction	trampolines
	forests made by children
ramps for skate boards	gardens to tend and harvest
kilns for pottery	animals to care for and play with
pits for bonfires	
climbing structures	ball and game fields
old cars, boats, planes	sports equipment

- How could you create an outdoor program where you live?

- Who could be responsible for upkeep and maintenance?

- How would you group? staff? supervise?

- What roles could families play?

Special-Interest Programs

Special-interest programs may be school-based, meeting before or after school. They may meet at a community facility or in a private home. They are staffed by persons who are interested and knowledgeable about the specific ventures. These groups may or may not meet every day, and their focus may evolve. For instance, interests may grow from creative writing to word processing, computer art, or film-making, or they may progress from the environment to city planning, farm techniques, or science. Children might attend several special-interest groups, meeting at different times. Pursuing personal interests leads to close friendships as well as lifelong abilities.

- Do you see groups such as these as an alternative to a standard school-age program?

- With what age child?

- How would they meet the needs for self-direction and physical activity?

- How could they meet family needs for out-of-school supervised care?

Jobs

What child is not pleased to be significant, important, responsible? Job programs may be developed as part of the established school-age curriculum or as a completely different approach to child care through community experiences. Jobs-for-pay or jobs-for-no-pay — a job is an important activity. Jobs give a sense of structure to children's time and help develop the sense of dependability and the ability to see things through from beginning to end. Jobs for pay encourage the increasing feeling of independence, for the money is something of one's very own; volunteer jobs encourage the developing desire for responsibility.

Jobs within a home or center might include responsibilities such as toy repair, painting and maintenance, clerical and telephone responsibilities, and food preparation and serving. Jobs in the community might include community gardening and clean-up, animal care, help with younger children, and errands and chores for the housebound or homeless.

- How would you make a job program work with the variety of ages of children enrolled?

- What jobs would kids enjoy?

- How could you budget for and arrange for jobs for pay?

- How would you present this program to families and the community?

Occasional Care

Often referred to as drop-in arrangements, these programs can meet the needs of children and youth who need supervision only on an occasional basis — a few times a week or just once in a while. Activities are age-appropriate, the staff is consistent, and schedules are defined among the staff and families.

- Why is this an effective service?

- How would you design experiences to provide familiarity and continuity?

- By what means will you get children involved in the planning of the program?

- What administrative factors must you consider?

Adventure Clubs

A program might be built around daily explorations—community trips. This approach may work best as part-time experience (two or three days a week) for families interested in part-time care. Think about the possibilities for a holiday, weekend, or afternoon adventure program to skating rinks, camping facilities, museums, parks, factories, concerts, etc.

- What does your community have to offer?

- What do you need to consider — age-range, budget, time, etc.?

- What are the transportation possibilities?

- How would you involve children, families, and community members in the planning?

New Places

Look around your own environment for spaces that have never been considered as sites for youth programs: museums, sport centers, libraries, parks, farms, health clubs, zoos, forests, theater sites, playgrounds, college campuses, shopping malls, office buildings, church or synagogue facilities, store fronts.

- What are the necessary essentials such as sufficient indoor and outdoor space, food preparation and storage areas, and telephones?

- How will you convince your contacts of the benefits of using the space?

- What would be the advantages and disadvantages of sharing such spaces?

- How would you achieve a well-rounded curriculum?

Create Your Own Design

Think of another unique approach to an out-of-school program.

- What is the mission or philosophy of your program?

- What are your main goals?

- Define the age range of the children.

- Describe the space, staffing, activities, and family involvement.

- What equipment and supplies will you need?

- What resources are available to help you?

- What are the particular advantages?

- What might be the problems?

- How will you determine or evaluate the quality of the program?

- Design a promotional brochure.

II. STRETCH YOUR MIND BEYOND THE FAMILIAR

There are many different kinds of home life and family situations. As you watch and listen to the children, you will learn about the variety of circumstances and environments they live in. Families from foreign countries may have customs and holidays unfamiliar to you; likewise, they may be unaware of the customs, values, and holidays of their new homeland.

The well-being of children depends on feeling respected and wanted. Be aware of differences in the cultural backgrounds of the children, who may avoid a group activity or react in negative ways because of cultural factors. For example, a child whose family does not celebrate Christmas may be very uneasy about participating in activities solely addressed to this holiday.

- How can you make a child who does not speak your language feel welcome and comfortable?

- How will you encourage language skills in a child from a home where verbal communication is minimal?

- How will you react to a child who is parented by two men or two women?

- How can you help a child who comes from a climate of violence, gangs, guns, and abuse?

- How will you relate to families very different from your own and where might you go for help?

NOTES

[1] The report of the *National Study of Before- and After-School Programs*, 1993, provides a comprehensive study of the prevalence, structures and features of "formalized before and after school programs" which have been developed, including data on the role of the public schools. Still other arrangements exist in the form of home and family child care and more informal settings such as community youth recreation and enrichment programs, tutoring and special skills programs and camps. (see pages xvi-xviii)

[2] You might be interested in this U.S. comprehensive demographic survey:

Casper, L.M., Hawkins, M., O'Connell, M., *Who's Minding the Kids?*, Child care arrangements: U.S. Bureau of the Census, Current Population Report, U.S. Gov't. Printing Office, Washington DC, 1994.

[3] For another study of where children are and what they are doing when school is closed, we recommend *The Serious Business of Growing Up: A Study of Children's Lives Outside of School.* by Elliot A. Medrich, et al. (1982), and *A Matter of Time: Risk and Opportunity in the Nonschool Hours.* (See bibliography at the end of this text for complete listings.)

[4] We refer you to *After-School Programs & the K-8 Principal:Standards for Quality School-Age Child Care, Revised Edition*, National Association of Elementary School Principals, 1615 Duke Street, Alexandria VA 22314-3483, 1999. This publication, originally developed in collaboration with Wellesley College School-Age Child Care Project, is a guide for developing quality programs within school settings.

[5] Perhaps as O'Connor suggests in *Assessing School-Age Child Care Quality*, Wellesley College Center for Research on Women, 1992, program quality can be evaluated on the basis of the following dimensions:

1.) human relationships among staff, children, and parents;

2.) indoor and outdoor space, materials, supplies, and equipment;

3.) activities and use of time; and

4.) safety, health and nutrition

[6] See Supplement 2 at the end of this text for a listing of the 144 NSACA Standards for Quality School-Age Care.

RECOMMENDED READINGS

Carnegie Council on Adolescent Development's Task Force on Youth Development and Community Programs. *A Matter of Time: Risk and Opportunity in the Nonschool Hours*. Waldorf: Carnegie Council on Adolescent Development, 1994.

Center for Youth Development and Policy Research. "Preliminary Issues in Strengthening the Field of Youth Development Work." Washington DC: Center for Youth Development and Policy Research, 1994.

Children's Defense Fund. *Opportunities for Prevention: Building After-School and Summer Programs for Young Adolescents*. Washington DC: Adolescent Pregnancy Prevention Clearinghouse, 1987.

Coolsen, P., M. Seligson, J. Garbarino. *When School's Out and Nobody's Home*. Chicago: National Committee for Prevention of Child Abuse, 1985.

Fink, D. *School-Age Children with Special Needs: What Do They Do When School is Out?* Brookline: Exceptional Parent Press, 1988.

Gabarino, J. *Children and Families in the Social Environment*. New York: Aldine, 1982.

Leach, P. *Children First: What Our Society Must Do and Is Not Doing for Our Children Today*. New York: Knopf, 1994.

Miller, B. and F. Marx. *Afterschool Arrangements in Middle Childhood: A Review of the Literature*. Wellesley: Center for Research on Women, Wellesley College, 1990.

Musson, S. *School-Age Care: Theory and Practice*, 2nd Ed. Ontario: Addison Wesley Longman, 1999.

National Association of Elementary School Principals. *After-School Programs and the K-8 Principal: Standards for Quality School-Age Child Care*, Revised Ed. Alexandria, VA: NAESP, 1999.

Newman, R. L. *Building Relationships with Parents and Families in School-Age Programs*. Nashville: School-Age NOTES, 1999.

Seligson, M. and D. Fink. *No Time to Waste: An Action Agenda of School-Age Child Care*. Wellesley: Center for Research on Women, Wellesley College, 1989.

—and M. Allenson. *School-Age Child Care: An Action Manual for the 90's and Beyond*. Wellesley: Center for Research on Women, Wellesley College, 1993.

U.S. Department of Education. "National Study of Before and After School Programs." Washington DC: U.S. Department of Education, 1993.

Zigler, E., and M. Long. *Child Care Crises: Balancing the Needs of Children, Families and Society*. New York: Macmillan, 1990.

Chapter Two
Who Are The Children?

"I can't go back to being a baby
and I can't get to be an adult so quick."

Chase, age 5

"You know what person I like
the very most? Myself. Because I'm
the only me. I'm smart. I'm nice. I'm
good at rugby. I have a grandmother.
And that's about it! Those are all good
things and I have them all!"

Ryan
age 7

"Growing up can be very
important. When you are young,
you wish you were older. When
you are older, you wish you were
young. I think that is funny."

Chris
age 11

"Caterpillar: 'And who are you?'
Alice: 'I hardly know, sir, just at present - at least I know who I was when
I got up this morning, but I think I must have changed several times since then.'"

Lewis Carroll
1832-1898

In this chapter...

➢ Basic Human Needs
 — A Sense of Identity, Good Relationships, Power
➢ Who Are The Children?
 — Meeting Physical, Social, Self, and Intellectual Needs
➢ Children Who Need Special Care
➢ Worries and Concerns: What's on Children's Minds?

There are many things to think about when we ask, "Who are the children?" There are so many similarities yet so many differences among children and youth of all ages. There are so many factors which make each of them the way they are. There are factors which relate to their development and to their age: the five- and six-year-olds, still family centered and intent on pleasing adults, still very much geared to preschool experiences and imitative play; the seven through eleven-year-olds, increasingly intent on seeking friendships, gaining feelings of independence, and mastering skills; and the twelve to fourteen-year-olds, who are fast approaching adolescence, with some degree of physical and psychological maturity and an emerging sense of the roles they wish to play in the adult world.

There are factors to consider that relate to the well-being of children in their homes, in their neighborhoods, in their schools. There are factors that relate to the societal expectations and changes at a particular time, in a particular place; factors about the impact of community services, legal systems, economics, and factors about their culture, the particular people, places, and experiences in each child's life. There are factors concerning children's genetic and personal development, their individual temperaments, and their perceptions of their own lives. All of these factors, and many more, have an impact on what a child is like and what a child becomes.

The focus of this chapter is on some of the human needs, the developmental characteristics, and the concerns of children and youth, as well as the ways through which school-age care can help children function safely, happily and effectively in a complex society. Society touches every child as every child touches society. Children and youth help determine the quality of society. The extent to which adults care for children and meet their needs will influence their adult behavior.

This chapter provides basic information about human development essential for working effectively with school-age children and creating quality school-age programs.[1] The chapter is in four sections.

I. Basic human needs

- the need for an individual to be recognized as a unique person, *a sense of identity*

- the need to belong, *good relationships*

- the need for personal control, *power*

II. Basic human growth and development

- physical development

- social development

- self development

- intellectual development

III. Children Who Need Special Care

IV. Worries and concerns: What's on children's minds?

- self • family • school • friends • loneliness • media messages
- gender roles • sex and sexuality • violence and crime • drugs
- death

Basic Human Needs

A SENSE OF IDENTITY — THE NEED TO BE SOMEBODY

The need to be "somebody" is a primary human need, common to all children and youth. It is the need to have an *identity*, a sense of self that is both worthy and capable. Each child wants to be someone special and important. In the earlier years of their lives, most children have had the care and direction which told them how to be and how to behave. Yet, increasingly, as children enter the school-age years, they want to be recognized as persons who are somewhat independent of home and family and important in their own right. While home may still be the base for security, the place to rely on when things are tough, the sense of identity is very much influenced now by how children believe their friends see them. Starting at about the age of five, the support of friends is quite important to help children gain the confidence to stand on their own.

There are several significant factors in the establishment of an identity. There must be a recognition on the part of the family and other significant adults in children's lives that they are individual, independent beings. This is a difficult task, especially for parents who often see their children as extensions of themselves. They are reluctant to have their children behave in unique, independent ways. It also is often difficult for teachers to allow for uniqueness and individuality because they expect classroom behaviors that conform to school expectations. Adults in out-of-school settings, however, have the time and opportunity to provide experiences that encourage and recognize individual identity.

School-agers also may have difficulty accepting and defining themselves. The acceptance of one's own identity means honoring all one knows and feels about oneself. For instance, it involves acceptance of the physical body, with all of its strengths and limitations. During the school-age years, this becomes increasingly difficult. If friends and peers are growing and developing earlier, more fully, more attractively, acceptance of self may be difficult. School-agers have to deal with the taunts of "You're too short" or "Move over, Fatso." It involves acceptance of variable levels and kinds of capabilities and skills. "Sure, I have a hard time with baseball, but I am really good at the piano." "I need a lot of help with spelling, but have you seen my juggling act?"

The process for the development of a sense of self-identity involves seeing how *different* people are from each other. Children can recognize differences in personalities, differences between the sexes, between adults and children. Their lives are touched by racial, religious, and cultural differences. They can see differences in behavior, in abilities, in interests, in school performance. They are aware of many different ways in which people approach and plan for their futures.

As children enter into preadolescence they become increasingly aware of how they are also *alike*, especially like others their own age. This often results in their wanting to be like each other even more, especially those persons they really admire and with whom they wish to be identified. This can result in common dress, interests, language, hair styles, and food preferences.

All of this behavior leads to identification with and a desire to be in select social groups — doing most everything together and alike. These peer groups are often at odds with the standards of the adults around them. While belonging to a club or being a member of a group is a source of self-identity, it can also interfere with the development of an individual sense of identity. The pressure for "sameness" is strong, but individual strengths also can prosper if they have been nurtured.

A complicating factor in this search for identity is the need for the child, beginning at about the age of nine or ten, to be different from parents and family. Preadolescents may try very hard not to be like parents or siblings. They often are annoyed or angered in situations where they must be with their families or even identified with them. It is wise for individuals who work with children and pre-adolescents to be cautious in how they state even positive relationships between children and their families. Statements such as "You're as pretty as your sister," or "You sound just like your dad when you speak," may interfere with the developing sense of personal identity. It is as if children temporarily have to give up some of their past in order to move forward.

A sense of identity: What am I like? At what am I really good? For what do I want to be known? Am I respected? Children who come to out-of-school programs often don't have good or clear feelings about themselves. They are not sure why they must be there. They may see their friends going home to families. They sometimes feel like excess baggage when they hear their parents struggling over child care arrangements. They have a hard time sorting out what they observe around them and what they feel about themselves.

It is a challenge for staff to help each child feel comfortable, wanted, and respected, to develop a strong and positive sense of self. It requires, first of all, a recognition of the constantly developing person. It requires building on children's strengths as they learn what they can do and do well, so each child can say "I'm good at this and this...I must be okay." It requires the development of school-age programs which allow for children's testing of a variety of roles and behaviors as they strive for self-awareness, self-acceptance, and their developing sense of identity.

GOOD RELATIONSHIPS — THE NEED TO BELONG

The need to relate to others — *to belong* — is another major need which consumes an enormous amount of children's energy, both physically and emotionally. Therefore it, too, becomes an integral part of program development. The need for relationships is closely related to the need for self-identity. Our sense of identity, our ability to think well of ourselves, develops to a great extent from all of our relationships with people in our lives. This begins at birth and continues throughout our lives. Through all of the people with whom we live, play, and work, we continually form pictures of ourselves. We come to feel a sense of connection; we imitate others; we learn from others. We gain security and support from others. We become who we are through all sorts of human relationships, starting from our family and reaching out into a constantly expanding social world. We define ourselves through all of our relationships.

The satisfaction of the need to belong, the need for relationships with others, becomes a primary motivator of behavior in an ever increasing way as a person moves from childhood into and through adolescence. During the school-age years, children's interests and allegiances gradually shift from a primary focus on the family to one which is built around peers and friends. The development of peer relationships and best friends may seem to be children's primary interest. In order to belong, they want to look like others, behave like others and talk like others — consequently "others" (peers and friends) become primary role models.

The need to belong and to relate to others becomes so strong that both children and youth may engage in risky and even potentially self-destructive behaviors to become part of a group. While many parents are concerned, they may have increasingly less influence, and when they attempt to influence they may tend to do so through harsh discipline, by being judgmental, or in other conflict producing ways. Parents may threaten their children about questionable friends and negative peer influence rather than helping their children deal effectively with these influences. Staff and families can provide guidance by helping children learn peer refusal skills (how to say "no" to peers), how to exit situations that the child recognizes as wrong or harmful, and how to establish the kinds of relationships which can lead to a satisfying sense of belonging.

Children function in the worlds of both peers and adults. Trustworthy adult relationships are essential. A sense of belonging cannot come from peers alone, strong as this bond may be. The sense of trust in others, which says to a child, "I, too, can be trustworthy," begins in infancy. It begins as parents respond to a baby's needs: "Can I trust someone to come? Can I trust someone to help me?" Then someone comes.

This sense of trust is the first task in forming good relationships. The foundation for trust continues as adults remain close to children and provide for their needs. Staff who care for school-agers may provide the most constant, consistent, dependable relationships some children have as many family relationships change and adults come and go. One of the greatest concerns of children is "Who will take care of me?" They need continued assurance that they are, indeed, well cared for.

Quality care implies meeting the need for good relationships and a sense of belonging: belonging in a family, belonging to a community, relationships with peers, chances to have friends and to be a friend. Quality staff helps to provide for those needs and in so doing responds to the question: "Who will take care of me?"

POWER — THE NEED FOR PERSONAL CONTROL

A third human need of school-agers is the need to have power, to have control in their lives. A strong sense of identity along with trustworthy relationships with other dependable human beings lead to an ability to have control over one's actions, choices, and responsible decisions. This personal control creates personal power.

Personal control is referred to here in a broad context. Self-control is an integral part of personal control. Self-control provides children with the essential ability to channel impulses and desires so that they can grow and develop into fully functioning individuals.

As children approach school-age, they begin to have more control over their own selves. They control their bodies, their language; they control intricate toys, complex rules to games; they choose their own ways of behaving. Despite the fact they are living with directions coming from many adults, they are striving for personal control. To have a sense of personal control, children must first believe they have the power to control. This comes after many experiences with personal choices and decisions, which lead them where they want to go.

School-age children frequently express the need to control through physical power, often inappropriately. Older youth may seek power through delinquent acts. When children do not feel a sense of power or control, they may strike out in inappropriate ways.

Children can learn to exert power through good verbal skills and the ability to both receive and send clear nonverbal messages. As control of communication skills develops, so does a child's ability to question the potentially negative influences of some peers and adults, as well as of some advertising and media presentations. Power also comes from having good problem-solving skills, good thinking skills, and, above all, self-assurance.

Children often feel a lack of control because of the many controlling persons in their lives. Children are controlled by parents, directed by teachers, bossed by siblings. There may be few chances for developing a feeling that they themselves have any capability to control.

Adults may or may not have children's best interests at heart. Sports-loving adults may push their unwilling sons or daughters into contact sports when they may prefer to spend their free time playing guitar. Children who hear television commercials that a specific kind of clothing will make them popular may believe that message and desperately want the item. If they lack the control to purchase this item because they do not have money, transportation, or parental permission, they may feel especially helpless.

Children can be helped with the skills and understandings needed to receive messages, think about their meanings, and thoughtfully come to decisions that keep them in control of their own lives. This often comes with balancing their own ideas with those of adults and peers: "Jane invited me over to her house, but Dad says I have to clean my room first. So I'll clean the room and then go to Jane's house." It involves weighing the value of one idea against another: "If I go out for soccer, I won't have time to learn tennis — I've got to decide."

Of course, children and youth cannot always be in control of situations because adults guide, set rules, and determine much about their daily living, whereas peers argue, negotiate, and compromise. But they can be empowered if they are allowed to help with plans, make choices, and express their own ideas.

Adults can be resources when children "lose control." Sometimes youngsters cannot find ways to exert control and to govern their own lives when they are discouraged by their environment or their relationships. When children feel no options are available, they may call for help. If help is not obtained, they may turn to such desperate solutions as running away, substance abuse, even suicide.

Staff respond to this important need for personal power when they share power with children and help them gain not only a sense of power but real control within their lives.[2]

Who Are The Children?

ESSENTIAL TO KNOW

No longer preschoolers and not yet teenagers, the school-age child is maturing in four major aspects of their being, through *physical development*, *social development*, *self development*, and *intellectual development*. Understanding and responding to these aspects of a child's life is the essence of quality school-age care.

The school-age child is making strides toward growing up — knowing more about the world, behaving in certain ways, acquiring a values system. All of these qualities are combined to create a unique individual.[3]

WHAT ARE THEIR PHYSICAL NEEDS?

Body changes

The bodies of both boys and girls are undergoing many changes in size and complexity during the period between the ages of five and fourteen. While five-year-olds are small, physically immature, and not yet physically well coordinated, fourteen-year-olds may be almost fully developed and well on the way to physical maturity. Girls may be maturing faster than boys, and they often are larger and stronger than boys of the same age. These physical changes frequently create curiosity and confusion for school-agers concerning their self-images and how others perceive them. They may also have concerns about how they will look as adult males and females. Concerns over whether they have facial blemishes, are too fat, too tall, too short, or flat-chested interfere with their self-images and make them more self-conscious. These are important considerations in terms of the activities boys and girls engage in together and may be responsible for their choices in relationships and group participation.

Muscle development

Muscle development, both large and small, is rapid during the early school-age years. Adequate provision should be made to encourage this development. Certain physical skills — throwing and catching, running, swimming, handling simple tools, writing and drawing — are important to acquire. Special attention should be directed to children who are not developing physical skills, for these skills are often essential to feeling accepted by friends and for developing a wholesome, positive attitude toward one's own body. The image school-age children have of their bodies is very closely linked to the self-concept or picture they have of themselves as a total person. Many children are quite adept as they use their bodies, maturing in strength, flexibility, and precision of movement. Others are very awkward because of uneven physical growth.

All children need experiences through which they will feel comfortable. For instance, a child may lack the coordination for baseball and yet be an excellent drummer. A child may be a fine artist and yet be unable to run or dance. Some children enjoy the physical outlet of rough and tumble play while others never use their bodies in an aggressive manner. Having an abundant amount of energy to use, children often choose strenuous activities. Since both endurance and energy have limits, provision is needed for adequate rest, relaxation, nourishment, and sleep.

Children may place themselves in physical danger, both in testing the limits of their physical capabilities and in accepting dares.

I dare you

Children may place themselves in physical danger, both in testing the limits of their physical capabilities and in accepting dares. Safety and supervision need careful consideration in planning activities and activity areas. Equipment must be well designed and kept in good repair.

Keep up with the checkups

The health of school-agers is generally good, but reinforcement of good health and nutrition habits is important. Checkups of all kinds continue: dental checkups to ensure proper care for the permanent teeth now appearing; vision and hearing screenings to identify problems which can be corrected before learning or behavior are affected; general physical examinations to ascertain that the body has developed sufficiently to allow participation in vigorous physical activities. Strenuous sports such as football, competitive swimming, and soccer require a certain physical maturity to prevent body damage. Medical reports should be available to staff for easy reference if there are any questions related to strenuous physical exertion.

Sexual development

Chemical changes occur during the middle childhood years of five to fourteen as youth progress toward sexual maturation. Boys and girls gradually begin to be differentiated as male and female sexual beings. From the beginning and throughout adolescence, energy is increasingly expended in the development of sexuality. Boys and girls become interested in each other and the visible differences which are present.

Much time may be spent wondering about body changes and feelings never before experienced. Interest in sex is to be expected, accompanied by much misunderstanding. Staff provide adult role models for gender identification. The process of gender identity is begun early and becomes increasingly important as the more obvious physical changes appear. A child usually models after an adult of the same sex. This may be difficult for the male child who has only female teachers and caregivers, and so effort is needed to provide male role models for boys.

Sexual development results in greater curiosity about one's own sex as well as the opposite sex. The development of close friendships with members of the same sex provides opportunities to share the intimate details of "growing up." From these friendships, children often gain a great deal of security in knowing that all the changes in them and their bodies are also happening to others.

The natural interest in all aspects of sex results in much talk about sex and experimentation with words having sexual meanings. The talk may lead to some sexual experimentation, which may result in guilt and embarrassment. Adults may help alleviate guilt and embarrassment by accepting the children's interests and providing accurate answers. Some older school-agers may have already been involved in sexual activities, and caregivers should be aware of which resources may be needed to deal with their behaviors.

MEETING PHYSICAL NEEDS - WHAT CAN ADULTS DO?

Provide a wide range of things to do

Because there is such a broad span of physical development there must be a wide variety of activities from which to choose. Younger children are physically unable to participate in many activities suitable for school-agers whose body skills and muscle strength are more developed. Older children may not be challenged by physical activities beneath their skill level. Even when activities are suitable for all ages (e.g. carpentry, swimming, ball games), physical differences influence the ways in which children participate.

Consider age groupings

The broad range in development not only results in differences in physical skills, but can affect how children feel and how they view themselves in relation to other children and youth in the program. The physical development of the twelve- to fourteen-year-olds may be so complete that they see themselves as adults and are embarrassed by being with those who are younger and less physically mature. Because of their physical development, their experiences, and conversations about sex, they may not interact with younger children appropriately.

Adults must be aware of how the physical development of older school-agers affects their relations with younger children. They also must be aware of how the immaturity of younger children affects their views of themselves if they are dominated by or must compete with ten, twelve, or fourteen-year-olds.

Parents of younger school-agers may be wary of the inclusion of physically mature older children. They need reassurance that staff are sensitive to this and will place children in age groups that will nurture their individual growth and development.

Provide space

Adequate space is essential, both indoors and outdoors: space to develop muscles; space for movement and active games; space for the equipment and furniture that increase in size as bodies grow larger; space for the materials that spread out as they are used and as ideas grow. At least 35 to 50 square feet per child of indoor activity space is necessary; 75 to 200 square feet per child for outdoor activities.

Provide "action activities"

After what may have been a long sedentary day of school, it is hard to sit any longer. It is a good time for choices of activities requiring movement: running, jumping, climbing, lifting, catching, throwing.

Provide opportunities for small muscle development

Present a variety of choices of experiences with table games, art media, writing materials, construction materials.

Provide supervision

Supervision helps ensure safety — but supervision without over-protection and over-direction. These children are eager for greater independence and personal control.

Provide opportunities for rest

When energy is temporarily spent, plan places for rest that are easy to find: comfortable furniture to flop on such as a bed, cot, or couch; the grass or floor or sleeping bags for stretching out; a tree to lean against; a box to crawl into; or a perch on top of a climber. Sometimes children may not be feeling well and need to lie down in a quiet, separate place.

Provide nutrition

Food restores energy and also provides comfort. Food may be supplied either as snacks or full meals. All children need a well-balanced diet and sufficient amounts of food and drink to satisfy increasingly bigger appetites and growing bodies. It is important to stress this with parents and consult with nutrition experts. Children can help with their morning and afternoon snacks, even lunch on full days of attendance, with careful attention given to nutritional value. As children help with food preparation and develop food preparation skills, information about nutrition is reinforced.

Food also carries emotional significance. The giving and receiving of food are expressions of caring. Eating together enhances a sense of family and of being a part of a group.

Provide play and other smart things to do

Here are a few activities relating to physical development. You will think of more:

ball games	dancing	jumping rope
bicycling	gardening	skating
carpentry	hiking	typing
crocheting		

Self-Care: What are the dangers to physical development?

* What protects children who are unsupervised from the physical risks of fire and accident, guns, assault from peers or adults?
* What protects them from dangerous sexual experiences?
* Who is there to assure nourishment, physical activity, rest, fresh air, sunshine?

WHAT ARE THEIR SOCIAL NEEDS?

Stepping away from home

A major part of growing up involves wanting and needing to interact with other people, especially those of the same age.

Before children enter school, their environment has been extensively controlled by their home life. As they move away from home for longer periods of time, other people have increasing control and impact: friends from school and the neighborhood, and adults in the community, such as teachers, religious leaders, and instructors of music, art, and sports. Although their family remains the single strongest influence, children may adopt many of the attitudes, skills, values, and beliefs of groups with whom they are in contact.

There's strength in numbers

Between the ages of five and fourteen the peer group of friends becomes an increasingly important part of a child's life. Friends provide the child with growth experiences and satisfaction of certain needs, along with some friction, confusion, and social problems. The peer group is generally a group of children of the same age who may have interests in common and who provide one another with the opportunity to gain self-understanding. Children start to view themselves as others see them. The impact of the peer group is so profound during this time that all adults need to recognize it and be prepared to help make the impact positive.

Staff recognize that by ages six and seven, school-age children want to belong to and feel a part of a group so much that they will do almost anything to belong, even though they may harm themselves in the process. A big part of belonging is learning how to join groups and how to leave groups when the situation or the behavior is not satisfying to the child. The six- or seven-year-olds may hover around the fringes of a group — watching, obeying the orders of the older children, but still seeking affection from the adults. By the time they're ten or twelve years old, however, school-agers transfer all their energy into being an accepted member of a peer group. The feeling of "strength in numbers" may also lead to an opposition to adults — talking back, arguing, protesting. Caregivers can learn to deal with these behaviors without feeling personally threatened.

With all the fighting, roughhousing, squabbling, and bickering among children, adults may question how much children need to be with one another. They do! Coping with loneliness is difficult. Loneliness is destructive, as is boredom. Both occur when children do not have peer contacts. Friendships with other children allow for the give-and-take experiences by which children find their own personalities and their own ways of coping.

Getting to know you

Preschool children play well with others as long as their friends fit in with their own plans. School-agers, however, increasingly like to play with others not for what they can do with them but because they really want to know other children — who they are, what they are like, and whether they will be a friend. In wishing to like and be liked, they are willing to change their ways to be accepted by a friend and by the ever-changing cliques of friends. As children grow older this may range from choice of toys to style of dress or to experiments with smoking, sex, drugs, and vandalism. Once children get to know each other, their relationships can be very intense.

Accepting and belonging

Acceptance into groups becomes increasingly important as children move toward adolescence. Yet discrimination by physical appearance, behavior, social position, intellectual functioning, culture, or race may have already begun, thus threatening social approval. School-age programs can aid in diminishing any developing social discriminations and help each child find acceptance and belonging.

Helping children find acceptability and self-esteem is a primary task for caregivers. There is a close relationship between self-esteem and prejudice. People who are satisfied with themselves tend to be more accepting of other people. This is true of children *and* adults, and is a clue for working with children, hiring and working with staff, and relating to parents. The members of a school-age group constitute a close unit through which children can get to know each other well and understand their differences of age, habits, values, culture, and personality.

Trying new language to make new friends

Since full acceptance is often achieved by conformity (being like others), children may adopt the language of "the group" — words, phrases, chants, even jokes and slang — in order to feel accepted. Even if the children do not know the meaning of the words, using group language may give them a sense of emancipation, and they may feel more accepted.

Making friends with staff and other adults

School-agers relate to adults on an increasingly mature basis. The social contacts with adults become more like friendships. As nine- and ten-year-olds develop social skills, caregivers will want to encourage the feelings of friendship while maintaining the role of the responsible adult. Older children may confide and share private information with adults outside the family, believing they will be less likely to get "preached at" or get into arguments than they would at home.

A time for one's self

The need to be with friends is strong, but the need to have private personal time is also important. School-age care usually implies a group situation, and this is healthy, especially for the older children. But there are many hours, and it is also important to have time and spaces in which to relax, think, and work on individual ideas.

Aspiring to be a "teen"

Much behavior of older school-agers, especially the ten- to fourteen-year-olds, can be regarded as a trying out of "roles" — imitating a friend, acting for the effect on others. One of the most common roles is to "already be a teenager." They style their hair, imitate the dances, use the same expressions — in a hurry to grow up.

MEETING SOCIAL NEEDS - WHAT CAN ADULTS DO?

Be sure every child has friends

Help children make friends through their activities. Consciously plan for this to happen.

- *Present ideas to be freely selected by each child* that can be enjoyed with old friends and new. Children may discover activities through their friends or their friends through activities.

- *Create activities which invite specific children to work together* in carrying out an idea or responsibility. It may take two to go on an errand or pump up the balls or write a skit.

- *Plan activities which lend themselves to varying numbers of participants.* Some children want to be with just one or two friends, others enjoy small gangs. Two or three can make a pie, six or seven can build a clubhouse.

- *Allow time for friendships to develop.* Friends need time to be friends — time and places to giggle together,

Friends need time to be friends—time and places to giggle together, share secrets and talk.

share secrets and talk. This cannot happen if every moment is scheduled.

- *Consider developmental levels of children* when planning certain group activities. Since interests may tend to be similar, it is likely close friendships may then develop.

- *Help preserve school or neighborhood friendships* with children who are not in child care. It may be possible to work out ways for children to visit with their friends who are not in the program.

- *Watch children who are on the fringes, who seem to have no friends.* These children may fight, argue, or sulk, or they may stick with adults believing them to be safer, kinder, more accepting than peers. These children may play down their interests, ideas, and skills, just to be accepted, or they may desperately seek attention through inappropriate language, dress, and behaviors.

- *Recognize that friendships involve various **types** of relationships:* good friends, "best friends," cliques and groups, and finally, in adolescence, "pairs." In the process of the evolution of these friendships there are times of acceptance as well as times of exclusion. Social living, with its ups and downs, may not run smoothly.

ANXIOUS MOMENTS, FRIENDSHIPS AND DEVELOPMENTAL NEEDS

by Rich Scofield

(School-Age NOTES, December, 1996, reprinted with permission.)

Rich Scofield, Editor/Publisher of School-Age NOTES, returned to being a caregiver two afternoons a week [1995-96] in a SAC program. The following are some of his observations.

Two recent observations in the after school program point to the subtle, yet important influence programs can have if they are sensitive and knowledgeable about the developmental needs of school-agers and allow for that in programming.

The first is the observation of how SAC programs can facilitate friendships and the importance of those opportunities. The ability to make friends, to deal with the conflicts that inevitably arise to maintain those friendships are obviously important life-skills. What I've seen in the after school program is friendships that are consistent and long-lasting - they were inseparable friends at the beginning of second grade last year and that friendship is maintained this year. Two sets are boys and one set is girls. I know these third graders best because they were my "group" last year. There may be other friendships that don't get seen because one of them doesn't come to after school.

What the after school program provides is the opportunity for those friends to choose together what they want to do and to be together as long as they want. What I often see is non-specific play and interactions rather than joining in an art project together or playing soccer together. It is more the opportunity to interact together that is important. Dramatic play they invent and the "drama" of friendships and school life often serve as vehicles for that interaction. If they were in a program with more adult-led, adult-directed programming, they would not have the same freedom of time to talk and play as long as they wanted to. There are social and emotional needs that are being met by these opportunities.

The second observation that points to the subtle, yet important influence programs can have if they are sensitive and knowledgeable about the developmental needs of school-agers and allow for that in programming has to do with "fear of abandonment." In preschool programs we are more likely to see "anxious moments" in the late afternoon when children worry whether their parents are going to pick them up. But, the same phenomenon of "anxious moments" can occur with school-agers. Often, it is brought to our attention because they keep asking what time it is. But some children display more subtle behaviors. It may be that a child is wandering through the program not engaging in any activity. It may be that they are hanging around an adult being "clingy." The untrained adult may chastise the child for these behaviors, which adds to the child's emotional burden.

I saw one of the kindergartners appearing to be sad and couldn't get much of a response. The associate director, who has been there 10 years, pointed out that we had just had the clocks turned back from daylight savings time, so it now got dark earlier and the child was worried about getting picked up. The younger children thought the darker skies meant their parents were really late. [So much for my child development specialist degree!] The child was reassured her mother was coming and staff were able to comfort and redirect her appropriately. Having staff ratios that allow for one-to-one interactions and a programming philosophy that considers individual needs helped meet those emotional needs of that child brought on by "anxious moments."

Importance of Friendships

In *Critical Issues for Children*, by the editors of the *Brown University Child and Adolescent Behavior Letter*, the importance of school-age friendships is examined.

The article "Friendships Provide Important and Lasting Lessons" begins with Willard W. Hartup's idea that " Contrary to popular belief, the best indicator of how well your child will adapt as an adult is not school grades, but peer friendships."

Hartup says that friendships in this stage of development provide four basic functions that help children in their journey toward adolescence and adulthood. These functions are: *emotional resources* - for having fun, and for dealing with stressful situations or events; *cognitive resources* - for problem solving, and for acquiring knowledge; *social contexts* - for acquiring and enhancing basic social skills, such as communication, cooperation, and group entry; and *relationship models* - as a context in which to understand subsequent relationships.

As emotional resources, friendships provide children with the security to meet new people, explore new things and tackle new problems, says Hartup. Friends set the emotional stage for exploring the surroundings, and support the processes involved in just having fun.

In addition, several studies have indicated that friendships actually help to buffer children and adolescents from the adverse effects of negative or stressful events, such as family conflict, illness or school problems.

Children also provide cognitive resources for their friends. Friends teach one another in a variety of situations. Mimicking - in speech mannerisms or in clothing choice, for example - is common among childhood friends. Studies of peer collaboration indicate that friends who collaborate to complete a task show greater mastery over that task than non-friends who collaborate. Friends talk more, take more time to work out differences in their understanding of game rules, and compromise more readily than non-friends do. These conditions make friendships a unique context for learning, Hartup says.

Recognize that a part of becoming socialized is to assume a gender role

Children in school-age programs are working on this aspect of social development. Caregivers need to be responsive to children's efforts at gender or sex-role development.

- *Accept children's gender role choice* and allow opportunities for both girls and boys to participate in activities of their preference. Girls may enjoy woodworking as well as jewelry making, and boys may want information on cooking as well as car racing.

- *Be aware of the marked sex differences.* For instance, most boys at six to eight are highly physical, active, full of movement and energy. Often they are acting out what they think is expected of a male in the culture. Many girls are not as preoccupied with the stereotyped feminine role as boys are with the stereotyped masculine role. Girls also tend to be more task-oriented. They may openly enjoy male-associated activities such as building furniture or playing soccer.

- *Know that sex differences, sex roles, and sex consciousness have a large and changing impact on the social life of these children.* Styles of play and play interests may change. Adults can provide activities that will effect a comfortable transition from the period when children play mostly with members of their own sex, maybe even having "crushes" on members of the same sex, to the time when boys and girls discover each other. Time may be spent being giggly, teasing, and trying to attract the attention of the opposite sex, often with embarrassment as to what to do with the attention once it is gained.

Adults can also help children and youth with social language skills ("Will you go skating with me?"), so they can make conversation when they are finally standing next to someone they admire. Adults can offer varied experiences so school-agers have plenty of topics to talk about.

Plan for some privacy

School-agers, very involved in getting along with others, may also need ways to be alone. Every moment need not be spent in social interactions; often it is good to get away from constant group interaction. Some ways in which children may find privacy are through:

- separate rooms for different activities

- room arrangement — corners, areas, levels

- equipment — large boxes into which to crawl, equipment to climb into or hide under, cots, easy chairs, couches, mats, platforms, lofts

- flexible programming — time to be alone in solo activities such as reading, games, construction, or experimental projects.

Capitalize on the important social learnings

Moving from four walls of school to four walls of child care can be a limiting and isolating experience. Provide ways for kids to go beyond these settings. No single community setting will be the sole source for interesting experiences. School-agers enjoy exploring the community, especially with their friends, but they may still need adult companionship for safety, security, and sharing ideas.

Arrange visits to places and people that represent various aspects of community living. These persons may also be invited to visit the children whether in a home or center.

Arrange for children to be an active part of the community by assuming responsibilities and participating in community activities. Contacts can be made with such resources as recreation and school personnel, colleges, youth clubs, scouts, 4-H, Red Cross, "Y" programs, film departments, theaters, libraries, art centers, museums.

Approximate the "real world" in all ways possible

School-age children want real responsibilities. They need to know about functioning in the larger world into which they will move. The school-age program is a growing one with abundant stimulation and opportunity for ongoing change. When children provide and plan for their activities, they assume a good deal of responsibility. This will encourage them to be comfortable with various aspects of the society in which they live and in which they will take an increasingly active role.

School-agers plan, organize, implement, make decisions, and accept responsibilities. They may wish to try a simple form of government for the group. They may plan parties and visits, they may paint, they may make costumes for a play or signs for a car wash. They can decide how to spend earned money and can plan for and make celebration refreshments. The availability of friends of different races, ages, religions, and cultural origins can create a sense of community and cooperation, which is essential for an effective society.

Get a head start on the gang

Children who are members of gangs state that the gang provides a feeling of belonging and a feeling of importance, that the other gang members "really care about them," that they learn to take care of themselves and be loyal to others, that they become powerful. Gangs surely serve these purposes. Supervised and well-planned out-of-school programs, however, attain these same goals for kids without the violence and dangerous behavior characteristic of the gang culture.

Provide play and other smart things to do

Here are a few activities relating to social growth. You will think of more.

Adopt a family, grandparent, city block
Backyard camping
Board games
Conflict resolution games

Meeting with visitors
Interest clubs
Neighborhood parties
Writing pen pals
Sidewalk fund raisers
Group sports
Volunteer experiences in the community

Self-Care: What are the dangers to social development?

* If children are locked in their homes, how can they be part of a peer group?

* If children are unsupervised and on the streets, what prevents early delinquent acts?

* If children are home alone watching television or out on the streets, who become the role models?

WHAT ARE THEIR SELF NEEDS?

Becoming one's self

As children and youth mature, they develop into unique individuals. They express, through behavior, their own emotions, attitudes, values, and beliefs. All of this is evidence of the development of self. Uniqueness of persons is determined in part by their physical being and in part by the environment in which they are living and growing. It is also determined by certain personal factors such as the learning style, the knowledge gained, the conscience that has been developed, the level of independence achieved, and the feeling of self-worth.

Maturing children are becoming more independent. As the ideas to which they are exposed become more extensive, they can relate to the world in many new ways. They have an independent store of knowledge and thus some authority to make personal choices. This is a time when older children sort out their thoughts about what their life is and what it could or should be. It is a time when the recognition of what is and what could be may lead to planning and requests for help, or to frustration and turbulence.

Reaching out

As youth become increasingly independent of family, they begin to find some of the security they need from other sources. Security is derived from their own performance level and their uniquely developing attitudes and beliefs. They may become closely attached to a particular adult outside the family and attempt to imitate this person's lifestyle.

In becoming more independent, school-agers learn to cooperate with adults outside the family. This necessitates learning what is expected — the "rules of the game" — and developing a set of values to make choices. This may also lead to a realization that adults can be wrong and ignorant as well as wise and sensitive. Conscience and a sense of morality are shaped by these experiences.

Expressing feelings

Personal growth of the school-age child includes emotional development. Younger school-agers generally express feelings freely – joy, affection, jealousy, shyness – and some still cry easily. As they grow older and worry about the opinions of others, they don't express feelings as openly; they don't talk much about feelings, and they hide the tears.

Sometimes it is difficult for children to express their feelings because their feelings are not consistent. Frequently school-agers are not really sure what their feelings are or should be. For instance, they are very dependent on their parents for care and may believe that they should love their parents, but they may be angry or confused by parental behavior and wonder what "love" feelings are all about.

As school-agers are more frequently exposed to evaluative judgments made about them, they may begin to question their own self-worth. They become sensitive to criticism, ridicule, and the opinions of others, especially peers. Their worries become more evident and may be expressed in behavior if not in words. Staff can help children handle their worry or frustration by encouraging them to recognize the feelings and by assuring them of their own strengths. Through acceptance and affection, hurt youngsters find confidence.

Assuming responsibilities

An aspect of the development of values, conscience, and morality is the assumption of responsibility for one's own behavior such as making thoughtful decisions and judgments and getting along with others — an important outcome of quality out-of-school programs.

The increasing desire to be oneself within a group setting develops feelings of responsibility to others as well as to oneself. The drive for independence also becomes a challenge towards self-reliance and self-direction. Both the feeling of self and the drive for independence lead school-agers into the quest for responsibility and usefulness, guiding them toward social responsibility, self-confidence, and self-respect. They begin to assume leadership roles and develop a desire for active and responsible involvement in their social world.

Meeting success

To be successful, to feel a sense of a "success-identity," school-agers need experiences *with* success, accomplishment, good relationships, and satisfactions. They need to know they can explore ways to find their own satisfactions through people, skills, responsibilities, and questioning without fear. Failing children usually have known few successes, and they may continue to fail unless they are helped to develop positive feelings of self-worth and adequate means of coping with their problems. School-age programs, every day, can provide many kinds of successes — small successes, grand successes. Each success encourages the confidence that even when there are failures, success is reachable.

Magic, justice, morals, and conscience

The combination of imagination, feelings, and empathy, along with the school-ager's sense of justice, contribute to moral development. They now have a fascination with the "pretend." They may conjure up witches, enemies, ghosts, and scapegoats so they can express fear of "something" when they are not sure why their real fears exist. They feel the pain of rejection by a peer and can now imagine other people's feelings. They try to help other children over bad times. They develop a sense of justice, and the cries of "It's not fair" are often heard. They see the inconsistencies of adult behavior, and they often become a harsh judge of others as they believe what's right is right and what's wrong is wrong.

The development of a sense of right and wrong, honesty and thoughtfulness, is a complex and continuous process. The tall tales of the six- to nine-year-olds do not mean they cannot tell fantasy from reality; they can. It does not mean they are intentionally lying; they are not. Tall tales like "This fifty foot snake ran right down our steps today!" are fun, as an outlet for imaginative thinking. They can be accepted with gentle humor and interest. (Ask what the snake was wearing!) Tall tales may say, "Please pay attention to me."

Actual lying is usually a sign of fear of punishment. Harsh punishment breeds lies. Children who must lie are often frightened of what will happen if they tell the truth. While they recognize lying as a "major crime," they may need to use lying as self-protection. But "magic" thinking, as well as literal and judgmental thinking, can help avoid guilt, because school-agers can now "justify" a misdeed. "You said not to say that word, but I heard you say it" or "We're not supposed to run – I was jogging!"

Stealing is also related to the development of conscience. Some children may do a certain amount of experimental stealing because they have seen others do it, or they may want to lure friends with stolen candy, clothing, or a new toy. Most children know this is wrong and as their own values and controls take over, stealing does not continue. Other children steal in order to find sources of comfort in material things when their own lives are not happy. They usually do not know why they steal. They may be insecure and angry and have problems acting on what is right. These youngsters may need attention, and even the punishment gains them that attention. They also may need teaching or therapy. Still other children may come from a gang culture, and to form identity with and be accepted by peers, they behave as the gang members do and so may steal. They are doing what is "right" in terms of the gang and can thereby avoid feelings of guilt.

The self and the future

As children and youth grow toward maturity, their feelings about their own strengths may determine what they do with their future. They may have strong abilities, but a poor opinion of themselves can prevent their recognition of these abilities. They may then drop out of school because of problems handling the pressures. They may so fear competition that they avoid school requirements, social contacts, or jobs that require skills they are unsure about. If school-agers feel secure with themselves, they can resist pressures from others to try drugs, sex, or even to go out for football when they prefer drama club. They can find the strength to resist values that are not based on good reason and humane thinking.

As school-agers feel secure with themselves, they begin to define themselves as part of the worlds of their family, friends, and community – but as separate, identifiable, human beings.

MEETING SELF NEEDS - WHAT CAN ADULTS DO?

Recognize that children are trying to discover themselves

Children's emotional reactions and sense of self come from the way they think others see them and from their actual feelings of competence and accomplishment. They are beginning to see who they might be and how they can be themselves, independent of their parents. As they play they are reaching into themselves and into their own society: the world of childhood.

Acknowledge the rites and rituals of childhood

Through interactions with their friends, school-agers find a testing ground for their uniqueness and worth as human beings. Staff acknowledge the rites and rituals of childhood and make useful interpretations of their meanings:

- the songs and chants: repetitive, some universal, some unique variations in different communities— but a symbol of belonging

- the collections: from incredible junk to carefully organized valuables — the beginning efforts of ordering the world

- the cliques and special groups: with the glory that comes in acceptance and the tragic moments that accompany rejection – the ability to present a society in miniature for children so they can begin to feel who they are and how they function

Provide for the growth of responsible independence

Maturity and responsible independence are the bases for democratic societies, communities in which citizens take responsibility for their own well-being and participate actively in meeting the needs of others. Responsible behavior and self-control develop when activities allow children to act on their ideas and when adults genuinely care about each child's strivings toward maturity. School-age programs establish a climate in which children are confident in assuming the responsible decisions that benefit their own lives and the lives of those around them. Responsibilities offered to children should be age-appropriate and attainable. In a quality program every school-ager is helped to feel like a responsible, effective individual.

Children with high self-esteem, especially as they approach pre-adolescence, are more interested in helping others and relating to broad social issues. They are not afraid to express or evaluate their ideas. They develop convictions and may act on them. Staff help all children recognize their own abilities, trust themselves, and trust relationships with others as they function within the freedom of the school-age program as well as their communities.

Recognize the school-agers' trial-and-many-error approach to solving problems

Although adults are available for support and help when needed, the child's growing sense of judgment and responsibility requires an environment in which:

- adults accept that through personal styles of behavior and communication children do the best they know how in meeting their needs;

- activities are presented without the adults dictating how they must be pursued;

- opinions and feelings can be expressed, and adults can be trusted to keep confidences and help children sort out their concerns

- guidance is offered, but it is not overwhelming – it's positive but not punitive, and it involves trusting children to gain more self-control over their own actions;

- trial-and-error is a learning experience that leads to the building of trust in one's own abilities to make responsible decisions, trust that helps children choose avenues to success;

- acceptance and confidence are always present in the form of "I'm glad you're here, and I know you will find things to do which you enjoy and do well."

Trial-and-error is a learning experience that leads to the building of trust in one's own abilities.

Nurture the strengths

It is easy to recognize the skills, talents, and interests of younger school-agers — they are good at drawing, sports, or playing the piano. They may be loving and loved, happy and humorous.

It is also essential to nurture the strengths of the older children, the pre-adolescents. They have particular qualities that should not go unnoticed amid their social desires for nonconformity. To encourage a strong sense of self and a hopeful future, caregivers can build on the positive qualities children have as they grow toward adolescence:

- The sense of altruism — wanting to help others, wanting to cure social injustice, and willingness to work to this end

- The desire to tackle problems — the motivation to display competence and do things well

- The respect for honesty — the awareness of people's just or trustworthy behaviors

- The sense of idealism — the belief that situations can be mastered, cured, made better

Provide play and other smart things to do

Here are a few activities relating to self-development needs. You will think of more.

Community service projects

Doing "nothing" together

Dramatic play

Family get-togethers

Pet care

Informal discussions

Self-affirmation games

Self-expressive activities — art, photography, poetry, writing,

Dramatic productions, dance

Self-Care: What are the dangers to self-development?

* How are the good feelings of strength and success developed when children are alone, threatened, bored, and fearful or when parent expectations about self-care exceed a child's level of ability?

* Who is there to applaud when a new skill is mastered?

* How can feelings of self-worth compete with feelings of desertion, loneliness, and alienation?

WHAT ARE THEIR INTELLECTUAL NEEDS?

A focus on reality

The school-age years are a time of intellectual growth — cognitive growth — and children and youth enjoy opportunities to practice the intellectual skills that accompany their cognitive development.

Many school-agers express a very serious, earnest attitude toward working and learning. They are focusing on reality —what they see, know about, can do. They are excited about creating things, making things work, discovering things. New knowledge becomes integrated with the familiar so ideas are understandable. The younger children deal best with concrete ideas and firsthand experiences. They gradually develop the capacity for abstract thought.

The use of skills

Attention span and an increased understanding of time make it easier for school-age children to plan ahead and act on their own in carrying out ideas. While there are wide ranges in abilities, children use the intellectual skills introduced in school, such as reading, writing and calculating, in practical ways: writing play scripts, playing games, using computers. The thousands of concepts being presented for learning need sufficient basis in experience to be understandable and familiar to the child. The challenges of problem solving, incorporation of new ideas, and curiosity are all important and do not stop when a child leaves school. In fact, the leisurely, noncompetitive climate of out-of-school settings is extremely appropriate for individual development in these areas and for relating the skills to personal interests.

When learning to think for themselves, many children attempt tasks still beyond their ability. But improving skills leads to a sense of mastery. An activity may be pursued over a long period of time, and finished products become more and more important to school-agers. They become ever more critical of their own performance and are sensitive to criticism.

Building on curiosity

These children are explorers, investigating the world and all its properties, making decisions, solving problems and puzzles, asking questions, and finding out how things work. They love new information, interesting facts, and ideas to ponder. They become familiar with the tools, symbols, language, and values of their particular culture and peer group.

Curiosity is the stimulus for all learning. When children's curiosity has been ignored or frustrated, they may behave in ways which inhibit intellectual growth — frantically rushing from one idea or activity to another, not stopping to understand what they are trying to learn. Or they may simply stop asking questions or stop trying to find answers to anything.

Knowledge plus know-how

Not only do school-agers enjoy knowing more about life around them, they also want to "solve" life's problems — finding creative ways to accomplish tasks and to get things to work. By the ages of nine or ten they enjoy selecting a task and seeing it through to completion. This reflects their developing sense of industry which has started by about the ages of seven or eight and has now intensified. They practice new skills by showing them off to people; they want others to be aware of their energy and their ability to think about the world around them in unusual ways. By preadolescence, however, the need for acceptance through conformity may lead some school-agers to play down their own ideas if they fear they are unacceptable to their peers.

And a sense of humor

School-agers are intrigued with magic, riddles, jokes, and teasing. Increased skills with language enable them to play with words and their varieties of meanings, to invent and recite puns, to tease and surprise.

Humor is actually an intellectual process, and its quality depends on the level of children's thinking, their vocabulary, experiences with imagination, and values of their particular culture. Humor has certain common characteristics that appeal to youngsters: the element of fun, the surprise ending, the nonsense and absurdity, and the appeal to peers and popularity. They are aware of the interplay between reality and fantasy. What is real? What is make-believe? They want everyone to know *they* know the difference.

Who's doing all that talking?

Younger school-agers understand more language than they are able to use effectively. So they may use verbal language inappropriately or aggressively. Most of their talking is about real subjects, though sprinkled with some make-believe and playful use of words. Older children may use words just to shock adults and test their reactions. They may use these words among themselves. The children who speak English as a second language may not understand the appropriate use of words, or as they learn more English, they may also teach the other children words and phrases, sometimes slang phrases, in their language of origin. Their language development reflects their ability to think more abstractly about all aspects of their lives, and being able to express ideas in words becomes more important. Conversation should be encouraged. And when children are with friends, there is usually plenty of talking.

MEETING INTELLECTUAL NEEDS — WHAT CAN ADULTS DO?

Recognize that intellectual development is not limited to the time spent in school

In a quality program, staff are responsive to intellectual needs. The out-of-school program may actually be more conducive to certain academic pursuits than the school setting. There may be more time, less pressure, less competition, fewer worries of evaluative judgments.

There are ample opportunities for language development: listening to and discussing a story or making up one, reading a book of one's own choice, using writing skills in functional ways, using a computer, listening to records or tapes, and, above all, talking with friends and adults.

There are opportunities for cognitive thinking and curiosity as children face and solve problems — social, mechanical, mathematical — as children explore materials and ideas, ask questions, find answers.

Recognize that intellectual development is not limited to times with adults, friends, or activities

There may be times when a child really wishes to be alone: perhaps just to tinker with a new project or think about something. Quiet moments alone sometimes allow a person to gain new perspectives, discover new solutions, and have great thoughts!

Encourage time for children to develop individual interests and skills

This is an age when special skills are emerging. Some kids are already showing a particular proficiency at sports, music, writing, art, or dancing. Sometimes there is intense interest in animals; some children are very interested in machinery. Since the school day has been multi-interest and multi-skill oriented, there has often been only token time for an individual focus. Now a child can pursue a specific interest. This might include such activities as individual or group music lessons, drawing or ceramics, an organized sports program, or a puppetry workshop.

Although the out-of-school program is relaxing and fun and not a continuation of the school day, a flexible program provides opportunity for children to complete any school homework if they wish. They may want to get away from schoolwork for a while or they may want to complete homework and then enjoy other activities. Sometimes it's fun to do homework along with friends; sometimes a quiet spot alone is needed.

Provide space, materials, and activities to support interest and curiosity

Provide opportunities for children to do things and work in ways not usual in school. Much of children's success will come because they can select what they want to do and decline what they do not like. Activities such as building a clubhouse, repairing a bike, or producing a musical all involve tasks that appeal to their sense of industry and involve selection, participation and completion. Children are neither judged nor evaluated on the quality of their performance, but rather are encouraged to try, to explore, and to expand their interests.

- Develop a library with many kinds of books, magazines, and other media. Children may share their own books as well as books they borrow from school and libraries. Books may be obtained in bulk from the local public library, and children can make their own selection.

- Provide materials to construct with, make discoveries with, change around, take apart, put together. Every element of change challenges powers of thinking.

- Plan display space for children to use for items of interest — their art work, "my sister's birth announcement," news items, etc. Children can be in charge of this space with help from adults.

There may be times when a child really wishes to be alone— quiet moments alone allow a child to gain new perspectives.

- Select appropriate television programs or video tapes. Sometimes television may be used for rest and relaxation, other times as a basis for discussions and follow-through activities. Adults help children develop selectivity regarding the amount and kind of television to view.

- Watch local newspapers and community calendars for announcements about auditions, performances, band concerts, motion pictures, fairs, exhibits, demonstrations and lectures, and nature tours. Many of these events may be suitable for school-agers.

- Above all, remember that a growing, inquiring mind reaches beyond the location of the program setting. Plan for trips and community experiences that expose youngsters to new ideas, new places, new information.

Be a believer in humor

Good humor grows in a comfortable environment where joy is evident and children are relaxed, where children are able to be imaginative and adults are fun. School-agers who are not afraid of being hurt or embarrassed are free to experiment with the surprise elements of humor. Humor can transform an atmosphere of stress or anger or boredom. Children perk up when adults tell a funny story and share a laugh. Humor helps make life *fun*, lighten a tense situation and pull a group together with a good laugh. Humor, however, should never slip into hurtful teasing, embarrassing, or ridiculing anyone.

Be on hand to support growth in ways of thinking

As children know more, they will question more. New ideas will spring from current knowledge. As you expand children's experiences, they are given a base for increased intellectual thinking. The more they know, the more they will want to know.

You can enrich school-agers' experiences by becoming more knowledgeable and sharing your own hobbies and interests with the children. You can be there for children to come to for encouragement, interpretation, and assistance.

Provide play and other smart things to do

Here are a few activities relating to intellectual development. You will think of more.

animal care

archaeological digs

block construction

collections

community trips

computers

doll house construction

electronic games

interest clubs

model building kits

nature trail

tutoring peers

visitors

Self-Care: What are the dangers to intellectual development?

* Who can extend a child's knowledge?

* Who is there to answer questions?

* Will preoccupation with personal safety interfere with learning?

* What are the learning experiences?

    • What kind?

    • Who knows?

    • Who seems to care?

Children Who Need Special Care

CHILDREN WHO HAVE SPECIAL NEEDS

The effective school-age program treats each child who walks in the door as special. Each child is unique. The term "children with special needs," however, is used in this text to describe children who, because of developmental, physical, emotional, behavioral, or medical conditions, may require specific care such as additional supervision, specific methods of treatment, supportive equipment, or modifications to a program.

Under the Americans with Disabilities Act (ADA) a disabled child is more specifically defined as one whose physical or mental impairment substantially limits that child from caring for her or himself, from performing manual tasks or from any other "major life activity" such as walking, seeing, hearing, speaking, breathing, or learning.[4]

There are developmental or medical conditions that may require neither personal restrictions nor any adaptations of the program but merely the staff's awareness of the condition: for children who have asthma, seizures, are mildly affected by cerebral palsy or mental retardation, or have a terminal illness. There are other conditions — severe heart conditions, blindness, amputations — which may prevent a child from participating in particular aspects of the program, such as active sports. Other conditions may require program, nutritional, or equipment adaptations: visual impairment, allergies, severe mental retardation, orthopedic or learning disabilities, chronic illness, neurological and behavioral problems, severe emotional disturbance, and multiple disabilities. A one-to-one adult-child ratio may be required for children with a severe behavior disturbance or acute physical disability.

A child's medical or psychiatric diagnosis is useful but it reveals only one aspect of the whole child. Without knowing all the implications of a given disability or birth defect or emotional state of being, staff should treat each boy or girl as a feeling, sensitive human being and then determine any special needs and provide for those needs. Physicians, educators, therapists, and other specialists seen by children on a regular basis are responsible for determining medical, educational, physical, and psychological progress. School-age program providers have a different, although related, charge to give children an environment in which to enjoy themselves, make friends, relax, try out new activities, and to grow in the belief that they have the capacity to function in their world.[5]

Human needs and special needs

The human needs for a personal identity, for good relationships, and for a sense of power also apply to school-agers with special needs. In addition to the basic developmental and human needs, youngsters bring their own personal life experiences. A specific developmental condition may or may not have contributed to their present personality. As in the case of every person, there are many contributing factors, and staff must look beyond the label, diagnosis, wheelchair, thick-rimmed glasses, or confusing behavior, to see each child's personality, ideas, feelings, and human needs.

Personal identity and children with special needs

Here is a perfect chance to help children have good feelings about themselves, to thrive in a joyful setting. There are no pressures to perform. The experience is not academic, therapeutic, or competitive. It is a chance to participate in activities that may not be offered during school hours, such as theater, dance, cooking, outdoors exploration, and field trips. It is a time to make friends and to be close to an admired adult. It is a time to dabble in, try out, or become proficient in activities that are easy for the nondisabled yet more of a challenge for the disabled. It may take more time, energy, and patience to give disabled children a try at experiences, but the program can make an important contribution to the development of children's good feelings resulting from being able to participate in their own way, in their own time, and at their own level.

Relationships with these children involve extra work, time, and imagination to expand their sense of their own identity, but as with all children staff begins by understanding each child's sense of self, home life, school life, friends, pets, and curiosity. Staff learn what children can do and what they would like to do, what they can do alone and what they need help with. Children often need help in recognizing their abilities. "Marcy, you play this game so well. Please sit with Anne and show her how to play it." "Bobby can't hear us. Will you show him where to go?" Staff can encourage children to feel as comfortable as possible with their disabilities and to feel comfortable in accepting assistance. "Here, try this walker so you can reach the easel." "I know you speak slowly, so take lots of time." "When you get so angry, come over to me, and I'll see how I can help." "It's hard to shuffle those cards. Ask Polly if she can finish the game with you."

It is good to let nondisabled children handle special equipment such as canes, walkers, or head protectors in order to feel comfortable with them. The environment can also include stories, videos, films, or pictures which show persons with special needs, so the children, both disabled and nondisabled, view themselves as part of the wide variation of being human.

School-age care encourages a sense of self by exposing children to many experiences so that they are comfortable in this busy, complex world. It helps them attain a realistic sense of self as they become at ease with their own particular strengths and capabilities. It expands their interests so they can achieve competence and success in a variety of activities through which to build future skills.

MANAGING THE DIFFICULT CHILD

10 Tips for Working with Children with Attention Deficit Disorder

(School-Age NOTES, July 1994, reprinted with permission)

Attention Deficit Disorder (ADD) and Attention Deficit Hyperactivity Disorder (ADHD) are two neurological syndromes whose symptoms remind people of "the difficult child." Many staff in SAC programs have difficulty working with children with ADD and ADHD. Not all children identified as having ADD are hyperactive. {ADD and ADHD has to be diagnosed by a medical doctor with ADD expertise.}

Some of the characteristics of children with ADD or ADHD are: -easily distracted; -doesn't finish projects or activities; -hears but doesn't seem to listen; -difficulty adjusting to new situations and changes in routine; -speaks out and acts out impulsively; -disrupts other children; -often talks excessively; -has difficulty playing quietly; -often loses things such as notes from parents, lunch money, homework; -disorganized, often cubby or locker a jumbled mess; -daydreams, "spacey;" -often engages in physically dangerous activities without considering possible consequences; -fidgets, wiggles and drums fingers or taps feet.

The following are tips and strategies for managing children with ADD or ADHD. Many of these tips are also good practices for working with all school-agers.

1. **Kids with ADD need structure**. They need external structure since they have difficulty structuring internally. Make lists. Create prompts and reminders. Do previews. Provide repetition. Give direction. Set limits and boundaries.

2. **Waiting is difficult**. Engage them in activities which constantly involves with no waiting such as dodgeball rather than kickball.

3. **Help children make their own schedule** of what they are interested in doing each afternoon and what they are suppose to do (homework). Scheduling with agreed upon prompts and reminders helps avoid one of the hallmarks of ADD: procrastination.

4. **Set limits, boundaries**. This is containing and soothing, not punitive. Do it **consistently**, **predictably**, **promptly**, and **plainly**. Don't get into complicated arguments which are just diversions.

5. **Provide an escape-valve to help gain control** and "save face." This may be saying they are going to the directors office; going out in the hall; or going to a special designated place in the cafeteria that has clay to pound and drawing and writing materials available to express their feelings.

6. **Break down large tasks into small tasks**. Helping to "clean-up" at the end of the day may seem overwhelming. Finding all the LEGO materials and putting them in the box is manageable.

7. **Encourage physical exercise**. Vigorous exercise helps work off excess energy and focus attention. It stimulates certain hormones and neurochemicals that are beneficial.

8. **Prepare for free time** with lists of suggested activities to help structure the ADD child's choices. Sudden unstructured time can be overstimulating.

9. **Repeat**, Repeat, Repeat.

10. **Look for and appreciate their specialness**. Children with ADD are often more sensitive, gifted, and talented than they seem. They are full of creativity, play, spontaneity, and good cheer. They tend to be generous of spirit and glad to help out. They usually have a "special something" that enriches the opportunities with them.

RESOURCES:

I Can't Sit Still: Educating and Affirming Inattentive and Hyperactive Children by Dorothy Davies Johnson, M.D., 1992, available from School-Age NOTES $17.95 (15.95 for subscribers) plus $3.50 S&H.

Driven to Distraction: Recognizing and Coping with Attention Deficit Disorder from Childhood through Adulthood by Edward M. Hallowell, M.D. and John J. Ratey, M.D., 1994, available at local bookstores $23.

PAY ATTENTION!!! Answers to Common Questions About the Diagnosis and Treatment of Attention Deficit Disorder by Craig B. Liden, M.D., Jane Zalenski, and Roberta Newman, available from Transact Health Systems for $15 plus $2 S&H send to: Atten: Sharon, Transact Health Systems, 2566 Haymaker Rd., Monroeville PA 15146.

Good relationships and children with special needs

School-agers with special needs may look differently, act differently, and think differently from other children. Staff need to examine their own feelings and reactions, because all children must feel accepted if they are to accept themselves. The accepting environment helps children not only in accepting themselves but also in accepting one another.

Some of these children have difficulty in developing close connections with others. Relationships within families may revolve around much concern on the part of the parent and dependence on the part of the child. Children may be keenly aware of being different from other family members. Relationships with teachers, doctors, and therapists may be so concentrated on the child's differences that it gets in the way of the normal give-and-take of adult-child relations.

Many of these children have had limited contact with adults other than family and the professionals responsible for their welfare. Staff can help broaden their understanding of the variety of adult personalities and roles in society, in both cultural and physical diversity. Expanded social relationships with other adults can be encouraged by visitors and trips.

Relationships with friends are particularly challenging. The desire to have and be a best friend and the feeling of being part of a group become increasingly important to school-agers. Many children with disabilities can not easily reach out independently for friendship, and so here is a significant challenge. Staff can help in much the same way as with nondisabled children by creating activities that require two children to work together in handling errands or responsibilities, by organizing children in small continuous groupings to create a family feeling, by providing spaces for even smaller groups to meet in and converse and hang out, by recognizing age and sex differences in choice of friends, by working with families to cement friendships through home visits, and by watching for children who share interests and abilities.

In addition, because of physical, emotional, medical, or developmental differences, staff may need to push wheelchairs over to the cozy, quiet, friendly spaces; a standing arrangement may be needed so a child can stand with a friend at a game table. Children can be encouraged to help each other with braces, crutches, writing, reading, running, and catching. The focus is on the children's personalities involved in the daily relationships. In encouraging friendships you, too, become a friend.

Personal power and children with special needs

"When will someone come?" "I can't keep up with everyone else!" "I want it, but I can't even pick it up!" These are familiar comments from many school-agers with disabilities.

We understand the feelings, because all of us have had them at one time or another, but most of us are agile, active, and healthy enough to act upon our wishes. Many youngsters with disabilities do not believe they have the power to take control of their lives. In many ways these children truly may be dependent — physically, socially, emotionally, or intellectually — yet the human drive for independence, autonomy, and control is still there.

Probably the easiest way to support children's need for control is to let them make their own choices. Choice by choice, one small taste of independence followed by another, they learn that they have power. "Wheel yourself over to whatever you want to do today." "Frank needs someone to hold the tools for him. Can you do that?" "Let's decide where to go tomorrow — the bowling alley, the mall, or the pool." As with anyone, children with special needs want to feel the power of control, and there may be many aspects of their lives that require both control and self-control: dietary restrictions to follow, physical limitations to overcome, behavior patterns to control, and cognitive problems to master.

Besides their special needs, staff should never lose sight of the usual developmental characteristics, especially in a multi-age setting. As children grow older, they expect to be more in control, more in power. "We're in charge of this now!" "No little kids allowed!" "You can't do that till you're in the fifth grade!" Although some children lack normal physical, mental, or behavioral skills, staff can recognize this need for power by giving older children responsibilities simply because they are older, regardless of the disability. "Only sixth graders will make the pizza today." "All the fourteen-year-olds are in charge of next week's video." Each such experience gives these young persons power and helps them prepare for the independence and control that they will need as they grow up.

Family of children and youth with special needs

Out-of-school care for children with special needs has not, historically, been a priority. Most of the children have not been home alone, because parents, recognizing the risks of self-care, have stayed home with their children. As a result, there have been few child care options for them. Over the years they have expressed these facts to child care advocates and legislative bodies, so programs are now developing for these boys and girls, and training is being designed for persons who wish to work with them. As programs respond to children with special needs, their parents, who heretofore have been overwhelmed with medical and educational considerations, are now more readily able to seek employment. For some families periodic respite care, in small blocks of time, is all that is needed, so a parent can leave home to attend to necessary responsibilities. For other families, part-time or full-time care may prevent placement of the child in a residential facility, an extremely expensive proposition for most families.

Whatever the child care arrangement, there is a close relationship between family and caregiver. Parents will make their needs known to policy makers, schools, and advocacy groups, as well as to the provider of the care. Staff may need a lot of help from families in order to understand and respond appropriately to each child with regard to individual routines, likes and dislikes, skills mastered, toileting and eating habits, interests, fears, curiosities, and medical procedures.

While families help staff learn about their children, caregivers can help the family by clarifying their role as nurturing, protecting, and recreational. Caregivers should also recognize the range of feelings experienced by these parents: uncertainty, helplessness, isolation, fear, exhaustion, guilt, anger, and depression, as well as acceptance, hope, and competence.

Getting information and training

Many families are now well acquainted with their child's illness or disability. They are able to explain medical and nonmedical procedures, nutritional needs and feeding techniques, and emergency care. When a family does not seem skilled in the care of the child, it is essential to seek assistance from others such as the child's doctor, public health personnel, child psychiatrists and specialists at mental health facilities, local medical centers, and respite-care associations, as well as the care center's medical consultant. In addition, several community groups are specifically related to children with particular special needs: United Cerebral Palsy, the Association for Children with Hearing Disabilities, the Council for Exceptional Children, and the Association for Retarded Children. Further information concerning disabilities is available from the personnel in colleges, universities, medical schools, libraries, and departments of special education and therapeutic recreation. Training specifically related to children with special needs in child care situations is currently developing in a variety of training institutions. Check your local community, and if none is available, advocate for this training.

Adapting your program

Again, parents know their children's interests, hobbies, and friends. Departments and organizations such as the local child care regulatory agency, public school special education department, recreation departments, and scouting can contribute ideas. Knowing each child's characteristics allows program modifications that let every child participate in the child care activities to the greatest extent possible. For instance, it may take more time to start activities, participate, and clean up. Many of these children move slowly, lose attention, and need extra adult help. It may take more time to eat, use the bathroom, and move from place to place.

With modifications in time, space, and procedures, an out-of-school program can provide experiences for all children to enjoy in their particular environments and cultures, even when it takes extra time, hands, and imagination. Familiar activities include snow play, gardening, cooking, painting, and carpentry. More ambitious ventures are boating, job-skill practice, fishing, bowling, pottery making, shopping, animal care, and swimming. In any event, these children should be involved in planning and discussion. Community experiences are particularly appropriate. Many of these boys and girls, particularly those who cannot go places on their own, will benefit from the recreational, social, and leisure time experiences that a community offers.

Providing adequate staff

We have discussed the necessity of appropriate training as well as the characteristics of successful staff for all school-age children. Staffing for children with special needs requires the same qualities: knowledge, flexibility, acceptance, optimism, and trustworthiness. In addition, program providers must have a sincere interest in working with these children and knowledge for handling special procedures. Successful care necessitates close supervision and a low adult-child ratio, perhaps even one adult per child. The ratios may vary depending on the activity.

For example, one-to-one for carpentry or swimming, one-to-five or -six for an art experience, one-to-ten or -fifteen for singing or group times.

There also must be enough staff if a one-to-one situation is required for toileting, eating, changing clothes, or walking, to assure the other children are appropriately supervised. Staff may be supplemented with additional adults at certain times of the day or periodically as needed. They may be part-time employees, regular volunteers from the community, parents, grandparents, siblings, students, or student teachers. Adults who have disabilities working with the program may be excellent role-models for the children.

Assuring that physical facilities are appropriate

Space: Do activity areas accommodate wheelchairs? Can children move around free from all hazards? Is there room for specialized equipment? Can staff and children move out easily in case of emergencies? Is the bathroom easily accessible?

Visibility: Can adults see the children? Can children see the adults? Are activity choices visible to children so they can make their own decisions?

Equipment: Is specialized equipment available so every child can participate in activities, equipment such as standing-boxes, guardrails, handrails, special feeding equipment, means for resting, sleeping, mobility and transportation?

Including children with special needs

We recommend including children and youth with special needs with other youngsters whenever possible, because this reflects the reality of the broader world. Such group activities require trained and sensitive staff and appropriate program planning. There may be times, however, when separation is appropriate.

Advantages of inclusion for all children

- Becoming comfortable and developing friendships with people who are different
- Sharing the variety of childhood experiences
- Accepting and giving help when needed
- Remaining together with one's siblings
- Recognizing the similarities of all people

Advantages of separation for children with special needs

- Closer supervision, more protection and attention
- Specially trained staff
- Fewer social problems like being teased, pushed aside, labeled, or harassed by other children
- More ease with others who have special problems or the same means of locomotion or communication
- Less discomfort in communicating personal needs
- Activities specifically geared to each child
- Development of empathy for others who have disabilities

Successful care of children with special needs necessitates close supervision and a low adult-child ratio.

Home care or center care?

This decision depends on the individual children, family circumstances, and neighborhood and community resources. Training should develop for providers in both settings and systems of information and referral are needed to help families locate programs that include children with special needs.

Advantages of home care

- Proximity to neighborhood friends
- One placement regardless of age
- Reduced tension and competition as a result of a wide age range
- Close supervision and attention
- Potential for personal attention to unusual behaviors and disabilities

Advantages of center care

- Likelihood of other children of the same age
- Large numbers of children for participation in activities
- Possibility of a variety of appropriate adaptive equipment
- Probability of trained providers
- Wider variety of activities

CHILDREN WHO ARE ILL

Care of sick children

How ill? How contagious? Can staff respond to an individual child who is ill, as well as to the rest of the group? Should children really be home when they are ill and feeling awful? Can trained adults take care of children in their own homes? Could children attend a separate get-well unit in their regular school-age program? What policies and licensing requirements are appropriate for care of sick children? Can consortiums be developed through which employers share the cost of emergency care? Can sick-child school-age programs meet the human needs of the child who is mildly ill and cannot be in school? All of these questions must be addressed by child care advocates, physicians, child-life specialists, and child care providers, as care for sick children becomes a part of the child care system.[6]

Care of sick children — whether in-home, family, or center care — is usually for youngsters who are mildly ill or recuperating from illness or surgery and who are unable to return to school. Some programs accept children with communicable diseases if isolation areas are available (most periods of contagion are early in the illness, before and after the first symptoms appear). A child usually should see a physician before returning to any child care program.

Before sick children are enrolled in care, it must be determined whether they could remain in their usual programs. What is the risk of contagion? Can the regular program meet the medical and comfort needs of an ill child? Will the needs of a sick child reduce the quality of care for the other kids in the group? The answers to the questions depend on individual situations and on whether state laws permit the inclusion of sick children in regular school-age programs.

Sick-child care can operate as an exclusive service for ill children or as a complement to other child care services. Programs are currently developing as in-home, family, and center-based care. Some are created at hospital pediatric units, others at parent work sites. Services may be connected to an employer sick-child network to which parents have access if a child becomes ill. Satellite centers for sick children may become connected to one or more family or center programs.

Certain criteria should be evident regardless of the form of service: a physically comfortable environment, trained and competent staff, appropriate activities, familiar setting, effective sanitation, nutrition, medical and emergency procedures, and supporting consultative resources.

When a child gets sick during the day

When children become ill or are injured during the regular child care program period, they need attention, rest, privacy, and medical treatment until their families arrive or emergency transportation is provided to a medical facility. Staff in school-age programs must be able to recognize children who need immediate medical attention and also must be familiar with the policies regarding care for mildly ill children. Policies relating to ill children should be written and shared with families. Staff must also be familiar with the procedures for reporting communicable diseases.

When privacy or isolation is required, children should be within sight and hearing of adults. Although kids shouldn't be required to participate in activities if they don't feel well enough, they should not be separated from the group with nothing to do if they feel well enough for quiet play, games, or companionship.

Isolation

While separation from a group, either within a regular program or a program for sick children, may be advisable for the child's comfort or because of contagion, behavior, or a special medical need, the child should never view it as punishment. Also, no one should ever be isolated from the others and then "forgotten." Sick school-agers need attention. They may want things to do or someone to talk with, and they are often anxious or frightened about their condition.

Family communication

Generally families visit a program with their children in advance so that it is a familiar place. They preregister and provide their children's medical history and immunization records. Written permission is provided for administering medication. Parents receive the written policies for admission, which identify the types of symptoms, illness, or injuries that the program can include or must exclude, along with specifying the staff's ability to monitor particular conditions.

Families share information about any restrictions of mobility, special diet, rest, allergies, or the need to be kept indoors. They should also share information such as their children's habits, tastes, interests, and fears.

Families are encouraged to be available for consultation and are assured that they will be notified should their children's conditions change during the day. They should feel free to call to check on how their child is feeling or to talk with their child. If a child becomes too sick to be cared for in the program, families are, of course, notified to pick up their child and are advised to seek medical treatment.

Staff keep written reports documenting each child's condition, medication, nutrition, and activities throughout the day. This may be given to the family at the end of the day with a copy maintained in the program's file.

Staffing

Child-life specialists are especially trained and certified through the Association for the Care of Children's Health to work with children in health-care settings. They may be selected to work with children in family, in-home, center, or hospital settings.

Child care providers who wish to work with sick school-agers should receive training that includes the same components necessary for anyone working with school-agers, such as child development, nurturing skills, and planning activities. In addition, they must be knowledgeable about components relating to children who are ill:

- the emotional responses of individual children to illness, medical treatment, and care;

- minimizing anxiety and stress and maximizing feelings of independence and competence;

- procedures for infection control;

- first aid and cardiopulmonary resuscitation (CPR);

- administration of medication;

- recognition and documentation of symptoms of illness and of child abuse;

- emergency procedures;

- knowledge of how to deal with the questions and concerns of children about their bodies, medical procedures, hospitalization, separation from family, etc.

Staff must have access to immediate medical help, consultation, and emergency care. At least two staff members should be present at all times, and staff-child ratios need should be carefully established and maintained. The regulations for the state of Delaware in addressing care for sick children require the following staff-child ratios:

> 0-12 months: 1 to 3
>
> 1-4 years: 1 to 4
>
> 4 years and up: 1 to 5

Equipment and activities

When kids are ill, they become less physically active, but if they are simply recovering from illness or injury or surgery, they may want to do everything as usual. They should be offered the same choices of activities available in any good school-age program: cooking, reading, games, opportunities to catch up on school work, music, crafts, props for role play, viewing and listening materials, and possibly some outdoor activities. The choice is important because unless school-agers are very ill, they still need some control by choosing activities, since being sick often implies losing some personal control.

There are a few special things to consider in designing the environment and the activity program for sick children:

- sufficient space (30-50 square feet per child is recommended by the American Academy of Pediatrics);

- surfaces that can be easily sanitized to prevent the spread of infection;

- areas for comfort, soft places for relaxing;

- availability of beds, blankets, and pillows for resting or napping without disturbance;

- activities that can be done at bedside as well as the usual age-appropriate experiences;

- a balance of child-chosen activities, adult-planned experiences, and quiet and moderately active tasks appropriate to the wide range of ages and physical conditions;

- provision of lots of fluids and small amounts of food throughout the day, since heavy meals may be hard to digest;

- experiences of being helped and cared for as well as opportunities for helping and caring for other ill children in the group and for pets and plants.

One ten-year-old stated as he left a program for sick children, "I feel okay now. Just a little play here and a great lunch made me feel good again. But I'd really like to come back tomorrow." A program like the one he described can help mildly ill children understand that they are well cared for even when they cannot stay home.

Worries and Concerns: What's on Children's Minds?

If we expect a school-age program to fit the child, we need to know what children are thinking. Sometimes that is difficult. School-agers usually don't talk much about their concerns, but sometimes children's worries stick out all over. They question and nag, cry or cling, or they come and pour out their problems. Regardless of how they deal with what is on their minds, when they come through the program's doors they do not leave their thoughts and worries behind them. As you tune in and watch and listen, you will need to know when you can help and when you cannot.

CONCERN FOR SELF

Most children are first of all concerned about themselves. They worry about what they can and cannot do. Are they likable? Are they "normal?" Will they be cared for? What will they be like as they grow up? The concerns underlying all these questions are addressed in the following sections.

FAMILY

"I love my family, but..." Living in a happy, secure family reinforces the need to belong. Most children experience a positive home life, yet there are hurt children, uncaring or hurried homes, deserting parents and those who are ill, family conflicts that may have led to separation, divorce, abuse, fighting and violence. School-agers do not know what to do about these conditions. They often believe they are the cause of the troubles. They may feel they should be able to solve the problems but cannot.

There may be worries about money: enough family money or one's own money, enough to eat, dress, and survive in separated or poor families, enough for a trip, college, or toys. School-agers may look for easy sources of money.

There may be the sadness and insecurity that comes when families move to new homes, neighborhoods, cities. There may be concerns about new schools and child care arrangements, new friends, separation from grandparents or other extended family members. There can also be worry about sibling conflicts or family illness.

These worries can be overwhelming and cause children to be either aggressive and angry or shy and isolated. They don't know how to bring up family problems or where to go for help.

School-age staff can be helpful by supporting the feelings, never denying their importance to the child: "So it makes you angry," "So it makes you sad" — never being judgmental, and never criticizing the family: "Oh, your mom must have really been upset that day," rather than "How could your mom talk to you that way?"

Listening attentively to a school-ager's concerns, without encouraging unrealistic expectations for what can or should happen in a home, is also helpful. Staff can assure a child of confidentiality unless the worry is about something serious and there is concern for the child's welfare, in which case staff have the right and obligation to seek professional or protective help.

Staff can also help by observing carefully and noting changes in behavior and attempts to communicate worries, being available when children want to share their feelings, providing experiences that allow children to reduce the stresses of home life and also feel good at succeeding in a variety of activities, so they will know that even when family life is difficult, they are okay.[7]

SCHOOL

"Will I make it?" "Will my grades please my parents?" "Why do I have to learn what schools teach?" "Why do I even have to go to school?"

There is no choice about going to school, and school for many children is no fun. They may experience a great deal of failure, feel judged and evaluated, and believe that they will not be successful in life since they are not successful in school. They may feel school is boring, that teachers don't like them or care about them. They even worry about how they can continue for all the remaining years ahead. They may think after school caregivers will act as their teachers do, so they may test, fear, or show anger toward staff. They may hope caregivers will be different, loving and accepting, but they may not be sure what to expect.

Staff can help children understand the reasons for various aspects of school and how these apply to their lives. A school-age program can supplement the experiences children have in school. For those children for whom school is a largely negative experience, the school-age program can reinforce necessary skills in a positive, more relaxed environment and can help parents appreciate the out-of-school skills of children who have difficulty with school skills.

The school-age program builds on each child's strengths and interests with encouragement and assures them they are successful at many things. It provides an enjoyable, relaxing, noncompetitive living environment so children can think through and express their worries and concerns about school. Friendliness, a listening ear, and some welcoming words are a wonderful relief after a "tough" day at school.

FRIENDS

"How can I make friends?" "Will I keep my friend?" School-agers worry about belonging — to someone or to a group other than the family group. They want close relationships. They develop same-sex and opposite sex "crushes." As they approach adolescence, they may pair off into couples, and may change couples. They want to be a "good friend," but it isn't always easy to develop friendships. In school there may be little time; neighborhoods may be unsafe to play in; and child care often separates children from their friends. They may, in fact, feel alone and isolated at a time when they need friendships for support, encouragement, fun, and a testing ground for their ideas and behaviors. But making and keeping friends is a big concern.

School-agers need plenty of time to work together in pairs or small groups.

Staff can help by watching for youngsters who need a friend: children who are not comfortable with peers, not only those who retreat, fight or argue, but also those who seem to relate only to adults; children who never express an idea and are always followers; and those who down-play their own skills just to be accepted.

School-agers need plenty of time to just be together and talk or to work together in pairs or small groups. As they share what they know about and what they like to do, children with similar interests can find out about one another. When children in a particular age group are not compatible, there are reasons. Is there no one their age? Are they intellectually incompatible, slower or more mature than the others?

Children with poor communication skills can be helped to talk more easily with others, to offer opinions and express their feelings. And they can learn to try new ways to approach others to become friends.

Friendships do not always go well. There are children who are "in" and those who are "out." Children will need consoling about their broken friendships: "Look around — you'll find other kids who need a new friend." "It feels awful, I know, but let's talk to Devon about it — would that help?"

LONELINESS

Loneliness is an ongoing concern. Sometimes friendships fail or families are in disarray, and children find themselves not really belonging to any one family unit or family member. They may have spent much of their early years cared for by many different persons, and they approach school age believing they are alone and on their own. When neighborhood violence is a major concern, they cannot spend time out of doors playing and exploring and being with friends. In crowded living quarters, children may need to find time and space for privacy, thereby separating themselves from others. These factors, and many more, create a sense of loneliness, of disconnectedness.

Children and youth may not be sure of who cares, whom to turn to when problems come up, who will be interested in their successes as well as their failures. The result is a feeling of isolation. Sometimes the feeling is so negative that they will do almost anything for some kind of attention. Getting into trouble at school or in the community may, in fact, be a call for the "world" to notice the loneliness.

Because the feelings of isolation and loneliness are so pervasive, children and youth often turn to one another for support and caring. This can be an acceptable way of feeling better, but it is also filled with problems. Lonely kids notice their peers who are cared about, who are popular. They then look for evidence of what makes those peers popular. Often, they see the "popular" person is someone who misbehaves in school, is a friend of older persons who invite participation in dangerous behaviors, or is someone who has more money, better looks, more clothes or the "right" clothes. When they feel they cannot compete, they believe they cannot be popular. Feelings of unpopularity only add to their other feelings of disconnectedness.

Loneliness produces stress and undermines school-agers' feelings of confidence about what they can do or can become. It can lead to engaging in dangerous behaviors or gang affiliation. In the extreme, loneliness and isolation can cause antisocial behaviors or even lead to suicide.

In school-age programs there is opportunity to help boys and girls feel less isolated, less lonely, and less worried about being lonely. They will not feel less lonely automatically. Staff must help to give them the feeling that they belong, are wanted, and have friends.

Children come to these settings with a variety of skills and abilities; it is important that they be able to share what they can do, what they feel, and what they know. When they realize they are valued members of the group, they will feel less lonely and in turn can help others overcome their loneliness.

MESSAGES FROM THE MEDIA

The various media — television, radio, music tapes and compact discs, newspapers, movies, magazines, books, and video — regularly reach out into society to inform, entertain, and influence. Children are exposed to the best and worst of the media. Researchers studying how the media affect children and youth suggest that the influence is powerful and has lifelong implications. Each form of the media has potential for good as well as for harm.

What have children watched? What have they heard? What do they read? What have they learned? How do children feel as they are exposed to the many varieties of the media and their messages? These are questions adults should ask.

The adults responsible for children — parents, teachers, caregivers — need to be aware of media influences on thought, values, attitudes, and behaviors. The media do not distinguish between adult and child audiences. Every topic and taboo is discussed in the interest of information and sensational news. School-agers are exposed to it all.

What happens when media content is beyond a child's level of understanding? How do children interpret the distorted messages of the talk shows and soap operas about human relationships? Do they receive the impressions that sex, sexual relationships, and sexual deviations are adults' primary focus? Do they view the adult world as violent and manipulative? Are there enough examples of persons who are concerned, caring, and responsible?

Television, particularly, has determined what we do, what we know, and what we think and talk about. On the one hand, television has been a wonderful tool, showing school-agers what they might not see in any other way: animals in their natural environments, rocket ships launching into space, governments in action, and racial, ethnic and religious groups celebrating their cultures. Some television programs geared toward children provide opportunities for them to understand how they are similar to and different from others. Television can present knowledgeable adults who enrich school-agers with new information, problem-solving and decision-making skills, goal setting, and development of values and attitudes. Television can certainly be a positive force.

On the other hand, because much of television is not so positive, the role of the adult is important in helping children use television effectively to enrich their lives and sort out their feelings about the messages they are receiving. Caregivers can help by staying aware of the media to which children are exposed and engaging in on-going communication with them in regard to their responses.

The media bring messages that are informative, confusing, sometimes frightening. The graphic realism of television, movies, and movie videos, assaults children with the immediacy of such problems as violence in cities and neighborhoods and often presents a distorted image of life. But it presents opportunities for adults to build on the information and to clarify issues and reassure children when the presentations *are* confusing or frightening.

A major problem is that children often observe adults passively and addictively watching television themselves. Television is not so addictive, however, when there are other inviting things to do. Television and movie videos should not replace time for other essential activities such as relating to friends and adults, learning and creating on one's own, being physically active. Programs should have a clearly stated policy on why and when television or movie videos are appropriate. These might be a choice included near the end of the day for school-agers who want to rest, unwind, or withdraw for a while from social interactions. These media might be used during a full day or in special situations, such as children's interest in a televised news event.

As children grow toward adolescence, they develop increasing interest in music, movies, and magazines. Many popular music lyrics and music videos present sophisticated, angry, disturbing messages depicting, and possibly promoting, violent, tragic, and cruel aspects of life. For youngsters whose own environments are frightening or whose lives are unsettled and insecure and for children who are not perceptive enough to make wise personal decisions or distinguish between real and unreal, these media may encourage participation in activities that are unhealthy, immoral, and even illegal. Curtailing exposure to this music in places away from the school-age program may not be possible, but staff can help school-agers interpret and evaluate the messages.

Other confusing messages are presented by movies, videotapes, and advertisements. Messages may glamorize and glorify guns, drugs, alcohol and tobacco use, sexual activity, and the purchase of clothes or objects of special brands. Given their mental, physical, social, and emotional levels of development, school-agers may be unable to make good judgments about what these media are saying and implying they should do. At a time when they are just learning healthy and acceptable ways to behave and express themselves, they frequently see and read about unacceptable and dangerous behaviors.

The main issue regarding the use of all forms of the media is that they be chosen appropriately and be viewed in the context of helping school-agers respect themselves and understand the world and their part in it. The media should not be allowed to confuse children about life or add to their real-life worries and concerns. Adults need not turn completely away from these media forms but should become familiar with what kids are watching, hearing, reading, and thinking.

GENDER ROLES

Changes regarding the roles of males and females in society have resulted in some confusion for young people. They are confronted with changes in the way men and women function and express themselves. It is no longer clear how a person is to behave based on gender, on being male or female. For example, there are many male nurses today; previously, nursing was typically a female profession. Women are fighting wars; men are home tending households.

As older school-agers worry about how to be attractive to the opposite sex, they also may want to pursue an individual style that includes behaviors which, in the past, were not characteristic of their gender. With more options available regarding what both

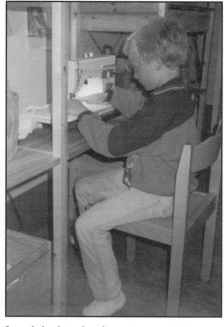

Boys and girls need opportunities and encouragement to try out many roles and develop all of their talents.

males and females can do, it is important for adults in school-age programs to provide many opportunities for personal choice and self-expression. It is also important for these adults not to judge or evaluate personal choice or expression.

Boys and girls need opportunities to try out different ways of functioning and, hopefully, arrive at personally satisfying behaviors and interests. All people can express feelings. All people can be passive or assertive. All people can aspire to excel physically and intellectually. Boys and girls can be encouraged to try out many roles and develop all of their talents. School-age staff can help them do this.

SEX AND SEXUALITY

"What's the big deal?" they ask so nonchalantly. However, sex and sexuality are topics that consume increasing amounts of mental, emotional, and physical energy as school-agers move from childhood through puberty and into adolescence. Interest in sex and sexuality starts by being very focused on members of one's own sex. This helps children establish their basic sexual identity of being either a boy or a girl. Young girls and boys prefer to spend time with members of their own sex and may make reference to how "terrible" the opposite sex is.

As bodies change and hormones are released, interest in the opposite sex increases, until it may become an all consuming concern. This concern may remain unresolved when adults do not talk with school-agers about their developing sexuality. Boys and girls want to know how their bodies work and they also want to know how to be attractive to the opposite sex, how to develop relationships with the opposite sex, and how to handle one's own sexual feelings and curiosity.

School provides formal learning experiences about sex. Families may provide some additional information, especially in the area of what *not* to do. In some instances family members may display inappropriate sexual behaviors, which encourage their children's early sexual experimentation. But for the most part, youth learn about sex and sexuality from one another, from the media, and from their own experimentation and so are often filled with confusion and misinformation. Caregivers, then, have to come to terms with their own feelings and beliefs about sex and sexuality. They first need to determine what they think children and youth need to know and can handle. They also should know where school-agers are in their thinking and their own sexual experience. Caregivers must be good listeners. In determining a policy on sex education in the school-age program, it is helpful to be familiar with family values and be willing to solicit opinions from parents, to openly communicate with them, and to know what is happening in the community. Finally, caregivers should be good providers of, and resources for, information.

What is the big deal? Children see sex on television, in magazines, perhaps in their homes. They often are misled into thinking it is necessary to have sex in order to have a relationship. In some environments school-agers under fifteen are already sexually active. In other environments they may not be sexually active, but sex is on their minds, partly because of the emphasis on sex in the adult world. Sexual activity risks pregnancy and a variety of serious, potentially deadly, diseases. Therefore, responsible adults need to alert school-agers to the consequences and dangers of sexual activity.

It is a big deal. With truthful and accurate discussions about sexuality, caregivers can help with decisions that are mature, responsible, and moral. Children have a right to know the facts and understand the feelings associated with sexuality so they can make good decisions regarding it.

A big deal is to help children be knowledgeable about their sexuality. It also involves, however, helping children develop self-esteem. Knowing they are important and worthy and on the way toward maturity helps build self-esteem. Children who have a real feeling of competence and self-worth can relate to each other in appropriate ways and fend off the pressures to engage in immature and irresponsible sexual behavior.

VIOLENCE AND CRIME

Many boys and girls feel threatened; they do not feel safe. Yet feeling safe is important to their ability to explore their ideas and their environment. Feeling safe is essential to functioning effectively.

Whether the increase in violence and crime — in homes, schools, and communities — can be attributed to specific causes such as poverty, family breakdown, drug use, or media subject matter, the fact remains that children are regularly confronted with violence and crime. It is a real concern to many of them. Most children witness violence only through the media, but that source still creates a lot of fear. Many children have witnessed real-life violence, and many have already been victims of violence.

Both violence and crime are frightening and may cause school-agers to ask, "Who can be trusted?" and "Should I be afraid of everyone I don't know?" A mother tells her children to lock the doors. A trusted father who taught his child how to behave is now in jail. "Don't talk to strangers" is a common warning. The questions and directives are confusing.

How can caregivers help with the confusion? School-age settings provide a safe haven from the frightening and confusing experiences, and within this protected environment staff can help children resolve their own conflicts and misunderstandings in nonviolent ways and by example, working with children's behaviors through supportive and nonviolent methods. Movies and other media can be carefully chosen, and their content can be discussed. Well-chosen activities do not permit the older children to take advantage of or to intimidate the younger ones. Experiences are included to help children feel safer and in control while at the same time not frightened further. Discussions might include how to keep possessions safe, handle money, deal with requests from strangers, contact resources for help, and deal with older siblings and their friends who try to bully.

It is equally important to listen, in a nonthreatening, nonjudgmental way, to school-agers' comments and their expressions of worries and fears. Listen to how they feel, neither dismissing nor exaggerating their concerns.

The worries are real, and so is the violence. But by starting with children who learn to reach goals and solve problems in nonviolent ways, it may be possible to curb the contagion of violence and crime.[8,9]

NATURAL DISASTERS AND HUMAN TRAGEDY

Most school-agers are exposed to natural and human tragedy through the media, but some kids have "been there." They have been victims of fires, bombings, air crashes, earthquakes, floods, and hurricanes. They have lost family or friends, homes or possessions. These events, when they occur, are certainly foremost among their concerns. Their lives have become destabilized. The concerns are real, whether the disasters are experienced, viewed, heard, or read about.

There may be questions that caregivers can try to answer, and the better they understand, the better they can deal with situations such as conquering fears of being alone, of separation from families, of recurrence of a disaster. There may be sleeping problems and nightmares and changes in behavior. Staff can explain and reassure.

Children's anxieties may mirror family anxieties. Staff may also be disturbed about the event. Everyone needs someone to talk with and share experiences. To offer support and help alleviate some fears and anxieties in school-agers when a disaster occurs, caregivers can:

✦ talk with children

✦ help them feel a sense of control

✦ help them settle their own conflicts in peaceful ways (see Chapter Four)

✦ create ways for families to share their concerns and needs

✦ refer families to available resources.

When disasters and tragedy strike, the school-age program can be a place of safe refuge, comfort, and predictability.[10]

ALCOHOL, TOBACCO AND OTHER DRUGS

"I'll never take drugs, so no problem!" Perhaps - but drugs, including cigarettes and alcohol, are a real concern to children. "Should I or shouldn't I? What will happen if I do or if I don't?" School-agers are exposed to the idea of drugs, drinking, and smoking and their harmful effects in the media, at school, and sometimes at home. They are bombarded with information whether they ask for it or not. In addition to being regularly exposed to the negative aspects of drugs, they may also be exposed to peers, adults, or siblings who either use regularly or experiment occasionally with dangerous substances. They may be part of family or peer-group discussions about the "fun" aspects of drugs. All of this makes it difficult for those who want to remain drug-free.

For children and youth in school-age programs, all drug use, including tobacco and alcohol, is illegal. In addition to being illegal, they are potentially very harmful to physical and mental development. Children may know this, but social and emotional pressures are strong, and children usually want to be one of the "gang." Children as young as ten and eleven are experimenting with drugs, and the age of first use tends to lower each year.

Staff should emphasize the negative aspects of drug use and support boys and girls in every way possible in their attempt to remain drug-free. Caregivers need to be good role models and teach a "no use" policy. It is helpful to know about the drug education children are receiving in school and at home and to be responsive to questions and concerns kids express about drugs and the pressures they may feel to use them.

Generally, even if a peer group does not pressure school-agers into doing something harmful, the individuals pressure themselves. At the ages of six or eight children say, "It's no problem. I won't do it!" But by the ages of ten or twelve, they say, "It's no big problem. I'll try it!" Then the big problems begin. Staff cannot control what happens at home or in neighborhoods, but school-age programs are protective environments and can also be preventive environments by emphasizing drug-free alternatives that help children and youth feel important, happy, and accepted.

DEATH

Death worries both younger and older children. During early childhood, the concern may involve the death of a family member or close relative. Gray or white hair or wrinkled skin might cause them to believe death is imminent. Although they do not want the person to die, they also worry about the effect of the loss on their own lives. "If my mother or father is no longer here, who will love and take care of me, buy my clothes, and feed me?" The fear is real, and there is not much that can be done to alleviate the fear except to allow children to express it and reassure them that provisions will be made for them in the event of a death.

As the child grows older, the concern involves the realization that all life forms die and they will die too. As early as five years of age the assumption of living forever suddenly changes to "When and how will I die? What does it feel like to die? What happens when you die?" These questions and worries often go unexpressed, and they can become obsessions. Many young children are afraid to go to sleep because they fear they will not wake up. Some school-agers feel guilty about the death of a friend or family member and believe themselves somehow at fault. Others feel anger or betrayal about the person who has died.

Worries continue as children move into puberty and adolescence. What is a natural fear and worry may become excessive and take huge amounts of physical and emotional energy. Sometimes the fear may result in behavior that looks like testing death. Youth often become big risk takers, pushing the limits of their physical and mental ability, often coming very close to killing themselves, perhaps in an effort to understand death.

The important thing to remember is that in *talking* about fears and worries everyone becomes better equipped to handle them. This is especially true with a topic such as death. But to talk about it, adults must understand their own feelings and beliefs about death and listen in a nonjudging, nonthreatening manner. Death is a topic that concerns people of all ages and beliefs. It should not be treated casually or dismissed but treated with great care and personal empathy.

When Things Are Going Well

Things are going well in a program when staff make a link between planning a school-age program and what they know about school-age development. They help children enjoy and be proud of their identity, to be liked by others. Staff respond to children's concerns and help them gradually gain more control over their own lives. Staff are sensitive to children's home lives and are a resource to their families.

In turn, school-agers demonstrate their liveliness and optimism, their spirit and energy and their growth in skills. They feel a sense of self-worth which may carry over into adolescence when things get tough. Their developing independence leads to wise decisions and responsible behaviors. They know someone cares about them and they are becoming persons who care about others.

Despite the wide age range, from the five-year-olds to the fourteen-year-olds, staff focus on each child. Activities are age-appropriate and the children are thriving.

When a school-age program offers its best, it will see the best in school-agers.

When Things Go Wrong

When children's needs are not met, their growth and development is affected. There are four kinds of behaviors which are often evidence that things are not going well for a child. These behaviors include aggression, submission, withdrawal and psychosomatic illness.

Aggressive behavior is generally obvious — fighting, hitting, calling names, destroying the projects and property of others. These are children who try to control every situation or prohibit others from participating in experiences. The aggression can be toward objects, toward persons, toward situations. When aggressive behaviors occur, peers tend to strike back and adults tend to stop the behavior without seeking the cause.

Submissive behavior is a more subtle way of indicating a problem. The child may appear to be totally cooperative and since it is easy to live with cooperative children, staff may not recognize there is a problem. However, cooperation taken to the extreme might be submissive behavior. Submissive behavior occurs when a child expresses no wishes, wants, or points of view of his own and does whatever is asked regardless of his own feelings and abilities, sometimes even when the request is dangerous. It is submitting to the will of another person.

When children do not feel powerful or important, when they do not feel anyone cares about them, they may think, "I will do anything to be liked, to belong, to be recognized." Submissive behavior results in a lack of independence or creative ability, and an inability to make choices and decisions which are maturing and personally rewarding.

Withdrawn behavior also indicates things are not going well. Shy, retiring children who "seek the shadows" are sometimes easy to miss, to lose, to dismiss as unimportant. Children who do not make themselves known may be hurting the most. They may go into a shell so they do not hurt as much. They may not trust anyone to help. They may, in fact, believe that the more they share about themselves, the more it will be used against them. The ultimate form of withdrawn behavior is a child or adolescent commiting suicide. The high incidence of suicide and suicide attempts among children today may be reflective of the great degree to which their needs go unmet. Caregivers should be vigilant in looking for children who are so shy and so withdrawn that they may be in real danger.

Psychosomatic illness is a process whereby children indicate unmet needs by becoming "sick." Children know that when they are sick they will receive attention and someone will take care of them. Unless school-agers' needs for attention are met, they may feel that if they get "sick," someone may notice them and care for them. Consequently, they pretend to be sick or develop psychosomatic symptoms, including fevers, stomach aches, headaches, and hives. Whether the source of the sickness is physical or psychosomatic, it deserves an immediate response: attention, love, support, making the child's environment safe and secure, and medical treatment.

These primary behaviors — *aggression, submission, withdrawal* and *psychomatic illness* — are clear signals something is wrong. An alert staff will look for what is wrong and try to find ways to meet the child's unmet needs.

When we are caring for children, we have taken on the job of trying to see that most things go well most of the time. That is why when we ask, "Who are the children?" we also must ask, "Who are the caregivers, the staff of school-age programs?" The relationship between the two is critical.

A child is like a piece of paper on which every passerby leaves a mark.
                                                    Chinese Folk Wisdom

---

Things to Think About

1. Select two activities: one a special experience, the other an ongoing, usual, experience. Using a chart like the one below, describe how each activity meets the basic human needs for identity, relationships, power.

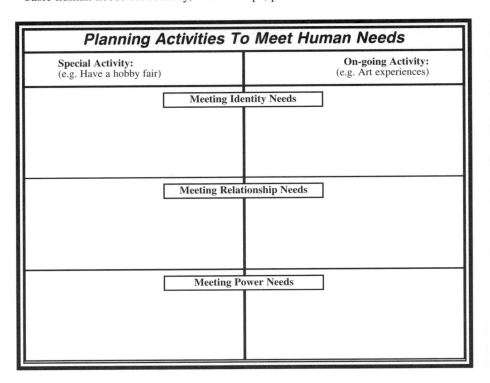

Planning Activities To Meet Human Needs	
Special Activity: (e.g. Have a hobby fair)	**On-going Activity:** (e.g. Art experiences)
Meeting Identity Needs	
Meeting Relationship Needs	
Meeting Power Needs	

2. Observe the same school-ager for at least three hours in a school-age program. Think about what it is like to be that child. Do you feel this child is off to a good start in life? Why? Have you any concerns? Why?

Physical Development

Describe this child's level of physical development. What evidence do you see of the child's physical skills? Body awareness?

How does the program appear to meet this child's physical needs? What else do you think could be done?

Social Development

How does the child relate to peers? To adults? Give examples.

Does the child always gravitate to others? Or sometimes seek privacy? What program activities are encouraging social interaction? What else do you think could be done?

Self Development

What evidence do you see of the child developing a feeling of self-identity? Give an example of the child's expression of feelings. Give an example of an observed success experience and of a failure experience. How do you think this child feels about himself or herself? What makes you think this?

Intellectual Development

What activities do you observe this child participating in? Does he or she seem interested in the experience? What evidence do you see of independent decision making? Do you observe attempts at humor? Describe. Chat with the child and ask what he or she is most interested in and most likes to do.

3. Think about three things that worried you when you were a school-ager. How old were you? How did these worries affect your behavior?

1. _____

2. _____

3. _____

NOTES

[1]We recommend further reading such as Dorothy Brigg's *Your Child's Self-Esteem*; Penelope Leach's *Your Growing Child: From babyhood to adolescence*; Ed Zigler's *Children In A Changing World: Development and Social Issues*.

[2]Readers may wish to explore further the emotional milestones from which school-agers build a sense of themselves. Child psychologist Stanley I. Greenspan, M.D. expands on this in *Playground Politics: Understanding the Emotional Life of Your School-age Child*, Addison-Wesley, 1993.

[3]These developmental aspects are more fully explored in *Yardsticks: Children in the Classroom - Ages 4-14* by Chip Wood, Northeast Foundation for Children, 1997.

[4] Your school-age program may be affected by the ADA. It is wise to be familiar with the components of the act. For information on ways to meet the needs of "children with special needs" and to be sure your program is in compliance with ADA, we refer you to *All Kids Count, Child Care and the Americans with Disabilities Act*. It also contains an extensive bibliography of resources.

[5] We also refer you to Dale Fink's *School-Age Children with Special Needs: What Do They Do When School Is Out?* This publication explores a range of recommendations and community responses to care for children with special needs.

[6] A report on this topic has been developed by BNA PLUS, a division of The Bureau of National Affairs, "Expecting the Unexpected: Sick and Emergency Child Care," 1992

[7]David Elkind's *Ties That Stress* takes a look at changes in the American family and the effects on children and youth.

[8]NAEYC has adopted two position statements: "Violence in the Lives of Children" (1993), and "Media Violence in Children's Lives" (1990). Both advocate public and professional policies and actions to help children cope with the effects of community and media violence. Both include bibliographies.

[9]For more on the effects of violence on children and how to counteract them, see NAEYC's book *Early Violence Prevention: Tools for Teachers of Young Children* by Slaby, Roedell, Arezzo and Hendrix, NAEYC, 1995.

[10]Also from NAEYC is a brochure addressing natural disaster called "When Disaster Strikes: Helping Young Children Cope." While the focus is on young children, the information is applicable to school-agers.

RECOMMENDED READINGS

Children Under Five

Allen, K.E. *Developmental Profiles*. Albany: Delmar, 1994.

Clemens, S. G. *The Sun's Not Broken, A Cloud's Just in the Way: On Child Centered Teaching*. Beltsville: Gryphon House, 1983.

Dodge, D. T. and L. J. Colker. *The Creative Curriculum for Early Childhood*. 3rd Ed. Washington DC: Teaching Strategies, 1993.

Fraiberg, S. H. *The Magic Years: Understanding and Handling the Problems of Early Childhood*. New York: MacMillan, 1981.

Galinsky, E. and J. Davis. *The Preschool Years*. New York: Random House, 1988.

Gordon, A., et al. *Beginnings and Beyond*. Albany: Delmar, 1994.

Hamilton, D.S. and B.M. Fleming. *Resources for Creative Teaching in ECE*. San Diego: Jovanovich, 1990. (through age 8)

Hymes, J. L. *The Child Under Six*. Englewood Cliffs: Prentice-Hall, 1966.

Hyson, M. C. *The Emotional Development of Young Children, Building An Emotion-Centered Curriculum*. New York: Teachers College Press, 1994.

Leach, P. *Your Baby and Child from Birth to Age Five*. New York: Knopf, 1989.

Miller, K. *Ages and Stages*. Beltsville: Gryphon House, 1985.

Read, K., et al. *Early Childhood Programs: Human Relationships and Learning*. Orlando: Harcourt Brace, 1993. (through age 8)

Seefeldt, C. *A Curriculum for Child Care Centers*. Columbus: Merrill, 1974.

Stallibrass, A. *The Self-Respecting Child*. New York: Addison-Wesley, 1989.

Children Over Five

Bjorklund, D. F. and B. R. *Looking at Children: An Introduction to Child Development*. Pacific Grove: Brooks/Cole, 1992.

Briggs, D.C. *Your Child's Self-Esteem*. New York: Dolphin, 1975.

Elkind, D. *All Grown Up and No Place to Go – Teenagers in Crisis*. Boston: Addison-Wesley, 1984.

—. *The Hurried Child*. Boston: Addison-Wesley, 1988.

Erikson, E. H. *Childhood and Society*. New York: Norton, 1963.

Gabarino, J. *Adolescent Development – An Ecological Perspective*. Columbus: Merrill, 1985.

—, J. Dubrow, K. Kosteing, and C. Pardo. *Children in Danger: Coping with the Effects of Community Violence*. San Francisco: Jossey-Bass, 1989.

Hendrick, J. *The Whole Child*. Columbus: Merrill, 1992.

Leach, P. *Your Growing Child from Babyhood to Adolescence*. New York. Knopf, 1989.

Lefrancois, G. R. *Of Children: An Introduction to Child Development*. 7th Ed. Belmont: Wadworth, 1992.

Papalia, D. E. and S. W. Olds. *A Child's World: Infancy Through Adolescence*. New York: McGraw-Hill, 1993.

Seefeldt, C. and N. Barbour. *Early Childhood Education: An Introduction*. 3rd Ed. Columbus: Merrill, 1994.

Stone, L. J. and J. Church. *Childhood and Adolescence*. 5th Ed. New York: McGraw-Hill, 1984.

Terry, S. G., J. M. Sorrentino and C. H. Flatter. *Children: Their Growth and Development*. New York: McGraw-Hill, 1979.

Wood, C. *Yardsticks: Children in the Classroom Ages 4-14*. Greenfield, MA: Northeast Foundation for Children, 1997.

Zigler, E. F. and M. Finn-Stevenson. *Children in a Changing World: Development and Social Issues*. 2nd Ed. Pacific Grove: Brooks/Cole, 1993.

Chapter 3

Who Are The Staff and What Do They Do?

"Mrs. Lopardi made me feel secure when my parents weren't home. Mrs. Lopardi was nice to be with because she was kind, loving, understanding. When she takes care of me it is almost like having my grandmother here."

> Kathleen
> age 11

"She was a model of virtue and wisdom: she had a natural elevation of spirit, a cultivated mind, an excellent heart; she was patient, gentle, cheerful, just, constant, and truly everything that could be desired in a person having to do with children."

> Catherine the Great
> 1729-1796

In this chapter...

➢ Who Is Needed to Do The Job?
➢ Staff Have Special Qualities
➢ Staff Have Special Interests
➢ The Commitment to Act Responsibly and Ethically at All Times
➢ The Right Match
➢ The Hiring Process
➢ Requirements for Staff
➢ Quality of Work Life: Keeping the Staff and Enjoying the Job
➢ What Do Staff Do?

Who is Needed to Do the Job?

Who is needed to help children like who they are, relate well to others, and feel a sense of control over their own lives? Who is needed to help the children be comfortable, happy, responsible, and interesting persons? That is what staff are all about.

How well school-agers thrive in out-of-school hours depends on the quality of care they receive. The quality of care depends on the caregiver being a warm, nurturing person who is challenged by a child's need for intellectual stimulation and the desire to accomplish. This adult cannot be threatened by school-agers' strivings for independence, their fresh ideas, and their super-abundant energy. The quality of care depends upon the adults' respect for a child's need to have a special friend along with the need to be part of a special peer group. These persons need the sense of humor to lighten up a crisis and help a child relax, as well as the ability to support each child in times of conflict or stress. Above all, they know how to help children like themselves.

That is what quality care is all about.

How well school-agers thrive depends on how well staff relate to families. They are interested in and capable of working with parents and family on behalf of each child, sharing with them the bright spots at the end of a very long day. They are able to soothe a child's worry when a parent is late. They accept a child's anger and fears if parents separate, are neglectful, disappoint, or die. What sort of person can help a parent teach their children self-confidence and personal control through positive support rather than harsh discipline? Who can do this without posing a threat to parental responsibility or making a parent feel inadequate? Who can search for just the right community resource for a family in need? Who will rejoice with parents over each child's successes and encourage families if a child falters?

Whoever can do this, that's who is needed. For that is also what quality is about.

How can we link up the children with the kind of staff who will help them to thrive? How can we link them up with truly nurturing caregivers? First, it will be important to spread the word that out-of-school care is a vital field. People who are interested in and well trained in child and youth development should be encouraged to enter the profession. The importance of these hours in the life of a child and the connection between nurturing, caregiving skills, and a child's entire future must be emphasized. Who is needed to do the job is a very important question.

This chapter will take a close look at the personal qualities, skills, and responsibilities which are essential in a caregiver. The terms *staff* and *caregiver* as used in this text describe an individual with the responsibility for the care of children five to fourteen years of age in the absence of their parents when school is not in session. This may refer to agency personnel who are accountable for school-age programs, directors, group leaders, assistants, family care providers, or caregivers in the child's own home. The term *nurturing* describes the ability to share oneself in ways which will help others grow, mature, and thrive. The words *nurturing* and *caregiver* cannot be separated.

Like children, nurturing caregivers come from many backgrounds, many cultures. Like children, nurturing caregivers are also in the process of maturing, as everyone is, both personally and professionally.

To be an effective and successful caregiver is to be comfortable enough with oneself to grow and work with other people in ways which will help the children. It is essential for staff to know themselves and be aware of their strengths and interests as well as their weaknesses and needs. It is part of the maturation process to be conscious of one's own feelings as well as the feelings of others, to be accepting of one's own individuality as well as the individuality of others.

Maturing, nurturing caregivers are a combination of the many stages in their own development. They still have the curiosity and playfulness of infancy. They still have their early childhood capacity for warmth and close relationships. They still have the humor, independence, and intellectual drives of their school-age years. But these are now combined with increased knowledge, mature judgment, the capacity to give and share, and a personal stability and sensitivity. These are the people we need. These are the *nurturing caregivers.*

All staff, whatever the setting, establish a unique relationship with the children in their care. It can be a very meaningful and lasting relationship. The influence on a child may be forever.

All staff are also providing a family service. The quality of the service has a strong impact on family life, stability, and functioning.

Caregivers, then, meet the needs of both children and families. In the process, they relate to other adults in the community, to other staff in a center, to agency representatives, and to other people in the child's life. They work successfully in a variety of circumstances with a variety of players.

Adults move easily and comfortably in their roles with the well-being of children and their families clearly in focus. Their roles are ever shifting, ever changing. Staff are parent substitutes when parents cannot be present, role models, program creators, activity directors, and "interior decorators" as they plan the out-of-school environment. Staff assume and combine a variety of complex responsibilities. The caregiver is a mediator and consultant when children need help and a leader who provides the new and interesting experiences which help a child thrive and grow.

How can we describe a person in this profession? Who is needed to do the job?

Staff Have Special Qualities

There are five basic qualities that are essential in order for a person to work well with the particular characteristics of children and youth. You may think of others to add to the list below as you work with particular children and families.

Each essential quality is discussed in relation to the growth and development of children: physical, social, self, and intellectual. Each aspect of growth and development requires the response of staff who are:

✧ KNOWLEDGEABLE   ✧ FLEXIBLE   ✧ ACCEPTING

✧ OPTIMISTIC   ✧ TRUSTWORTHY

HOW DO YOU MEASURE UP?
10 Staff Indicators of Quality

by Rich Scofield

(*School-Age Notes*, September 1991. Reprinted with permission.)

This September 1991 article from School-Age NOTES *highlights staff indicators of quality from three resources which were published in 1991. They were* Developmentally Appropriate Practice in School-Age Programs *and* Quality Criteria for School-Age Child Care Programs, *both published by Project Home Safe. Today both a re out-of-print. The third resource was a draft copy of* Assessing School-Age Child Care Quality *(ASQ) by the School-Age Child Care Project at the Center for Research on Women at Wellesley College. (The SACC Project is now the National Institute on Out-of-School Time.) The publication ASQ which was a mainstay of the field for many years was revised and is now a part of the accreditation kit from the National School-Age Care Alliance (NSACA).*

The original introduction to this article contained the following comment: "These documents are exciting contributions to the school-age care field. From the three documents 35 pages related to quality staffing were pulled. This did not include the environment and programming which can be considered a function of staff. From the 35 pages 10 factors about quality staffing common in the three documents were identified."

1. Staff Interaction — How staff interact with each other, with children and with parents is a critical factor that Michelle Seligson in Wellesley's ASQ says distinguishes a mediocre program from one of high quality. Adults are models at this stage in the child's development when the children watch them closely to figure out adult roles and responsibilities. The personal qualities of warmth, flexibility, enthusiasm, and a sense of humor are a part of this modeling. Staff should also have a repertoire of knowledge, skills and abilities that are interesting and engaging to school-agers.

In 1979, Meg Barden Cline reported that meaningful conversations with adults was one of three things that happened spontaneously, every day in her program, and therefore must be meeting an important need. The Quality Criteria document states this as one of its criteria. "Staff actively seek meaningful conversations with children and youth about their lives and their world." The staff do not see the developmentally appropriate emerging sense of independence as a problem that has to be managed and controlled.

2. Child-Centered Approach — In a developmentally appropriate school-age program the staff implement a child-centered approach. Self-selection, rather than staff selection, of activities, experiences and playmates predominates. Staff facilitate rather than direct or instruct. Children and youth can initiate their own activities without waiting for adults to direct them. Staff respect decisions by children and youth to participate or not, even if a child or youth chooses to do nothing.

3. Atmosphere — What does the program feel like? What tone for the program does the staff set? Do staff members enjoy interacting with the children—watching them, listening to them, and participating with them? Are children relaxed, involved in activities, and enjoying themselves? Are staff members having fun?

Or on the other hand: Does the staff look bored? Are they shouting? Are children screaming or shouting beyond normal involvement? Do children seem extra hyper? Does the staff gather at one end of the playground ignoring opportunities to be involved with the children?

"The way children act and interact with each other and the staff can be a reflection of program quality and an indicator of how the children feel about the program and the staff."

4. Balance — Providing a balance of experiences and fulfillment of needs is very developmentally appropriate. "The school day, which is fairly structured for most children, often is filled with limits on choice and requires participation. It provides little opportunity for self-selected activities. To provide balance in their total experience, children and youth require many experiences at the other end of the control-and-structure continuum." The self-selected activities should be varied and balanced, contributing to all aspects of a child's or youth's development.

5. Positive Guidance — Staff guide children in positive ways by:
- heading off problem behaviors,
- encouraging, modeling, praising positive behaviors like cooperation, problem solving, sharing, honesty, and affection,
- responding with logical consequences if rules are broken or if problems arise,
- giving children the opportunity to solve their own conflicts, helping when needed to clarify issues and work on compromise/negotiation.

6. Staff Relationships — Staff should:
- greet parents warmly and see them as partners in the program; keep them informed
- exhibit support for each other by listening and responding to each other
- work well together by communicating frequently and being clear about who is responsible for which tasks

7. Staff Qualifications — These are set at more than minimum.
- Activity coordinators directly responsible for a group of children or youth should have at least 2 years of academic preparation in child development, elementary education, physical education, recreation or related field.
- Director or administrator should have appropriate degrees as well as at least 3 years of direct experience.

8. Staff Ratios — should vary from 1:10 for younger children to 1:13 for older children. Group sizes should be small enough that children do not have long waits to get staff help or to use materials and equipment. Small group sizes also mean that children are not being moved about like large herds.

9. Meeting Staff Needs —
- Are salaries and benefits adequate to be able to bring down the turnover rate to at least below the national average of 40%?
- Are the staff given adequate support to provide quality care in the program?
- Do staff have adequate time to consult with the director and with other staff, to do program planning, to set up space and activities, to communicate with parents, and to evaluate the program and set goals?
- Do staff have adequate opportunities for training and use of resource materials and books?
- Are staff meetings satisfying the range of staff needs for problem solving and sorting out of policies and procedures?

10. Sense of Humor — "Staff maintain a sense of humor as they implement planned activities." Certainly humor is an unmentioned key to a successful program.

STAFF ARE KNOWLEDGEABLE

A knowledgeable staff person is someone who:

◇ is thoroughly trained, experienced, and interested in child and youth development and family dynamics

◇ knows how to plan, organize and implement appropriate experiences for children and youth

◇ knows about the community resources which can be used to enhance the lives of both children and families

◇ knows how to communicate the needs of children and youth to parents and help them understand their children's behaviors.

Staff who are *knowledgeable* apply this knowledge to *meeting children's developmental needs.*

Physical Needs

Knowledgeable staff know:

• what behaviors to expect from children whose basic needs are for physical movement, nourishment, and rest

• which activities develop healthy growth

• which activities help boys and girls relate comfortably with each other

• how to adapt to the wide range of physical skills

• how to provide supervision for safety without over-control

• how to care for children with special physical or developmental needs.

Knowledgeable staff know how to provide many experiences and share enthusiasm, interests, and skills.

Social Needs

Knowledgeable staff know how to:

- encourage friendships and how to share themselves as friends
- create a close group feeling
- maintain the influence and importance of family ties
- interpret and deal with children's often fluctuating loyalties, unfinished activities, and confusing and complex social relationships.

Self Needs

Knowledgeable staff know:

- how to help children feel protected but not overly directed or imposed upon
- how to apply sound principles of working with children's behaviors so their feelings, thinking, and goals are respected
- how to teach *what* to do rather than what *not* to do
- when to participate, intervene, or simply step back
- how to keep children in touch with their own strengths and feelings.

Intellectual Needs

Knowledgeable staff know how to:

- accommodate for the intellectual stages of different age levels, different interests, different approaches to activities, and the varied ways of thinking
- provide many experiences and share enthusiasm, interests, and skills
- provide children and youth with opportunities for stretching their thinking and for personal expression and feelings of accomplishment
- make use of the resources in the community to enrich children's lives.

STAFF ARE FLEXIBLE

A flexible staff person is someone who:

- ✧ adapts with the children as they assert their emerging independence
- ✧ is able to change plans with ease
- ✧ can stand back as kids work out problems with each other
- ✧ offers help without changing or imposing on children's own ideas
- ✧ is willing to help them carry out their plans.

Staff who are *flexible* apply this flexibility to *meeting children's developmental needs.*

Physical Needs

Flexible staff recognize:

- that as children and youth function according to their own growth calendar and physical schedule, they may not conform to adult expectations
- that the best of plans may need to be altered or postponed
- that as children react to body needs such as hunger, thirst, or fatigue, appropriate programming must be provided.

Social Needs

Flexible staff:

- switch gears and rethink plans
- incorporate a child's immediate social need to please a friend or assert an idea into activity planning
- demonstrate the idea that flexibility can make life easier and more enjoyable
- lead without rigidity
- help children think about their own beliefs and values while accommodating and respecting the ideas of others.

Self Needs

Flexible staff:

- watch, listen and feel what boys and girls are trying to say, do, and be
- move with the children and not against them as children express their ideas
- initiate activities and offer opinions.

Intellectual Needs

Flexible staff:

- plan activities which flow with the changing interests and skills as children question, explore, and gain knowledge
- do not allow pre-arranged plans and outcomes to get in the way of children's own discoveries and curiosity.

STAFF ARE ACCEPTING

An accepting staff person is someone who:

- ✧ welcomes children as they are and recognizes children bring with them all their previous life experiences (understandings, impressions, fears, likes, dislikes)
- ✧ is able to give warmth and acceptance like that of a loving home

✧ remembers childhood feelings of anger, loneliness, adventure, loving and being loved

✧ accepts mistakes as a part of growing up and learning

✧ accepts a variety of family cultures and values

✧ accepts both child and family, neither blaming nor shaming as they work for their happiness, welfare, and rights.

Staff who are *accepting* apply this acceptance to *meeting children's developmental needs.*

Physical Needs

Accepting staff:

- respect all physical variations in children and therefore help children respect themselves
- accept children's feelings, understandings, and misunderstandings about being male or female
- accept sexual interest and curiosity as a part of growing up
- accept children's growing awareness of what they look like and what they would like to look like.

Social Needs

Accepting staff:

- know how much children and youth wish to be accepted
- understand, without condoning, the experimenting with "forbidden" language and rebellious and boisterous assertive behaviors as expressions of feelings
- understand that loyalty to family puts children in the difficult position of choosing between family and staff expectations.

Self Needs

Accepting staff:

- respect children as they are, either confident and happy with themselves or perhaps hurt, angry, and troubled
- understand that behavior may be an outcome of those feelings and refrain from labeling or blaming: "It's because of school pressures" or "It's because his father left home."
- accept the joyous situations by sharing in children's pleasures
- accept the stressful situations with guidance, friendship, and support.

Intellectual Needs

Accepting staff recognize:

- that children learn through trial and error, making mistakes and trying things out in their own ways
- that children's thought processes are right for them depending

on their age, developmental level, biological makeup, and environment

- that intellectual growth is fostered in school and interests stem from school experiences
- the humor children are developing and laugh with them, but do not laugh at them or their ideas
- that children think in individual ways — different from adults and different from each other and plan appropriate activities to accommodate these differences

STAFF ARE OPTIMISTIC

An optimistic staff person is someone who:

- ✧ wishes and strives for what is positive and attainable
- ✧ believes healthy growth is most likely to occur when the best is expected to happen — whether in helping children change behavior, develop responsibility, or make friends
- ✧ uses a consistently positive approach, believing in children's own desires to do what is good and right
- ✧ knows optimism is contagious and children sense it in those who care about them.

Staff who are *optimistic* apply this optimism to *meeting children's developmental needs.*

Physical Needs

Optimistic staff:

- give reassurance based on knowledge of physical development that helps each child manage physical growth and change as part of healthy living

Social Needs

Optimistic staff:

- allow children to try out new social skills, behaviors, and responsibilities
- have real hopes for children and are not "I told you so" authoritarians
- recognize that when kids feel frustrated or rejected, their social behavior may be inappropriate as they try to be accepted and approved.

Self Needs

Optimistic staff:

- believe children are doing their best to fit into their community, home, school, and programs during out-of-school hours

- know that in spite of overwhelming obstacles for many children, healthy emotional growth and good personal feelings can be possible.

Intellectual Needs

Optimistic staff:

- know children and youth need someone to believe in them in order to develop their ability to think clearly and attain skills and knowledge
- encourage and assist children in completing tasks, in exploring and implementing their own ideas, and in initiating activities
- help youngsters share and follow up on school experiences to make them personal and easier to understand.

STAFF ARE TRUSTWORTHY

A trustworthy staff person:

- ✧ is dependable, helpful, truthful, and trusted
- ✧ is there each day and becomes a source of trust, especially for a child who has had untrustworthy past relationships.

Staff who are *trustworthy* demonstrate trustworthiness *in meeting children's developmental needs.*

Physical Needs

Trustworthy staff:

- are dependable and responsive when children have physical needs that require immediate attention, such as falls, thirst, hunger and rest
- are available as children need help coping with such issues as menstruation and the concerns of sexual development
- can be relied on to present factual information or to guide children to knowledgeable persons to talk with about body changes or sexual matters
- can be depended on to help the child who has difficulty seeing, hearing, or walking, making sure children in the group understand and respond to the needs of a child who is physically different.

Social Needs

Trustworthy staff, by their own examples of dependable behavior:

- help children become trusting and therefore trustworthy

- help children and youth see themselves as being important to other people and being able to be counted on

• encourage children to realize the advantages of dependable, trustworthy relationships

Self Needs

Trustworthy staff teach children:

• to trust in their own decisions

• to trust in their own ability to be dependable and trustworthy persons.

Intellectual Needs

Trustworthy staff encourage children to:

• trust in their own ideas and seek out many people and a variety of resources as they acquire knowledge and explore ways of thinking and doing

• look for the dependable, trustworthy persons who can enhance their lives.

Staff Have Special Interests

Adults who choose to work with school-agers need to have a broad base of related interests. They are interested in how children grow and develop. They want to share with children the joys and discoveries of living. They recognize that many factors are essential for providing a comprehensive program. An effective school-age program requires a responsive staff who are interested in:

✧ GROWTH, DEVELOPMENT, AND INDIVIDUALITY

✧ ADULT-CHILD RELATIONSHIPS

✧ ACTIVITIES CHILDREN AND YOUTH ENJOY

✧ FAMILIES

✧ WORKING WITH OTHERS TOWARD GOALS FOR THE CHILD

GROWTH, DEVELOPMENT, AND INDIVIDUALITY

Effective staff are interested in how school-agers grow and develop. They not only like children but also are interested in them, not only enjoy children but also understand children. These caregivers are interested in the relationship of the school-age years to a child's total growth and personality and are interested in all kinds of children — the bright and not so bright, the attractive and the unkempt, the cooperative and the rebellious, and the responsive and those who are harder to reach. They all will be there when school lets out, ready and eager to continue their living and learning. They need a person who is interested in each one of them.

Nurturing staff may be the only consistent, dependable persons in some children's lives at a point when their families are in stress, at a point when they need to feel someone cares about them. It is important for children to know people other than their family who understand and like them and enjoy being with them.

School-agers' lives now proceed into wider circles of relationships with more and more contacts. Children will need to be dependent in many relationships and depended upon in others. They may have family who are close and can be trusted; they may not. They may have family who let them know they are respected and loved; they may not. They may have a perfectly wonderful family life which leads them to take for granted that they are also cherished by others. They may, on the other hand, test and tease and argue in their attempt to be accepted and recognized. If you are really interested in their growing years, children will know you enjoy sharing these hours with them.

Nurturing staff also are interested in the "whys" of behavior — why children act, think and feel as they do. They are interested in using this knowledge to plan activities which promote healthy growth. They are able to use this knowledge to guide children's efforts toward self-direction and maturity. They know children's behaviors are caused by all that has happened in their individual lives. They know behaviors are an attempt to meet individual needs to be recognized, confident, liked, and capable of making good decisions. They are interested in why school-agers behave as they do.

They tune in to both boys and girls. They tune in to their particular age, interests, skills, and concerns. They are alert to bright, curious, questioning children and know how to respond to angry or sullen children, as well as children who do not believe in their own worth. Since staff are interested in and know about children, they do not feel threatened by their actions, words, or moods.

ADULT-CHILD RELATIONSHIPS

Staff look at their own behaviors, language, and values and ask themselves, "Will a child be enriched by these?" Children and youth are watching and listening to the grown-ups in their lives. Their families continue to be the strongest adult influence but other adults are gaining in importance — their teachers, clergy, police officers, the clerk in the video store, as well as questionable or frightening persons in the neighborhood. They are all contributing to the development of children's attitudes toward the world, other people, and themselves. Children are introduced to views and lifestyles other than their family's. They incorporate some of these into their thinking and behavior while rejecting others. Knowledgeable, flexible, accepting, optimistic, and trustworthy are all words that describe a good adult role model. They describe traits for children to incorporate into their own lives.

Both men and women are important in working with children and youth. Men play a particularly important role in the lives of children who see no consistent father role in their homes. Women role models are important when mothers are absent or behave inappropriately. Both sexes help children with their own sexual identities as adults accept and enjoy their own male and female roles. Both sexes help children develop trust in the adults outside their homes. Both sexes help children feel safe and comfortable as they form their own relationships with boys and girls, men and women.

Staff are interested in and aware of their own relationships to a child. The role of caregiver is neither parent nor teacher. The role is different from either of these, yet it is some of both. In addition, staff are friends, confidantes, coaches, instructors. The nurturing adult knows some children need to be freed, some need restraint, and others need encouragement. Some simply need to have family attitudes and roles reinforced. Others, from multi-problem, disorganized or limited homes in which child guidance is minimal, require help in developing moral thinking and responsible behavior.

Authoritarian persons have a difficult and unhappy time with school-age children and youth. People who always must be in power and authority repeatedly will find themselves in struggles and skirmishes with children. As children approach preadolescence, the power struggles between them and adults tend to increase because the preadolescent is striving to be independent. So it is essential to allow children to make decisions, express opinions, and introduce ideas.

Successful school-age care workers are sensitive to children's attempts at independence. They will pull in the reins gently when behavior is unacceptable so the children themselves will want to change the behavior rather than engage in a power struggle with the adult. Successful staff remember that children look to adults as examples of acceptable behaviors and how to relate to others. Adults who understand and develop appropriate relationships have good times with these children. Those who do not understand or accept the variety of their roles deprive themselves of enjoyment and good companionship with school-agers.

Adults know the strong influence they may have on a child's life. It may not be too late to instill trust in a child whose early foundation at home was weak or nonsupportive. It may not be too late to interest children in exciting activities to replace a steady diet of television or misbehavior with inappropriate companions. It is never too late to encourage a child or show love and affection.

ACTIVITIES WHICH CHILDREN AND YOUTH ENJOY

Staff in school-age programs are interested in a lot of activities which also interest children. Just like the children, they are persons with varied and increasing abilities and learnings. They are able to ask questions and encourage children to ask questions, able to learn and to teach. They are able to teach weaving, carpentry, swimming, or chess because they know the skills involved. They acquire these skills and share them. If they are not able to further a child's interest, they find someone who can. As you help children you may act as "consultants." Having presented children with the time, space, and materials, you may function in a consultative role, giving help when needed. You will also continue to develop your own skills so you can expand those of children.

When you are a caregiver, you have interests from your personal life which can be shared with children. You may have skills you haven't really thought about which children will enjoy, such as storytelling, cooking, playing games, quilting, sculpting, using modeling kits, or skating. Everyone has memories of what they liked to do during out-of-school time. Share those ideas. Everyone has things they enjoy doing as an adult and this is a profession where you need not leave your own interests at home. Share with the children about the theater, ham radio, needlework, winter sports. This is a profession where enthusiasm is contagious!

FAMILIES

Each of us is a particular person coming from an individual family. Our families to a great extent have influenced our lives. As adults you can see children as part of their particular family. Aware of the family situation, you understand its impact on the child. Your words and actions reflect your interest in and understanding of the particular stresses which both child and parent may have faced.

You are aware of family hopes for their children, pride in and emotional bonds to their children. Nurturing adults do not criticize, complain, or blame as they relate to families. They do not "tattle-tale" to families about children's behavior, but work to help them understand their children's points of view and enrich their children's lives.

Staff support each child as they support each family. They refrain from criticizing family actions to the child. They do nothing which might weaken the child's ties to the family. Should, however, the family situation be potentially dangerous to the child, all staff members are obligated to contact appropriate resources or authorities. They must see that the family is helped whenever possible so the child can grow up in a safe, healthy, positive, and nurturing environment. The school-age program may be the only child-rearing support available to a family.

WORKING WITH OTHERS TOWARD GOALS FOR THE CHILD

Staff in out-of-school programs are not alone. They are part of the many people who help children become whom they wish to become. They work with the wider community for the well-being of each child.

It is important to communicate with teachers as well as parents. In knowing about a child's school life you will be aware of the activities and special events taking place in school. In knowing how the child is functioning in school, you can include specific appropriate activities during out-of-school hours. There may be other agencies serving a child with whom you will cooperate, such as mental health groups if the child is receiving counseling; hospital clinics or pediatricians if there are physical problems; social agencies if there have been early problems

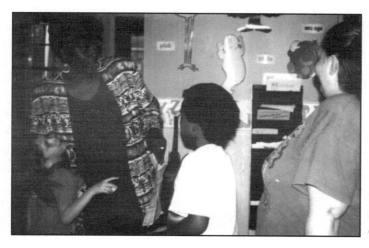

The school-age program may be the only child-rearing support available to a family.

with the law. Understanding your role as a team member, you may contribute to an action plan implementing any professional recommendations relating to the care of the child.

As you work with professionals or other agencies you may need to share with members of your program the development and implementation of any plans to meet the needs of the child. Persons who are the sole providers of care will work closely with both family and professionals in relating to the child's needs. Consultation about a child may relate to such things as dietary needs, appropriate guidance techniques, requirements for special care, or particular learning styles or difficulties. This kind of information is essential to know for all persons who work with the child.

The Commitment to Act Responsibly and Ethically at All Times

Anyone who cares for children is acting in the interests of the children and their families. This means acting responsibly. It means behaving in ways which strengthen each child and the family. It means sticking to what is known about good school-age programming, the right kind of living for children and youth. It means acting in an ethical manner.

Persons who act responsibly do not look for the quickest, easiest responses. They do not jump into the newest fad or trend which promises an immediate solution. Each word and action is well thought through in light of what is believed to be a just and wise decision that supports a child's personal growth. The implications of a word or action are considered thoughtfully. "What will a child feel and think as a result of what I do?" "How will families feel and what may they do as a result of what I say?"

Working with children requires a personal commitment to a truly humanitarian profession. It is a profession in which one is responsible for human lives. It demands a personal and professional commitment that requires specific obligations to the children and their families.

THE OBLIGATION TO SUPPORT CHILDREN'S RIGHTS TO A DEVELOPMENTALLY APPROPRIATE PROGRAM

All providers base their plans on respect for each child's physical, social, emotional, and intellectual well-being. It is an obligation to know children's interests, abilities, wishes, and any unique problems they may have. It is an obligation to provide safe, healthy, and interesting settings in which growth and good times can take place. They must know what school-age children are like. They must apply this knowledge and continue to expand it and expand their understanding of human behavior.

In order to support children's rights to a developmentally appropriate program, it is also essential to know, and abide by, all applicable child care laws and regulations which protect and enhance the quality of children's lives. It is useful to periodically review child care laws and regulations to be certain they evolve and change as needed. It is imperative to develop and support standards which are based on what is right for children at particular age levels and in particular settings.

We owe it to school-agers to constantly evaluate the quality of their programs. The quality of programs must not be allowed to slip and slide, to be compromised or diminished by changes of place, people, seasons, or children. We owe it to our children to preserve what is good living, what is a good childhood.

THE OBLIGATION TO RESPECT CHILDREN'S FEELINGS AND BELIEF IN THEIR OWN SELF-WORTH

Nurturing adults who respect what is right for children will help them feel good about themselves. You watch, listen and try to help each child be successful. You help children in ways that do not require competition. They are not compared with their friends or siblings. You are committed to encourage them to be comfortable with their friends and family and happy with themselves.

It is an obligation, too, to talk with parents in ways that will help develop their respect for their child's uniqueness and value. It also may be necessary to relate to parents in ways that will protect their child from excessive parental punishment.

We owe it to children to adhere to sound practices which are based on the belief that each child is acting in the best way he or she knows how. Such practices never shame, embarrass, degrade, intimidate, or cause any physical or emotional harm to any child. We protect each child from neglect or abuse of any kind.

We owe it to school-agers to create a climate of trust and cooperation with families and co-workers so everyone who is a part of children's lives behaves in ways which will enhance their sense of well-being. We owe it to school-agers to let them know we are on their side and by their side, that they are valued and important.

Nurturing adults who respect what is right for children will help them feel good about themselves.

THE OBLIGATION TO PRESERVE CONFIDENTIALITY

The rights and personal privacy of each child must be respected and balanced with the needs of both caregiver and family. The rights and personal privacy of each family must be preserved as you live with their children and use community resources in working with their children. This means an obligation to protect confidentiality. A climate is created where both children and family members can confide personal information or problems. This should be confidential information. Relationships are created with community resources and agencies to safeguard the well-being of both children and families. These may be confidential relationships.

In some instances, however, it may be necessary to share information in order to help or protect a child (for instance when a child is neglected or abused). This will require wise, sound, and thoughtful judgment. We owe it to both children and families to use all the skills we have in maintaining a relationship with them based on openness and trust while using any resources which are necessary to protect and preserve their best interests.

THE COMMITMENT TO INTEGRITY AND SELF-DEVELOPMENT

Based on your body of knowledge about child and youth development and what you believe to be beneficial for a child and family, you will be making thoughtful, helpful, and often personal decisions about children and families, co-workers, and your own professional life.

Does any of us have a complete body of knowledge on which to base convictions? As knowledge about caring for children expands, our professional growth and competence must continue to develop. You will continuously learn from many people and sources. In working with school-agers, you will maintain an openness to new ideas and learnings and will find ways to maintain your enthusiasm for the responsibility. Your obligation is to your own professional development.

In the process of development, you will be aware of your skills, interests, moral codes, and values so your own personality and integrity are preserved in any setting in which you work. With further training, you will continue to develop your skills and qualifications. You will recognize the difficulties of working in settings where children are not respected and settings which do not coincide with your beliefs and commitments. As you develop professionally, you will become increasingly able to help other persons to achieve and maintain the highest of standards. Your integrity and your commitment will be tested as you respond to various situations:

- What do you do when a supervisor or parent requests you to act in ways you believe are not in the best interests of a child or family?
- How do you respond when you see a parent or staff member act in a destructive manner toward a child?
- What do you do with information about possible neglect or abuse or illegal acts which you have observed or learned from a child or family?
- What do you do when child care regulations are not adhered to at your place of employment and children are at risk?

There will always be challenges to your commitment and beliefs. There will always be questions to ask and answers to find, opinions to express, and solutions to design. Remember your knowledge, your values, and what you believe is right for children.

The Right Match

Making the right match between any program and the right person to do the job is a two-way affair. In selecting staff, an employer needs to find applicants who will be comfortable additions to the program. They will be working closely together. They will need to be compatible.

When applying for a staff position, a person will want to be sure the setting is a good choice and there is a good match between philosophy, personality, program, and employer. The applicant needs to feel at ease in the setting.

As relationships are created, it is important for the children and the potential staff to meet. From this meeting the employer will be able to observe how comfortable the applicant really is with school-agers and the applicant can get a feel for the children as well as for the employer's current policies and procedures.

The quality of care a child receives depends on the persons who provide it. Utmost attention must be given to the selection of staff in relation to the particular position. This is a difficult task. It may be hard to make a judgment in one interview. It may require several contacts in different situations such as an interview plus observations with the children. Training and previous work experience also will need to be documented and references explored. The right match is important.

Mistakes in selection on the part of the employer should be corrected. If an employee's performance is not as appropriate or effective as expected after a reasonable length of time has passed and after guidance and training experiences have been provided, then this is not a good match and a change must be made. The quality of the daily program is significant and memorable to each child. Poor quality may cause irreversible harm in a child's life.

If staff find they are not comfortable with the program they have chosen, they should express their feelings to the employer. If it is not possible to work out the differences, it is best for them to seek positions where they are happier and to which they are better matched.

Who is needed for any particular school-age program? It certainly is important for someone to have the personal qualities and interests which are essential for fostering healthy development in children. But the special needs or particular focus of a program also requires consideration. For example, programs with a focus on visual arts, theater arts, or sports will look for staff who have abilities in these areas. If adults are skilled in one of these areas, then, in seeking employment, they might ascertain whether any of their special skills will be utilized. Programs which focus on play and social relationships will require staff members who know what children learn from rich, self-directed play situations and will know the quality, quantity, and value of materials which need to be provided. They will know how children's close — but ever changing — relationships with each other enhance their total development in social, emotional, intellectual, and physical growth.

Center or other group programs may want to augment and balance their team by employing individuals of different ages, genders, and ethnic or cultural backgrounds, especially caregivers with unique skills or interests.

Family child care providers may have their own skills and interests to add to those of the children and also may bring in other adults as visitors who can enrich the program.

In-home providers will blend with the expectations of the parents since they have been specially selected by the family and will have a major role in the development of their child.

The Hiring Process

Every program will involve sensitive judgment in selecting personnel. In-home care involves the selection of someone to come into one's home, perhaps more than one person, to cover a full day. Family child care providers will need to select substitute persons to be with the children in case of emergencies. Group care providers have continual judgments to make as centers develop, expand, and as staffing and scheduling changes occur. In each case, the process of choosing may be different. But for both employer and employee attaining the right match may involve some or all of the following steps:

MAKING CHOICES

For in-home care, both parents and other family members may wish to participate in the choice of the caregiver under consideration. In family care, the provider will choose carefully among possible substitutes. The children's families may participate in the choice and should certainly be introduced to any substitute caregiver. In center care, depending on the position to be filled, the selection may involve the director, members of the board, agency personnel, and current staff members.

Applicants also make choices. They will want to select appropriate employment and, after meeting employers and observing programs, will decide on where they will be interested in working.

CLARIFYING THE JOB POSITION

Employers need to furnish a clearly written, concise job description defining such aspects of the position as:

- job qualifications
- responsibilities and activities
- salary and benefits
- hours of employment

Applicants need to be prepared to share any of their own requirements such as:

- hours, days or seasons available for employment
- special interests or hobbies
- salary requirements

FINDING THE RIGHT PERSONS

Both employer and employee will have a variety of ways to find each other:
- word of mouth from friends, families
- notices in college placement offices, employment agencies
- notices in PTA, church, community newsletters, or bulletin boards
- ads in newspapers

SCREENING CHOICES

Employers may begin by looking at resumés, conducting interviews, observing candidates with children, or all of these. They will check the possible employees to be sure the candidate meets the particular needs of the home or program and any specific licensing, registration, or certification requirements. It is good to develop a standard interview form so that similar information is obtained and impressions can be recorded immediately. Decisions may be made on the basis of training, education, experience, interests, and personality. References should be checked.

Applicants may visit a variety of programs and respond to many advertisements before selecting the place of employment. They, too, will make the choice based on where they feel they will best fit in among a variety of school-age situations they have observed.

MAKING THE FINAL DECISION

The final choice is crucial for both employer and employee. If the first choice is not possible, consider the second choice. If, as employer or applicant, you have real doubts about your options, look further by beginning the employment process again. You may not have discovered your best match yet, and you may regret a wrong choice.

Requirements for Staff

State and local regulations may determine the minimum requirements for child care personnel. Individual programs, however, may develop their own personnel policies according to factors such as age, education, and experience. Their personnel policies may exceed legal minimum requirements. There is certain basic documentation which most personnel may be expected to submit:

- proof that minimum age requirement is met
- physical examination and tuberculosis test results
- first aid and/or CPR training certificate
- criminal background check
- verification of previous job experience
- references or recommendations
- verification of attendance and degrees in high school, college, graduate school
- verification of courses required by regulations
- other relevant personal information

MAKING CHOICES: GUIDES FOR INTERVIEWING

Keep in mind the personal attributes previously described. The interview as well as observation are ways for both employer and employee to be sure their choice is a good one.

The following pages may help guide your thinking as you employ staff or, as an applicant, you seek a sound match for your own skills. The pages include suggestions for:

Questions for employer to ask applicant
Questions for employer to ask oneself

Questions for applicant to ask employer
Questions for applicant to ask oneself

As you look at the sample questions, certain items may not apply to you. Additional information may be needed which you may wish to add. You will be most comfortable, of course, as you put the ideas into your own words.

You will have your own questions, both as employer or applicant. But remember, job relationships and job responsibilities are important in your life. Your satisfaction is an essential part of finding the right match. In turn, finding the right match will help create an environment which is right for the children.

Interview Guide for the Employer

Questions an Employer Might Ask the Applicant

1. Now that you've observed the children, what do you think about what you saw?

   What did you see that you particularly enjoyed?

   What concerned you?

   What suggestions would you have in terms of the room, the program, the play materials?

   What did you think of the program schedule? What would be your ideal schedule?

2. How do you like to work with children?

   With what age children are you most comfortable? Why?

   What do you like best about school-agers? Why?

   What do you like least? Why?

   Do you have any special hobby or interest you would like to share with children?

   What activities do you think school-agers should be doing when they are out of school? How would you plan for these?

   What activities would you really enjoy doing with children?

   How might you help a child who has no friends?

   How might you plan for children in one group whose ages may vary from five to eight, or even five to fourteen?

   How do you think a caregiver is different from a teacher?

   What aspects of out-of-school care would you like to learn more about?

   What specific things would you like to learn to do with school-agers?

3. How do you feel about school-age behavior?

   What kinds of behavior might upset you?

   How would you feel if a child spit at you? What would you do?

   When children use language which offends you, what would you do?

   When a child says "no" to you, will not obey you, how might you handle this?

   How do you think children would feel if you scolded them?

4. Have you ever worked with other adults?

   How do you feel about working under supervision?

   Describe any experiences supervising other persons.

   How do you handle disagreements?

   When talking with parents, can you describe your feelings? When do you feel uncomfortable?

   How might you keep parents involved with their child in the program?

   How would you answer a parent who asks, "How was Michael today?"

Questions an Employer Might Ask Oneself

1. Does this applicant seem to have the personal qualities and interests which I consider important?

2. How knowledgeable is this person about the development of school-age children?

3. How knowledgeable is the applicant about appropriate activities?

4. What skills does this person have which will be good for children?

5. Is this person willing to develop new skills to apply in working with children?

6. What are the person's feelings about children in general?

7. How might this person work with school-age behaviors?

8. Would this person work best with younger or older children?

9. Is this person open and accepting to new ideas and information about working with school-agers?

10. How flexible does this person seem in terms of respecting children's ideas and their own thinking?

11. Does this person's previous work record give me confidence?

12. Are certain qualities leading me to make incorrect judgments about other qualities or abilities? For example, does dress style or physical appearance make me question the ability to relate to children in supportive ways?

13. Will the applicant be a positive influence? In what ways?

14. If I were a school-ager, would I enjoy being with this person?

15. As a co-worker, would I enjoy being with this person?

Interview Guide for the Applicant

Questions an Applicant Might Ask the Employer

1. Who plans for the children's activities? What will be my role in planning for the activities? What will be the children's role?

2. Could you tell me about your schedule? (This will help to find out something about the program and the philosophy of care).

3. How do you handle behaviors such as fighting, bad language or "talking back"? (This will help you find out how much they understand children and what you will be expected to do).

4. What is my role with parents?

5. What do I do if I need materials?

6. Who will help me with my questions and concerns?

7. What is the salary range?

8. What are the benefits such as sick days? Medical insurance? Vacations?

9. What are the expected hours?

Questions an Applicant Might Ask Oneself

1. Is this a situation where I will be comfortable?

2. Can I bring my own interests to the children?

3. Are tasks to be assigned to me within my vision of what I want and am able to do?

4. Are methods of dealing with children's behaviors acceptable to me in terms of both children's growth and development and my own philosophy?

5. Are there enough materials both indoors and outdoors for children's effective use of out-of-school hours?

   How free would I be to see that adequate materials are provided?

6. Am I comfortable about being supervised by others?

   Supervising others?

7. Will this job fit into my personal schedule?

8. Will this job satisfy my need for continuing professional growth?

Quality of Work Life: Keeping the Staff and Enjoying the Job

Continuity of care is a key factor in the quality of care because it is important for children to be assured that someone familiar and dependable is taking care of them. Constant changes can be confusing; the child, the adults, and the program are all losers.

In order to maintain a continuity of care, staff must be comfortable, challenged, and enthusiastic. Otherwise, they may not work well with the youngsters or their co-workers and will eventually seek other employment. Two ways for achieving good quality of work life are considered here: professional development and personal working conditions.

PROFESSIONAL DEVELOPMENT

A later section in this text looks closely at the training component for staff development and suggests some criteria for coursework.

A successful program depends on knowledgeable, competent supervisors plus the close support from parents. There are several essential components to begin and encourage professional development.

Orientation to the job

When a good match is made and the new staff persons are hired, these adults need to know what is in store for them. What will be their role? Just what does the job entail? An orientation has many aspects depending upon the setting and may cover such factors as:

- Observation of the program before participation
- Introduction to the children, parents, other staff
- Tour of the facility
- Explanation of work responsibilities
- Sharing of personal interests and abilities
- Information about relating to children in positive ways
- Information on children who need special care
- Procedures to be followed for evacuation, health and safety, emergency phone numbers (911, poison control, protective services, available adults, licensing agency), dress requirements, parking areas, message systems
- Policies and government regulations
- Resources for continuing educational development such as reading matter, workshops, courses, in-service training, conferences

Individual supervision

Good supervision provides someone to walk with, someone with whom to share, ask questions, and think through problems; someone to help staff trust themselves, believe in their own competencies, and become better at caregiving.

Good supervision makes the work of staff less difficult and more interesting as they learn from others and respect new ideas. Supervisors may not have all the answers, but they listen. They negotiate solutions. They deepen the staff's knowledge about the job and help them implement the principles of child and youth development into program design. They clarify job goals and policies. A supervisor may be a licensing worker, a site coordinator, a director, or the parent in an in-home care situation. Good supervision, readily available to staff, always involves mutual respect and a trusting relationship.

Supervisors are able to see the particular situation — the room, the materials, the children. They will observe the staff's specific style of working, relationships with children and design for activity areas. The staff can address individual questions or concerns and know the supervisor has a first-hand understanding of the particular situation.

Both supervisor and supervisee are essential to each other. Neither can do the job alone. They are both interested in preventing problems and alert to solving those problems which arise. They both strive to increase their own capabilities through their exchanges as they work for better services for each child and family.

Supervisors depend on staff to observe carefully, report accurately, and interact with children, fellow staff, families, and supervisor in open, thoughtful ways. They depend on the skills and patience of the staff to try and try again in working through solutions. Staff persons depend on supervisors to listen to their ideas, recognize their feelings, and be willing to see them as individuals with their own working styles. Together they broaden their knowledge and define their goals, philosophy, and progress.

Supervisory conferences

Conference times may be planned both spontaneously and on a scheduled basis. New employees especially benefit from frequent access to supervisors during the first few months of employment. Conferences may be both individual and with small groups of staff. The purpose of scheduled conferences is to maintain a two-way exchange of ideas and help staff make thoughtful decisions about their work.

Performance evaluation

The respect between staff and supervisor is the foundation for both good supervision and continuing performance evaluation. Staff become increasingly aware of how they are doing, what they do easily and well, and what is more complex and difficult. Evaluations from supervisors are part of the supervising process. They are based on factors such as clearly defined job expectations in relation to quality of performance, adherence to philosophy and policies, and relationships with children, parents, and co-workers. Evaluations are part of a staff development process. They are meant to help individuals recognize their strengths, apply their interests, and realistically consider methods of growth and improvement.

Staff can also get help as they consult with co-workers, parents, and children. Evaluations from others, as well as self-evaluation, may be achieved in many ways and always should be thought of as part of the helping and learning process.

Staff meetings

Regularly scheduled meetings provide a time when all staff can meet to share information, opinions, successes, and failures. This may be a time to resolve problems and announce proposed changes in policies as well as in short or long range plans. They serve the purpose of providing a forum where everyone can bring gripes and concerns to be aired for consideration. They help build a feeling of a cohesive group working for the welfare of every child. Staff members should be included in planning the agenda for the meetings.

In-service training

The purpose of in-service experiences is to expand information, skills, and ideas. They are usually provided for the staff in a specific center or group of child care home providers, and may be conducted by agency personnel, experts or consultants in the field of school-age programs, the director, or staff members. Methods such as hands-on workshops, role play, problem-solving techniques, lectures, films, or discussions may be included. Content areas may cover topics such as art, music, sports, room arrangement, child and youth development, staff-child interaction, or parent involvement.

Ongoing professional development

All staff should be aware of conferences, coursework, workshops, lectures, and seminars which are relevant to the profession of providing out-of-school programs. The more knowledgeable staff are, the more they will want to know. The more competent they become, the more enthusiastic they will be about their position.

Observations of other school-age programs

As communities encourage and develop quality, visits can be arranged to observe a variety of programs and exchange ideas. You will observe programs of superior quality as well as notice situations which you question. You may learn a lot from visits into homes or centers. You will expand your sensitivity to children as you objectively observe what is or is not going well in settings other than your own workplace.

Increasing professional responsibility

Job satisfaction requires a personal commitment and interest in what you are doing, a feeling that your worth is appreciated and effort is valued. Staff may assume new and interesting tasks, based on their particular abilities, to help others become proficient also. Family providers may help others through consultations, workshops, and publications. Center providers may be challenged to develop and carry out new curricula and unique activities. Compensation for increased responsibility may take many forms such as job promotion, financial reward, and professional and community recognition.

PERSONAL WORKING CONDITIONS

We all function at our best when we are at ease in our roles, feel comfortable with our co-workers, and have a certain amount of gratification about what we are doing. Satisfying personal working conditions, as well as methods of professional development, contribute to maintaining job satisfaction and steady staff. The following are a few suggestions which encourage staff through personal job satisfaction:

- personnel policies which conform with all legal requirements, including policies such as salary, work hours, insurance, and other benefits

- group sizes small enough to make it possible for staff to work comfortably and know each child, and staff-child ratios which encourage personal relationships

- easy access to persons who **(a)** can be of help in immediate crises such as children's accidents or need for special attention, and **(b)** who can answer questions and give support as requested

- a non-threatening environment for provider input into program policies, such as suggestion boxes, committee participation, and staff meetings

- space where personnel can conveniently park their cars, store their personal belongings, and relax away from the children when not assuming responsibilities

- social get-togethers such as picnics, suppers, theater, or field trips

WHEN STAFF CHANGE

There will be changes in staff which occur for many reasons. People have professional needs to consider and personal needs to fulfill which cause them to leave a position. Employers, too, have different reasons for making changes in staff. These may be personal, financial, professional, or philosophical. Center staff simply may be assigned to a different group of children or their hours of employment may change and this will affect certain children. Adults should be prepared for changes; so should children.

When a new staff person is to be employed or a familiar adult is to leave, it is only fair that both staff and children be alerted to the change. Surprises are fun on special occasions; however, neither children nor adults want a steady diet of surprises. They want their lives to have a more predictable pattern.

When staff change, the children should have ample preparation. They should be told about it well in advance of the actual time the staff person leaves and well in advance of the introduction of a new staff person. Everyone feels some uncertainty about new experiences, new relationships, and new situations. It is particularly difficult for children because their need for relationships is so vital and their ways to cope with or verbalize about separation and disappointments are still so limited.

However, if children know what to expect and have time to live with their feelings and express these feelings, they are more likely to feel less apprehensive about changes in staff. It is especially useful for them to meet their new staff before that person assumes responsibility. Staff persons may be able to overlap for a day or more and be together with the children. This is helpful to both children and the new employee as they get acquainted and share information and routines. It makes this transition period somewhat easier for the children, allowing them to transfer their interest and affection to someone who is not a stranger. They also can talk about any feelings related to the person who is leaving as well as to the new person. This will help both children and the new employee start out with some ease.

Sometimes children do not realize their feelings until a staff person has left. Only then are they aware that the person will no longer be there to greet them and help them feel comfortable. If departing staff can return for a visit, the children can be reassured and will feel less deserted. This reunion will give both the children and the adult who left a chance to "catch up" on what everyone has been doing.

Children may need some time to adapt to new people. They don't know yet if the new staff can be trusted and they may act out in ways to challenge the new persons. They may act out so they can get a feel for what the adults' reactions will be. They may ask a lot of questions. There must be time for getting acquainted. Changes in staff, as with any changes, require our patience and our best ability to plan.

What Do Staff Do?

All staff have some of the same responsibilities. This is true regardless of the type of out-of-school program. It is true whether they are directors, group leaders, assistants, family or in-home caregivers. They have responsibilities to the program, the children and the families. They also may have responsibilities to an administration or an agency or to the community. They all have the responsibility to maintain the personal qualities of caregiving: knowledge, flexibility, acceptance, optimism, and trustworthiness.

They all have the tasks to build children's good feelings, interests, and confidence; help them trust and enjoy other people; and support their decision-making skills. They all have the task of working well with a variety of family and community situations and the obligation of confidentiality. And throughout the range of responsibilities and expectations, the well-being of the children and families is clearly in focus.

There are many patterns and kinds of out-of-school programs depending on the families and personnel who design them. Personnel policies and staff responsibilities will reflect individual situations. In settings where there may be only one adult, such as in-home or family child care, the adult provides the total service; the program should be geared both to sound principles of child and youth development and to the wishes of the families. In school-age centers, program responsibilities usually are delineated and consequently are shared.

We discuss here some of the functions and tasks which program personnel may expect.

STAFF IN CENTER PROGRAMS

You have seen advertisements such as this:

Unfamiliar work hours? Unusual age range? What kind of experience? What kind of training? What are the responsibilities?

Yes, the hours are unique. The age range is challenging. The training and experience are stated in a very general way. Actual responsibilities are not mentioned. It is hard to tell what this job is all about.

The following listings of job responsibilities are suggestions to help persons who are employing center staff as well as to help personnel who are interested in knowing what responsibilities must be assumed. The kind of training and experience required will depend on both individual center policies, supervisory agency regulations, and the particular goals and characteristics of the program.

Guides for staffing

Center Care: Multi-Site Director

In programs which have several locations, persons may be assigned responsibility for the overall operation of all centers operated by a single administrative body. These persons must be aware of all administrative policies as well as the operation, focus and philosophy of each program. They must know business management. They must also have the basic knowledge of child and youth development in order to judge and supervise the direction and success of each center. In addition, they will be supervising a wide array of persons and personalities with a wide range of training and experience. Good supervisory relations and professional supervisory skills will be essential.

A multi-site director or coordinator assigned to several sites may assume some of the program-site responsibilities such as billing, ordering, and certain record keeping. A multi-site director will be in close contact with each individual program director or site leader. The director who lives intimately and day by day with all the details of program life may need this support. Both site leader and multi-site director may be dealing with factors such as staff performance, family problems, designing the program, and developing each particular child's self-esteem and skills.

Center Care: Director

The success or failure of the program largely depends on the director. It is this person who establishes the tone and ensures that warmth, acceptance, and

vitality permeate the program. Staff attitudes and performance are dependent on the director's personal qualities and abilities to supervise, guide, and manage. This person has knowledge of the children, parents, and community, knows good programming, and has the skills for its implementation. The director is a model for other staff members. In a center which cannot support a director with administrative duties only, this person is also responsible for a group of children. In addition to appropriate educational background related to child and youth program development, experience with school-age children is essential for this position.

The success or failure of the program largely depends on the director.

Responsibilities of the director

The director with the staff

- sets the tone for a warm and nurturing environment
- recruits, selects, orients, schedules, supervises, supports, evaluates all staff and substitutes, and dismisses when necessary
- provides in-service training on a regular basis
- plans for and conducts staff meetings on a regular basis
- shares program planning with staff
- collects, develops, and shares professional materials
- participates with staff in continuation of professional development and maintains records of completion
- supervises all aspects of the program
- verifies that room design, activities, and materials support the program
- procures and maintains requested supplies
- discusses and resolves problems
- shares information or procedures such as medical and emergency information, child abuse reporting, phone numbers, fire evacuations

- ensures staff follow required health and safety measures such as health examinations, freedom from contagious disease and substance abuse, knowledge of CPR, first aid, and handwashing procedures
- provides information on children and families as needed
- confers with staff regarding individual child or family problems
- provides substitutes as needed to maintain staff-child ratio at all times
- ensures all staff work with children in positive and supportive ways

The director with the children

- introduces and welcomes each child to the setting
- responds to feelings children and youth bring to the center from home or school
- observes children and youth, their interests and abilities
- ensures activities meet children at their own developmental levels
- works with groups of children and youth as needed
- fosters children's community involvement
- counsels and supports individual children and youth as appropriate
- ensures children are safe, healthy, and comfortable in the program setting
- works to preserve the positive self-esteem of every child

The director with the families

- creates a warm and friendly welcome
- interviews, orients, discusses policies, procedures, center philosophy, and any pertinent codes and regulations
- obtains essential family information
- discusses information such as a child's interests, abilities, personality, likes, dislikes, worries
- plans for special needs of a child or family
- plans for financial arrangements
- coordinates meetings with families to involve their input
- maintains a system of communication through bulletin boards, newsletters, suggestion boxes
- informs families about field trips
- participates in special family projects and occasions
- resolves any problems of scheduling, personality conflicts with staff, feelings about the program
- invites families to visit center whenever they wish

The director with the community

- establishes good relationships with teachers, principals, custodians, and neighbors

- ensures contacts with community resources for enrichment of children's program
- establishes connections for family referrals
- maintains cooperation with regulatory agency personnel
- interprets program to the public and contributes to community projects
- uses consultant services as needed and available

The director as administrator
- is present in the center on a daily basis to administer, observe, and supervise
- maintains close contact with any governing board
- maintains compliance with all regulations and policies to ensure children's protection from developmental and environmental risks
- implements business management procedures
- procures and maintains equipment and materials
- administers nutrition program
- maintains property
- publicizes center
- prepares invoices
- prepares reports
- keeps records on all staff and children including supervisory observations, medical and emergency information, participation in training by staff
- prepares and implements budgets
- collects fees and maintains records of fee payments
- reports communicable diseases
- respects confidentiality with children, families, and all associates

Center Care: Group Leader

The person in charge of a group of children may be called by any number of titles such as "counselor," "leader," etc. "Teacher" is not recommended as the program is not an extension of the academic day nor are program personnel usually required to meet "teacher" qualifications. How the children address this person varies as well. Whether Ms., Mrs. or Mr. or first names are used depends on what makes the staff and children most comfortable. Whatever the title, this group leader, with the director and any assistants, plans and implements the program.

As with children, leaders come in many varieties: old, young, adventurer, artist, sports-oriented, science-oriented, geared to the arts, geared to community service, male, female. All have skills and talents which are incorporated into rich programming. Group leaders are the staff in a center setting who are closest to the children and most important to the families. They are consistent figures in the children's lives and are present each day. Consistency in staff scheduling is essential; rotating or changing staff is confusing to children and erodes the quality of their experience. Rotating or changing staff makes it difficult for parents to develop relationships which encourage sharing of information and observations vital to cooperative efforts on behalf of their children. Regardless of the background of group leaders, relevant training and experience in school-age child care is essential for success in this position.

The responsibilities to the children, families, and center may include the following as well as other specifically assigned responsibilities.

Responsibilities of the group leader

The group leader with the program

- plans and implements the program based on the needs of each child
- maintains an attractive, organized, inviting environment, both indoors and outdoors, which responds to children's interests and developmental levels
- ensures the availability, good condition, and cleanliness of equipment and materials
- adheres to all center regulations, policies, procedures, and philosophy
- operates in a professional manner in terms of behavior, appearance, language, accepting responsibilities
- participates in continuing training opportunities
- responds to new ideas and seeks out consultation and resources to further professional growth
- supervises assistants and volunteers
- attends staff meetings
- respects confidentiality with all associates, family members, and children

The group leader with the children

- gets to know each child in the group, establishing a friendly, personal, supportive relationship
- involves children and youth in planning the activities, listens closely, respects and responds to their feelings, moods, ideas
- helps children and youth solve problems when consulted
- handles sensitive topics with honesty and understanding
- communicates quietly and effectively with individuals as well as large and small groups of children
- helps children and youth resolve their conflicts by positive, non-punitive methods in order to preserve the positive self-esteem of each child
- encourages curiosity, inventiveness, discoveries
- is sensitive to children's thinking, opinions, and humor
- facilitates friendships between children
- keeps records of incidents, such as accidents, changes in behavior, and achievements

The group leader with the families

- welcomes and encourages family visits and involvement in the

program
- interacts easily with families in ways which respect their particular roles, cultures, and values
- communicates regularly with families to help them respect their child's achievements and individuality
- learns about the children from their families

Center Care: Assistant to Group Leader

The assistant to a group leader has the same personal qualities as the director and group leader. This position may not require the knowledge or the extensive training of a director or group leader, but the assistant may have some competencies and abilities which are lacking in other staff. The assistant must be selected with great care because this person is very close to the children and is as significant in their lives as any other staff member.

Responsibilities of the assistant

The assistant with the program
- is consistent in attendance to maintain appropriate staff-child ratios and to provide continuity for the children
- works under the supervision of group leaders and director and has a good working relationship with all staff
- attends staff meetings and is aware of program plans, schedules, policies, regulations
- knows who to go to for concerns or answers to questions about activities, children, or families
- participates in training experiences so interest in and understanding of children and program are enhanced and maintained
- helps prepare arrangement of room, activities, and materials for children's involvement
- performs housekeeping responsibilities as needed
- respects confidentiality of all persons

The assistant with the children
- finds time to be with each child in order to be in touch with individual interests, and to develop personal relationships
- respects children's feelings and relates to them in friendly, positive ways
- understands children's behaviors as expressions of feelings and does not get into power struggles with them
- enjoys the energy and talkativeness of school-agers
- uses appropriate language, dress, and behavior and is aware of being a role model for the children
- maintains a sense of humor, sharing humor with children but never laughing at them, lightening up crises, and creating a relaxing environment
- listens to children's ideas and opinions with respect and helps them plan and carry out their own ideas

The assistant with the families
- communicates with family members in a friendly, easy fashion
- is not judgmental about families or their children
- confers with the group leader before discussing a child's problem or any sensitive issue with the family
- relates any comments about children in positive ways
- helps make the transition from the program setting to home so hurried parents need not wait unnecessarily

Center Care: College Students and Other Interns

Students, with enthusiasm and a strong desire to use newly acquired knowledge and skills, can be effective staff members because they are often familiar with and interested in the school-agers' favorite activities.

Consistent attendance should be required as well as on-going in-service training. Students can help plan for and work with the children and will interact with supervising staff as well. Staff requirements will apply.

Center Care: Adolescents

As with college students, adolescents can bring zest and energy to a program since they are often still interested in many of the school-age child's activities. And as with college students, it is wise to discover and capture their particular skills and interests so their enthusiasm is transmitted and the assignment of unrewarding or uninteresting tasks is avoided.

Clear directions must be provided outlining responsibilities and responses to children. Supervising staff need to understand where adolescents are developmentally. In some ways they are very close to the children with whom they are working and interactions could become counter-productive. Because adolescents are still intensely concerned with fulfilling their own needs, they may not always be sensitive to the needs of others. Therefore, they may be threatened or confused by what younger children do. For example, school-age children tend to "explode" easily if the adolescents are not yet sure of their own actions and are unsettled within themselves, and most adolescents are neither sure nor settled. Adolescents may need a lot of help in evaluating their responses to children's behavior in order to avoid being drawn into angry power struggles, which can only end in more hostility than resolution.

Since they are still establishing their own identity, adolescents work best at the assistant level, under sensitive supervision with ongoing training and support.

Center Care: Older Adults

Older citizens in a community may have much to offer the school-age child. Again, some training relating to school-age development is essential. But an older person who is accepting of lots of physical movement, talk, possible rough language, and emerging sexual interests and independent behavior may work well with school-agers. A senior can tell a good story, enjoy a good laugh, and give hugs when needed. Many children do not have grandparents nearby and are comfortable and happy to be with such caring persons. Older people can share their life and love with children in activities such as hiking in the neighborhood, using

127

Older citizens in a community may have much to offer a school-age child.

woodworking tools, playing games, sewing, and shopping. In participating, these adults will need to respond flexibly to the school-age child's growing need for freedom, individuality, and peer friendships.

Center Care: Volunteers

Volunteers, who are at least 16 years of age, can be a real asset to the program if their roles are clearly defined and if their volunteer interests match the needs of the center. They can assume many tasks for which staff often cannot find adequate time — one-to-one caring time, unhurried and uninterrupted social time with children, clerical jobs, hosting family events, preparing refreshments, developing instructional materials, making telephone contacts and returning calls, training other volunteers, and helping with fundraising.

Trained volunteers are useful as substitutes and frequently become regular staff members. Volunteers are used successfully on a regular basis if a few considerations are made in planning for them:

- pre-service orientation
- ongoing in-service training
- keeping them up-to-date on children's daily experiences
- requirement of regular attendance
- meaningful assignments relating to their skills and interests
- inclusion in staff meetings as appropriate
- consistent supervision by a staff person
- opportunity to discuss experiences with a staff supervisor

Substitutes

The effective use of substitutes is crucial whether the setting is in-home, family-based, or center-based care. Substitute personnel is essential due to staff illness, vacation time, or unexpected emergencies. Consistent, well-chosen, and well-functioning substitutes ensure a feeling of security for both children and regular staff.

Substitute work is often a good way to begin for anyone who wishes to work with children and youth. It offers employers a chance to get to know potential employees so if a permanent opening occurs, these substitutes are familiar with the setting. It offers substitutes the opportunity to observe many programs so when they seek permanent employment they will know where they will be most comfortable. To the children, a kind, cheerful, and understanding substitute is as meaningful a role model as the regular staff members.

It is essential for employers to have a current list of available persons. Qualifications should match, as closely as possible, those required for the regular staff member who is being replaced. Substitutes also may be required to submit information such as a criminal background check, medical reports, references, and resumés. Substitutes should be interviewed before employment so the employer is aware of their abilities and personal qualities.

Substitutes, whenever possible, should have visited the program, become familiar with the policies and physical facilities, and met other staff and children. They may participate in any applicable in-service training and may receive literature about school-age development and ideas for activities. They should certainly receive a copy of the particular philosophy and policies about dealing with behavior, routines, etc. They will be made aware of food service procedures, children with special needs, the location of materials and supplies, and any special plans for the day. A small handbook may be created containing all essential information for substitutes.

Board of Directors

Programs which have a Board of Directors may allocate responsibilities to this group. The group also may act in an advisory capacity and include parents, staff, and youth. Responsibilities may include setting and reviewing program policies, budgets, goals, and fundraising. Members should be well informed about components of quality care as well as all licensing requirements.

Sources for Supplementary Staff

Sufficient and appropriate staffing is a continuing responsibility for long term employment, short periods of time, or emergencies. It also may be useful to supplement regular staff with persons who have special qualities which add variety to the setting. Out-of-school programs also may serve as sites for training experiences. Think about the resources in your community:
- parents
- field placement students from high school and college
- students from youth employment programs
- community residents who can share specific skills
- volunteer and job service agencies
- senior citizen programs
- friends and neighbors

FAMILY AND IN-HOME CARE

We have mentioned that staff in family and in-home care "do it all." Most of the job responsibilities we have delineated will apply. In addition, as staff become familiar with family expectations, their roles expand. They also may be transporters to and from school via walking, driving, or meeting a bus. They may be coordinators who ensure that dental appointments are kept or that a child gets to a dance lesson or sports practice. They may be social directors when children visit friends or friends come over to play.

We discuss here some of the specific tasks for family and in-home staff in relation to planning time and space.

The staff In family child care

Many newspapers carry want ads such as the following:

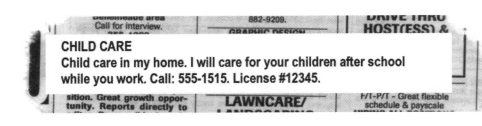

How much does this advertisement tell a parent? Not much — except that there is a license and that this is a legal operation in a state where family child care licenses are required. When a parent calls, it is important that the provider and family meet and clearly communicate their expectations. Is the family comfortable with the provider? Do the provider's plans and goals for school-age children meet the needs of their particular child? Will their child enjoy both the home and the caregiver? The caregiver, in turn, decides if she can provide both the experiences and the nurturing program the child deserves. With few exceptions, the program in a family child care home is a one-person operation. The provider sets the tone, plans and carries out the activities, makes use of the community resources, and complies with any state or local regulations. It is this person who communicates with the parent to ensure that the child's needs are met and that support for the family is there as well. It is the caregiver who is the "mother," the "friend," manager, bookkeeper, purchaser, and cook. The provider schedules the day so her own family responsibilities such as housecleaning, laundry, or family meals, do not interfere with the amount and quality of time spent with the children in the program. The provider must be aware of and sensitive to the needs of her own children who may be present as well as to the needs of those school-agers in her care.

In a growing number of communities, family child care systems are developed which provide support such as supervision, respite care, training, and methods of assistance which foster communication among providers.

Planning the Time

How does the day move along? As providers schedule activity times they may need to consider a wide span of age groups, perhaps as diverse as infants through school-agers. They may need to plan their time in relation to the dependent six-month-old, the assertive two-year-old, and the energetic school-ager. Each of the children's schedules, attention spans, and activities and interests may differ. Yet, each child, regardless of age, deserves an adult's full attention, involvement, and companionship.

Other factors also relate to scheduling time, such as the particular youngsters present on a given day, weather conditions, special activities, or community experiences. Time plans may relate to each day or many days. Flexibility, however, is a key factor in planning time. The schedules for school-age children and youth are discussed in a later section of this text and include suggestions for organizing the day to include indoor, outdoor, and community experiences.

Using the Space

Family child care providers consider the layout in the home, rooms to be available, outdoor play areas on the property, and play areas in and around the neighborhood. They will decide which family furniture and objects can be shared with the children. They may put aside those which are not part of the child care program as they provide the equipment and materials appropriate for a variety of school-age activities and interests. They use their home and neighborhood creatively. Providers need not replicate the extensive activities of a group center but they, too, find ways and means to give the children opportunities to develop and expand their social, physical, and intellectual skills. For instance, there may not be a full size playing field nearby nor space for a complete art studio, but there are certainly chances for physical activity and a good variety of art and craft materials accessible. There may not be an entire library of school-age appropriate books, but there is a good and changing selection on hand. Children both at centers and in home care require the same kind of developmental experiences regardless of the available space.

The caregiver in in-home child care

What about this ad?

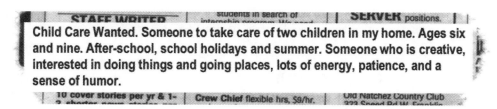

Who will answer it? Who has all of these qualities plus some...? Caregivers who come into the child's own home are solely responsible for the welfare of the child, or children, in the absence of the family. They ensure each child receives time and attention, and that household tasks or their own needs do not lead to neglect of the child's experiences. These staff talk with the parents about their ideas. They may suggest materials, activities, places to visit, things to see. If younger children are also in their care, they ensure the school-age child gets his fair share of personal time and appropriate experiences.

Parents will need to share special information with caregivers, such as health problems, medical procedures, medication, allergies, or need for more or less exercise. Caregivers need to know what the children like to do, where they enjoy going, any activities they should attend, such as music lessons, ball practice, art classes. They will also need emergency information such as telephone numbers for parents, neighbors, and doctors.

Caregivers become an integral part of the family. Their mere presence in the home setting encourages opportunities to develop close and meaningful relationships with the children in the family. As consistent family figures, in-home caregivers are important role models. They become real friends and children can look forward to talking with them, doing things with them, and coming home to them.

Planning the Time

In-home staff also consider scheduling for time. This means considering the wishes of both the children and the caregiver and the family's own plans. They will follow through on any plans the family has made, such as a shopping trip, Scout meeting, special classes, the beach, museum, or having friends over to play. They will need to know the family's wishes regarding time with television, homework, visiting with friends, or any cultural or religious experiences which the family wants the child to practice. Planning for time is a joint venture with the child, family, and caregiver.

Some plans can be spontaneous and others will be made in advance. A balance is good. Generally caregivers will organize the home around indoor and outdoor activities, mealtimes, and particular experiences at home or in the community. Plans can be flexible depending on many factors such as the mood of the children, the weather, and visiting friends.

Using the Space

In-home staff will need to know from the family which rooms may be used for children's play, where accessible materials are to be kept, and where extra play materials are stored (books, art supplies, construction toys, games). They may need to find out where meals and snacks are kept and where food is or is not allowed. They will need to know acceptable neighborhood activities and how far away from home the school-ager is permitted to go without supervision.

THE FAMILY CONNECTION

Connecting with parents and other family members

Children and youth may seek time, attention, and relationships with staff in out-of-school programs, but regardless of the amount of time spent with other adults, parents and family remain the most important people in each child's life. It is essential, then, that the connection between staff and families remain close and strong. The close relationship is on behalf of the children as they move from the security and familiarity of family to the new people and experiences available through out-of-school programs.

The art of connecting with parents and family begins with recognizing that the family relationship is powerful. It is always present and is an important aspect of each child's life. Children come from very specific, personal, and different family circumstances. Our partnership with parents is based on our acceptance of their differences. Just as we think about our children's lives, we also think about their families. Are the family's human needs being met? What are their feelings about themselves? What family relationships are thriving or fading? Are they achieving what they wish to achieve? We may not know the answers, but we will see each family as distinct human beings, like their children.

We avoid competition between ourselves and the families as we work with their children. We avoid judgment of different families who may or may not be parenting in appropriate ways. We recognize the pressures on parents, the sense of competition they may feel with the provider, the guilt about not being at home. We're aware of rushed lives, financial problems, good days, bad days, expectations about themselves or their children which are not materializing.

We are teaming up with families to help their children have a good life, now and later. Staff persons are not therapists, but they connect with families in other ways.

Staff connect through warm greetings as parents arrive and depart with their children — sharing the day's events, noting developmental strides in their child's maturity, finding a positive incident to relate. They connect as they keep families informed about children's interests, clubs, developing hobbies, and good friends. Staff connect as they listen to what is happening within the family as they deal with work, school, homework, and child care. Staff are supportive by listening. They support through good-natured humor. They do not discourage families by dwelling on their children's problems nor do they create an atmosphere which will cause families to react defensively rather than cooperatively. They may say "Max is having a hard time dealing with the younger children and we're trying to help him be more comfortable with them," instead of "Max is hitting all the little kids."

We also connect through specific child care practices which keep families a part of their children's lives while they are in out-of-school programs. Parents are given clear information regarding the policies, practices, and philosophy of the provider or the center. In-home providers share with families their personal requirements, skills, interests, and any information which a family needs in order to feel confident about the arrangements.

Parent information from family care or center providers might include schedules for the calendar year, daily schedules, discipline procedures, family involvement requirements, field trip procedures, nutritional programs, and the best times for parent-staff discussions. Newsletters, bulletin boards, and parent meetings are discussed. Parents get introduced to the staff who will care for their children and invited to visit whenever they wish. *Families must be knowledgeable about where they are leaving their children.*

Staff will need to know from the families such data as medical information, emergency information, special skills and interests of children and their families. *Staff must be knowledgeable about whom they are taking into their care.*

Information shared between staff and parents is confidential. Discussions about children should take place in privacy and in a relaxed setting. For instance, the end of the day, while often timely and convenient, may not be the best time to discuss a child's problem. At this time both parents and staff are usually tired and in a hurry, other children are present, and after a full day of work families may be overwhelmed by yet another set of problems.

Share positive happenings, share humor, share the good parts of growing up. Look at any problem together and do not assume you have all the answers. Devise a mutually satisfying plan for approaching a problem. It may or may not be useful for the child to be present. This will depend on the individual situation.

Parents as policy makers

When children are cared for in their own homes the family can direct the experiences and activities which they wish the caregiver to provide. The parent oversees the quality of the care and connects easily with both caregiver and children to assure the quality is carried out and maintained.

When children are in family care, the providers implement both family expectations for care as well as their own philosophy, policies, and procedures.

In group centers, families also have many opportunities to oversee the kind of care which their children receive. Many centers have parent group meetings, suggestion boxes, and boards of directors on which families serve. Open invitations to visit assure that parents can observe the program first-hand. Methods of program evaluation may be created throughout the year so the families feel included through their comments and suggestions. Parents should be encouraged to talk with their children about their ideas and feelings. Center personnel periodically check back with families as the program proceeds to see if they believe their suggestions have been considered and followed. If family suggestions are inappropriate or impossible to implement, then they are told why this is so.

Parent development

Just as children become better at doing things with practice and staff continue to improve with training and experience, so too can families get better at the job of parenting. As the relationships between families and staff grow, parents may confide joys; they may share concerns; they may question. Parents may be competent and confident about their parenting and relationships with their children or they may ask for and welcome assistance along the way. A good staff person provides all families with the kinds of environment and materials that say to families, "Here are ideas to explore as we live with children."

As schedules permit, family members often can keep connected and involved with their children by participation in the program.

A place is provided for parents to sit down and relax, read, browse. There are helpful books related to parenting, child and youth development, child care, school-age behavior, the effects on children of death, divorce, illness, or disabilities. There may be magazine articles, copies of interesting news items, or child care regulations and policies. There may be information shared by other families, such as recipes, trips to take, or holiday customs. There may be pictures of the children. A bulletin board is useful to post messages, announcements, notices of community activities for parents and children, or sitter and carpool resources.

Staff also respond with whatever help is needed to the family who requests guidance, counseling, legal advice, job training, or financial assistance. There is information about community services, resources for help, medical, psychiatric or psychological services.

Parents as helpers

Family involvement expands the number and kinds of activities and relationships which are offered to the children enrolled. As schedules permit, family members often can keep connected and involved with their children by participation in the program. Children's contacts with families of their friends enrich their view of the adult world as they are exposed to differing personalities as well as differing vocations and professions. From brief visits to talks and demonstrations, contact with families adds enrichment to the program for the children.

Special parent expertise may be discovered in areas such as substituting for staff, creating materials for special activities, clerical work, fundraising, or collecting scrap materials. Parents also may be able to assist with trips and special events, provide transportation, participate in repairing or creating equipment, development and maintenance of playground.

Parents and social events

Families need friends just as children do. As parents and other family members feel increasingly comfortable with the program, staff provide ways and space for them to develop friendships with each other. Sitter plans may be exchanged, carpools formed, child-rearing problems shared. Friendships among children can be nourished and strengthened as plans are made for exchanged visits.

Families and staff can share pot-luck suppers and picnics. The children in care can prepare food for the dinner. Informal opportunities to become acquainted over a meal, on a field trip, or even at a special occasion party strengthen communication and connection among families and also between families and the staff members.

The joint responsibility

Together with families, staff have an impact on what kind of adult each child will become. Families teach skills, values, identity, and behaviors. So do program staff. Both families and staff see the children implement these teachings through children's relationships with both peers and adults. As a staff person you may question, worry about, or admire the families' achievements. Together, however, you are both essential in enriching and nurturing the life of each child.

If you see a child without a smile, give him yours.

Talmud

Things to Think About

I. **Are you a nurturing person?**

If you were a child, would you like to have yourself as a caregiver?
...If you were five-years-old? Why?
...If you were ten-years-old? Why?
...If you were 14-years-old? Why?

Think of the last time you tried to help a child feel good about his/her own self? What was the situation? What did you say or do? If you could do it over, what would you do?

II. **Can you recognize nurturing persons?**

a. Observe, for at least two hours, one or two staff members as they work with children or youth. What evidence or lack of evidence do you see of:

- Knowledge?
- Flexibility?
- Acceptance?
- Optimism?
- Trustworthiness?

b. What evidence do you see of adults respecting the feelings and opinions of children and youth?

c. Describe someone you know whom you really admire. What characteristics of this person appeal to you?

III. **Bring yourself to your job**

What did you like to do when *you* were a child?

What do you like to do *now* that you can include in your program for children?

IV. **Where will you go from here?**

a. What do you consider your current strengths in working with school-agers? Where do you feel you need improvement?
Who could be the greatest help to you?

b. Make a list of the activities you want to learn more about doing with children or youth. Choose three. Get the help you need to be proficient at these. Describe where you went for help.

c. What are the most important goals you want for children in your care? How will you try to achieve these goals?

d. Are you comfortable under supervision? Why? Why not?

e. Are you comfortable supervising others? Why? Why not?

f. What have you learned about yourself as a result of having read the first three chapters of this text?

RECOMMENDED READINGS

American Academy of Pediatrics. *Caring for Our Children, National Health and Safety Performance Standards: Guidelines for Out-of-Home Child Care Programs.* Elk Grove Village: American Academy of Pediatrics, 1992.

Arns, B. *Survival Guide to School-Age Care.* 2nd Ed. Huntington Beach: School-Age Workshops Press, 1994.

Bloom, P. J. *A Great Place to Work: Improving Conditions for Staff in Young Children's Programs.* Washington DC: National Association for the Education of Young Children, revised, 1997.

Bumgarner, M. *Working with School-Age Children.* Mountain View, CA: Mayfield, 1999.

Click, P. M. *Caring for School-Age Children*, 2nd Ed. Albany, NY: Delmar, 1998.

Cuffaro, H. K. *Experimenting with the World, John Dewey and the Early Childhood Classroom.* New York: Teachers College Press, 1995.

Doggett, L. and J. George. *All Kids Count, Child Care and the Americans with Disabilities Act.* Arlington: The Arc, 1993.

Fink, D. *More Alike Than Different: Including Children with Special Needs in School-Age Care Settings.* Trenton: New Jersey Office of Child Care Development, 1991.

Harms, T., E. Vineberg Jacobs, and D. R. White. *School-Age Care Environmental Rating Scale.* New York: Teachers College Press, 1996.

Katz, L.G. and E. H. Ward. *Ethical Behavior in Early Childhood Education.* Expanded Ed. Washington DC: NAEYC, 1992.

Koralek, D. G., L. J. Colker, and D. T. Dodge. *Caring for Children in Family Child Care.* Vol. 1 & 2. Washington DC: Teaching Strategies, 1989.

—, R. L. Newman and L. Colker. *Caring for Children in School-Age Programs.* Vol. 1 & 2. Washington DC: Teaching Strategies, 1995.

— and M. Gibbons. *The New Youth Challenge, A Model for Working with Older Children in School-Age Child Care.* Nashville: School-Age NOTES, 1988.

National Association for the Education of Young Children. *Child Care and Ill Children and Healthy Child Care Practices.* revised. Washington DC: NAEYC, 1994.

Newman, R.. *Keys to Quality in School-Age Care.* (Video and Guide). Union Bridge, Summerwind, 1993.

Richard, M. M. *Before and After School Programs: A Start-Up and Administrative Manual.* Nashville: School-Age NOTES, 1991.

School-Age Child Care Project. *An Intergenerational Adventure* (Curriculum Guide for Training Older People to Work with School-Agers) Wellesley: Center for Reseach on Women, Wellesley College, 1985.

Sciarra, D. J. and A. G. Dorsey. *Developing and Administering a Child Care Center.* 2nd Ed. New York: Delmar, 1990.

Sisson, L. G. *Kids Club: A School-Age Program Guide for Directors.* Nashville: School-Age NOTES, 1990.

Wolery, M. and J. Wilbers, editors. *Including Children with Special Needs in Early Childhood Programs.* Washington DC: NAEYC, 1994.

Four
Children's Behaviors and Helping Relationships

"Don't yell at me! I'd rather just talk about it
because I feel bad when someone hurts my
feelings and it makes me want to hurt someone
or break something. And that would not help
much at all."

Jesse
age 9

I have come to a frightening conclusion.
I am the decisive element...
It is my personal approach that creates the climate.
It is my daily mood that makes the weather...
I possess tremendous power to make a child's life
    miserable or joyous.
I can humiliate or humor, hurt or heal.
In all situations it is my response that decides
    whether a crisis will be escalated or de-escalated,
And a child humanized or dehumanized.

Haim Ginott
1922-1973

"One of the most important things we can do
is to send a child home in the afternoon liking
himself just a little better than when he came
in the morning."

Eda Leshan

In this chapter...

> ➤ Staff As Helpers
> ➤ Behaviors And Feelings
> ➤ Why Children Behave As They Do
> ➤ Guiding Behavior
> ➤ War or Peace: Building Foundations For Peace
> ➤ Dealing With Behaviors Means Remembering Human Needs

Staff as Helpers

The more we know about people, the more we realize just how complex we are, how different, changing, and unpredictable. The more we know about people's behaviors and the causes of people's behaviors, the more difficult it is to state that any one approach to helping others, any one solution or activity, will solve a problem. But we know we must recognize the uniqueness of each person and accept children and youth as they come to us, behaving in their best ways as they try to meet their own needs. We know we must observe and listen carefully to understand each child's particular self. With this sensitivity, we can help enrich children's lives and reduce their problems. We can help them have confidence in their own capacity for finding personal satisfactions and relationships.

We also know that caregivers are helpers — concerned with people, responsible for helping school-agers achieve the best life they can possibly have. They are interested in helping because they believe that children can grow up to be sensitive, responsible, well-informed people, capable of acting with intelligence and independent thinking in ways that contribute to the welfare of themselves and others.

As helpers to children, staff look at many things. They look at the program, the total environment. What changes might be made which would contribute to a school-ager's well-being? They look at their own relationships with children and youth. How can they work with a particular child? What techniques work best with groups of children? What can be accomplished through fostering children's cooperative relationships with each other? In addition, good caregivers look at the other persons who may be a part of children's lives — families, teachers, and community people. What part have they played and how might they help now?

This chapter will discuss the helping relationships between staff and children and youth. It will discuss ways to help children and youth through their relationships with adults and each other. It will include creating cooperative environments, preventing behavior problems, and exploring positive ways to deal with behaviors. It also will discuss the destructive aspects of negative methods of discipline — punishments. Finally, it will include a discussion about dealing with conflicts among school-agers and between school-agers and adults.

Behaviors and Feelings

Behavior simply means *what children are doing*. Usually what children are doing is clear to us. They run, eat, talk, giggle, cry, play. Sometimes, however, their behaviors are not easy to live with; they puzzle us and make us angry. Some behaviors are not useful to the child and may be harmful to other people.

We recognize how we feel about children's behaviors and we distinguish between how we feel, when the behavior is simply part of a normal developmental growth process, and when there is a real problem. We need to be aware of our own acceptance level. Are you bothered by noise, loud voices, squabbling, whining? Some people are, others are not. Can you tolerate roughhouse play, bad language, sulking, talking back? Some adults can, some cannot.

We all recognize, however, that most behaviors are caused by children's feelings. Happy, easy-going behaviors have positive feelings behind them and angry, hostile behaviors have negative feelings behind them. They all have children behind them who want to be loved and cared for. So we will deal with a variety of behaviors in a variety of ways. Our methods are the result of our knowledge and experience and recognize the children's feelings as well as our own feelings. Our main goal is to encourage the children's good feelings about themselves so they don't need to behave in ways which harm themselves or others.

In dealing with any kinds of behaviors we must be patient. We are neither magicians nor miracle workers. We try and try again. No one phrase or technique is the magic wand.

Your own behaviors with children will be affected by your own feelings. On some days you will feel on top of the world, on others you wonder if anything you do is right. You have feelings of pleasure and feelings of anger and tension. On some days personal problems are hard to shake off. On other days the children's problems seem to be impossible to live with. There are days when you wonder if you are being too harsh, too lenient, too distant, too buddy-ish. At these times you may ask yourself, "How do I think the children see me? If I were a young person, would I like myself as a caregiver? Am I coming across in an honest way, as authentic, as real?"

Your feelings may affect your relations with the children but you would not be authentic if you were flat, unexpressive, unfeeling. We neither deny nor get trapped by our personal feelings. If we get angry at a child, we attack the problem, not the child. When something delights us, we share the joyous, generous feelings it has evoked.

In addition, we know that since behavior is based on meeting human needs, this also applies to us. Children's behaviors change and so do adult behaviors. Behavior is not static. Feelings fluctuate. As we recognize how feelings affect our own behavior, we will be aware of the children's ups and downs, highs and lows. We know feelings need not pile up, explode, or cause harm to others. We respond best to children when we recognize our similarities to them and when we deal with both our own feelings and with theirs.

Why Children Behave As They Do

Children want to do what they believe is right and what the world, as they know it, thinks is right, in order to be loved. Their behavior must be understood as the best they can produce at a given moment. Yet what children believe is the way to behave depends on many factors.

Their behaviors depend on what their own lives have been like up to this point. How have they been treated by others? How much satisfaction and security have they experienced so that they can pass along comfort and friendship? How much damage may have already occurred to their feelings about themselves? How much anger and rebellion is expressed because children have been hurt repeatedly, see all life as threatening, and now need to hurt others?

Children's behaviors change and so do adult behaviors. Behavior is not static. Feelings fluctuate.

Their behaviors depend on whom they are imitating. Children want acceptance so badly that they copy behaviors. If others, especially the adults in their lives, hit, hurt, yell, or are out of control, children believe this is what human beings are supposed to do. If adults tease and shame, children imitate. They imitate what they know, see, and believe to be true. Staff may need to help children interpret and deal with the behaviors they observe.

Children's behaviors depend on developmental growth. They grow and seek independence in stages. Each stage declares a new separation from the past, a declaration of independence. The two-year-old strikes out by saying "No." So does the ten-year-old. So does the adolescent. They all want to try out their own ways as they search for their own identities. This is normal, healthy developmental rebellion, although not always easy on adults.

Behaviors depend on whom children are trying to please. There are so many people in children's lives with different values, modes of behavior, and expectations — parents, teachers, caregivers, friends. Children's behaviors change as they relate to all the different persons in their lives and try to please them all.

There are children whose behaviors are caused by either minor or serious emotional, developmental, or neurological disabilities. These children may be incapable of understanding how they are expected to behave. Their behaviors may be caused by factors over which they have little or no control. Staff may need specialized training in working with these youngsters.

In developing a belief about how to behave, many school-agers experiment and test our reactions to their behaviors so that they can determine which are acceptable and which are not. They behave in ways to get our attention — hitting, spitting, cursing. They may cling, continually ask to do things for us and with us. From our responses, children develop their own convictions about themselves and about which behaviors will help them meet their particular needs.

Guiding Behavior

GETTING TO KNOW CHILDREN

If we are to help, we need to know whom we are helping. Children need to feel at ease enough to let us get to know them. Because out-of-school programs are informal, nurturing, and generally free from time pressures, they provide a good time for adults and young persons to get to know each other.

Be generous with yourself as you work with children. Share your own ideas and experiences. Loosen up, give smiles and affection. Use children's names as you talk with them. Recognize the new shirt, compliment the new lacrosse stick. Don't overreact to the bad jokes and crude language. Talk about what *you* like to do. Let the youngsters know you so you can get to know them.

To make a friend of children we need to be a friend. Make a point of having one good conversation each day with at least one or two children. Find a time and a place to talk and to listen. You will hear all kinds of clues about their behaviors — things they have seen and heard, things they like to do or not do, what they have read, where they have been, what their families do, what they are afraid of, and who are their friends.

Spending time alone with a child is very valuable. Invite a child to sit with you at snack time or in the reading area. Help a child learn or improve a skill. Just the two of you can try a game of chess, work with a yo-yo, or practice hitting the baseball. It is particularly valuable to spend time alone with a child who does not seem at all open to being a friend. These may be the least likable youngsters. They may be aggressive, dirty, loud, sullen, or withdrawn. They are the hardest to get to know. Yet they may want friendship very badly. You will see other sides to these children as you become a friend. You will discover their problems, but you will also find their strengths.

We can talk with children and we can learn about them by observing them. In order for this to be useful, the environment must be set up so that there is something to observe. This means quiet areas for conversation and a good selection of activities and materials that encourage interaction and self-expression. Whom do the children choose to be with and what do they choose to play? What do they talk about? What are they drawing? Who often seem alone? Who seem curious, adventurous? Who seem to be hesitant about trying out ideas, afraid of making mistakes, being "wrong," or being laughed at?

Other ways to get to know children are through structured activities planned just for this purpose:

⬦ children interview each other and audiotape or videotape the interviews

⬦ children share facts about themselves such as "My favorite dessert is..." or "What I hate most is..." or "On Sundays I..." or...

As a guide for obtaining personal information create an interviewing form like the following questionnaire, "Let's Talk About You!":

Let's Talk About You!

When you are not in school, what are your
favorite things to do?

What do you like best about school?

What do you think you do very well?

Is there something you don't know how to do
that you wish you could do?

What would you like to do when you grow up?

If we can take trips here, where would you like
to go?

Children who are too good

Are there school-agers who are so conforming they are never noticed, so fearful of adult displeasure they dare not display any signs of independence? These children want so much to please, are so in need of love and adult approval, that they seem to recede into the background. Others are constantly clinging or doing favors as they beg for acceptance. Staff know that this type of child is in need of just as much attention as the child who requests it by aggressive and out-of-control behaviors. The pressures can build up inside these quiet, conforming school-agers, many of whom do not communicate easily and never rebel or express their feelings. Because these youngsters, often quite troubled children, are more difficult to spot, it is harder to respond to them in ways which will help. They may be hurt, angry, or frightened children. Give them confidence in their own special identity by encouraging them, without pushing, to express opinions, to take on interesting responsibilities, and to have and be a friend. Confidence comes about as children are given assurance that they really are good.

Children who can ruin your day

There are school-agers who haunt you after work hours because of their behaviors — their rudeness, loudness, fights or their fearful, sullen, hostile faces. These are the children and youth who are far from having their needs met — persons who may have unmet physical needs (for food or sleep) or unmet self needs (for human closeness, understanding, security).

It is easier to deal with satisfying the physical needs because we can identify the problem — the child craves food, is irritable, is lethargic or falls asleep. It is more difficult to know about the self needs because they are not as visible. A child may not be aware of a problem nor be able to express it except in behaviors. Behaviors are where the problems become visible.

Most children in school-age care are nurtured, loved, and respected by the people around them, but many are not. Yet school-agers, troubled and wounded though they may be, are still reaching for what they need. Their methods, however, of reaching for nourishment, nurturing, and satisfactions are so frequent and so exaggerated that they wear you out. It is easy to put them on a constant diet of "No," of begging, appealing, or punishment. Many behaviors need to be stopped for a child's protection as well as the protection of others. Some harmless misbehaviors can be ignored, or you may exhaust yourself.

The hardest job is to understand the *why* behind the behavior and the children may not be able to help with this. Only the behaviors — lying, stealing, hurting, fighting, or even crying — give us the clues that all is not right. Now it is up to adults to observe the behavior more closely and try to find ways to help.

"All he wants is attention." Yes, true, he wants to be important. He wants people to notice him. Adults are good at giving attention to the pretty, pleasant, smiling children. It is much more difficult to meet the hopes and needs of troubled children. But with these children you can try to reverse how you would deal with most youngsters. Instead of giving praise and attention only for good behavior, try to give these children praise and attention, in all ways and whenever possible, to enable them to *achieve* good behavior. Welcome them warmly when they arrive. Assure them that you are glad to see them. Praise can be given for things as simple as a smile, particular skill, neat back-pack, new hair style, warm handshake.

In knowing that children need love, stability, and approval in order to grow well, you are simply following good principles of human development. You can give the love, stability, and approval — which they need — so they *can* behave well.

Destructive, offensive behaviors will not change right away. School-agers will keep resorting to the only behaviors they know until their particular needs are met. There will be ups and downs, the testing of adult reactions. However, slow as the job may seem, the children need the understanding and attention they crave. You try to offer these children what was not offered to them when they were infants, preschoolers, or the day before when a family crisis occurred. A helping relationship with any child is dependent on sensitive judgment. It requires practice and patience.

PREVENTING BEHAVIOR PROBLEMS

The better we know children, the closer we come to knowing the reasons behind their behaviors. Reasons differ with each child. Behaviors differ with each child. Yet most school-agers actually want to please adults and get along with their peers. We need to believe most children and youth are acting in the best ways they know how. When we believe this, we can aid them in creating environments built on their own strengths and for successfully obtaining their own goals. In preventing behavior problems which can be self-defeating for a child, we reassure children that we are truly sources for help.

The following discussion of appropriate planning versus poor planning may serve as a guide in preventing behavior problems. It is useful to check all factors of school-age programs regularly whether in a center or home. Such factors include schedules, activities, materials, physical environments, groupings, adult-child interactions, and competitive versus non-competitive climates. It is important to remember that each factor relates to meeting school-agers' needs for identity, good relationships, and power. Thoughtful planning will help prevent disruptive and destructive behaviors. Poor planning may contribute to behavior problems.

The program and appropriate planning

Appropriate planning means activities which are developed through cooperative rather than authoritative decisions. Children have been included in planning the experiences.

> *Inappropriate planning* means planning so tightly there is no room for children's ideas. School-agers may resent always being told what to do and they may rebel at the lack of independence.

Appropriate planning includes materials and activities which school-agers enjoy and are appropriate to the range of ages, interests, and developmental levels.

> *Inappropriate planning* is providing experiences without regard for the particular children enrolled and continuing with activities when children have become restless, bored, disinterested. This can lead to problem behaviors.

Appropriate planning provides cooperative experiences which give children mutual goals. Working toward something in common facilitates a sense of community and cooperation: designing an adventure playground, earning the money for a trip, participating in a community service activity, learning the skills of helping and supporting each other.

> *Inappropriate planning* emphasizes activities that create winners and losers, weed out the weaker players, or pit child against child. These experiences encourage comparisons and lead to resentful behaviors.

Appropriate planning means activities which focus on fun and group spirit, where success is easy to achieve and mistakes are okay.

> *Inappropriate planning* focuses on individual or team competitive activities. Competitive feelings may lead to competitive behaviors.

Appropriate planning means enough materials to go around, so children can pursue individual interests or work together without conflict.

Appropriate planning means enough materials to go around, so children can pursue individual interests or work together without conflict.

Inappropriate planning means providing so few materials (art supplies, blocks, books, carpentry tools) that nothing worthwhile can be accomplished and participants must compete and squabble for the few available choices.

Appropriate planning includes arrangement of the activity room, so choices and work areas are clear and materials are accessible, easy to put away, and kept in good repair enabling children to master the tasks.

> *Inappropriate planning* lets everything get all mixed up or thrown into cartons, so participants cannot see what is there, find what they need, or know where to work. These obstacles incite negative behaviors due to frustration.

Appropriate planning means alternating experiences that are both active and quiet, so children are physically able to participate without restlessness or fatigue.

> *Inappropriate planning* means expecting children to sit or be quiet for long periods of time or participate in so much physical activity that they become irritable from fatigue.

Appropriate planning includes evaluating the time schedule to check out those times which seem to encourage behavior problems such as waiting times with nothing to do, transitions between activities, times for sitting still, or after participation in competitive games.

> *Inappropriate planning* is expecting every moment to go smoothly without observing the rough spots when things seem to go wrong.

Appropriate planning allows for children's free choice of activities and encourages experimentation, trial and error, and personal expression.

> *Inappropriate planning* presents all activities as group projects everyone must do. When comparison, competition, and feelings of inadequacy arise, children try for recognition in undesirable ways.

Appropriate planning provides quiet places where children who need to be away from group interaction and stimulation can have things to do in comfortable, private areas.

> *Inappropriate planning* expects all children to react easily to group situations. The noise, bustle, and physical proximity of lots of other people may cause distractions and distress which lead to behavior problems.

Appropriate planning eliminates excessive and confusing noise by utilizing space dividers and soft fabrics and by scheduling for experiences with small groups.

> *Inappropriate planning* is the designing of activity areas with no thought about sound distractions, expecting all children to hear or function well in noisy situations. Noise can produce tensions which lead to troublesome behaviors.

Appropriate planning provides space for activities that are appropriate in both amount and arrangement, so children are not in the way of each other, can move easily from one area to another, and can successfully work on chosen tasks.

Inappropriate planning allows pathways from one activity to another to become confusing or cluttered. Trouble can brew when children constantly bump into each other or have to wait to reach a destination.

Appropriate planning provides reminders ahead of the time when an activity must end or be put away, making it clear when and how it may be continued or completed.

Inappropriate planning means interrupting children's work or play abruptly or without reason, causing disappointment, resentment, and anger.

The human environment

A good human environment is a cooperative environment in which everyone is respected; children respect each other's strengths and skills, ideas and differences, and function without regard to stereotypes of sex or culture.

A poor human environment can make everything a competitive challenge. Casting children in roles ("Since Sean is our greatest runner...") or comparing children by praising one over another ("Watch Marcy, see how neatly *she* does it") makes the praised children wonder if they can live up to the role and makes other children feel that they are lesser and cannot compete. Casting or comparing children may provoke bitter behaviors.

A good human environment has rules and limits designed with the children involved as part of cooperative living and learning. Children understand the reasons for having the limits. Rules are clear and in positive language: "Clean up our own spills." "Ask someone for help if you need it." "Roller blades are used outdoors."

A poor human environment always surrounds children with "don'ts" or negative reminders posted on charts or walls: "Don't run." "Don't yell." "Don't push." All of this says, "Don't be a child. Don't be yourself!" Confronted with so many "don'ts," children are challenged to act out when no one is looking.

In a good human environment interaction with children is frequent but not obtrusive. Groups are small enough that adults have time for each child — to share the happy moments, respond to those that are stressful, and express affection through smiles, facial expression, words, and touch. Personal contacts encourage personal respect, and behaviors will reflect that respect.

A poor human environment considers interactions as directions (giving orders, yelling across the room, using whistles or loud speakers to get attention) and schedules so tightly that adults are tied up with managing and directing with no time available for casual or purposeful interactions. Uncaring behaviors thrive in an atmosphere of impersonal adults and uncaring demands.

In a good human environment problems are anticipated. Adults stay close to the action where problems may occur. You can watch children's body movements and facial expressions and listen to their words during tense situations. You can quickly and calmly evaluate what might happen next and how to help before a real problem occurs. You can divert interests, use humor, try a gentle reminder (a wink, an arm around a shoulder). Don't hover over the kids, but be aware of what is happening in the whole group even when you are occupied with just one or two children.

> *A poor human environment* lacks sensitivity to signs of inevitable trouble. Staff are isolated from the needs of the group because of involvement with personal interests or those of just a few children. Children appreciate caring, alert, and understanding supervision.

In a good human environment feelings are respected. Responding to children's feelings helps prevent behavior problems. It is helpful to respond to the feelings behind the behaviors, to recognize needs which led to the feelings. "I know you're disappointed about not being able to go swimming today. I guess you're mad about that." In observing children, be alert to the feelings that may lead to troublesome behaviors. Help school-agers identify with the feelings of all living beings, animals as well as human beings. Share your own feelings. Help children understand that the same situations may make different people happy, frightened, angry, or sad. Helping youngsters see things from different points of view leads them to understand why people feel differently.

> *A poor human environment* denies children their own feelings and labels feelings which may not be sincere. "You're not scared!" "I know you're sorry you hit Trese; now tell her you're sorry." These are not honest ways of dealing with feelings and behaviors.

In observing children, be alert to the feelings that may lead to troublesome behaviors.

In good human environments children are helped to feel comfortable in their relationships with adults and understand the role of the caregiver. Children watch adults carefully. They imitate the way staff handle problems, differences in opinions, conflicts, sadness, anger, and aggression. They tend to believe the ways adults handle situations are the ways they should be handled. Children may have acquired strong feelings about authority from parents and a variety of other adults. Authority figures may be respected, feared, or may just seem to get in the way of the school-agers' "declaration of independence." Often older children feel that it's the grown-ups against the kids. The strength in a peer group may make it feel safe to test resistance to authority. "Do we have to do that again? No way!" Their point is, "Can we stand up to grown-ups and still be okay?"

> *A poor human environment* resorts to behaviors you would not want children to imitate. It considers children's resistance as personal attacks when their behaviors simply reflect the many complex experiences with the adults in their lives. You can help prevent difficult behaviors by setting good examples of respected behaviors.

Good human environments allow for individual situations. Circumstances sometimes require flexibility, understanding, and exceptions to the rule. Be ready to tailor solutions so all children know their personal needs can be recognized and met.

> *A poor human environment* means insisting on applying all rules to all children at all times. Inflexibility on the part of adults will only encourage inflexibility in the children.

Good human environments build children's confidence. We need to prepare children for life's future competition by building their self-confidence now. We help them participate and function in enjoyable ways as they meet their own goals and respect their own personal abilities. Personal satisfaction will come from enjoyment in participation, whether the school-ager is fast or slow, talented or not, skilled or unskilled. Do, however, respect children's own games of competition which they create among themselves. "Who's the fastest?" "Can you jump as high as me?" "I challenge you to a game of chess." This is a part of growing up.

> *A poor human environment* means falling into the trap of believing that since the world is a competitive place we must prepare children for competition by pitting them against each other. Such competition may build them up if they win but risks breaking them if they lose. When we surround youngsters with a competitive climate created by adults in authority, it can promote jealousy, anger, hostility, aggression, withdrawn behaviors, tension, distress, or even symptoms of emotional illness.

Good human environments provide for carefully chosen words. Words can hurt. Words can make children want to cooperate or rebel and misbehave. We need to keep our words within the understanding of children so the meanings are clear and not a source of threat or misunderstanding. We use language which does not ridicule or make fun of anyone and choose words which lighten up a situation.

"Hey, take it easy. You'll beat all speed records," is a better choice of words than "I told you to stop running. Now go sit by yourself until I tell you to move." Be patient and prepared to repeat and reword. Children forget. Sometimes they haven't even heard our words or understood them. It is also important to choose honest words so you can be trusted.

> *A poor human environment* is using words which confuse children ("It was not my intention to have this activity disintegrate!"), belittle or embarrass ("You'll never learn, you never listen!"), or words which blame, scold, frighten, or make fun of a person. These only attack the self-esteem which a child needs in order to behave appropriately.

In a good human environment staff are generous with honest praise. Praise children for what they accomplish ("You really worked hard on that skit. You must be proud." "Thanks for helping the younger kids out on the ice today. I appreciated that."). Praising the event helps the children evaluate themselves in terms of feeling capable, appreciated, and respected. By positive self-evaluation school-agers build positive self-esteem.

> *A poor human environment* consists of praising by personal evaluations or comparisons ("Terry, you are wonderful. You are our best actress.") The personal evaluation of "wonderful" may make the child worry about living up to the expectation. Being "best" may make children feel they must maintain this position or lose respect, and it may make everyone else feel inferior. Praise used as personal evaluation ("Robert, you're so smart") causes embarrassment and breeds resentment in others. It also makes a child doubt the adult's sincerity, since the praised child may not feel deserving of such praise. It puts the adult in the role of judge. It also tends to cause denial in older children ("No, I'm not really so smart... or kind... or generous"). So the evaluative praise has done little to provide positive self-esteem.

> Avoid praise which sends mixed messages. ("Josh, you did a great job setting up the tennis net, but why didn't you sweep up the court?" or "That was a good poem. Now watch your spelling.") Mixing praise and criticism leads children to expect criticism as part of praise. Negative behaviors may not improve when praise is mixed with criticism.

In good human environments school-agers are given acceptable choices in deciding about appropriate behaviors, so they become confident in their abilities to work out solutions to problems. Let children assume responsibility in deciding between alternative solutions. ("You could talk to Brent about how to share the volleyball or you could use the basketball until Brent is finished.")

> *A poor human environment* presents choices which are really threats ("You apologize to Brent or leave this gym."). This humiliation does little to help children take responsibility for their behaviors.

Good human environments allow school-agers ways to vent their concerns through regular group meetings, suggestion boxes, gripe sessions, private talks with staff, or writing up an incident or idea and presenting it to the adult or group.

> *A poor human environment* creates a climate which assumes everyone is happy. It condones tattling instead of dealing with the incidents which have encouraged it. It ignores the quiet, conforming, non-complaining children and doesn't provide time and ways for them to express their opinions. Dissatisfaction can result in resentful, sullen, angry behaviors.

A good human environment encourages developing independence and personal control through appropriate experiences with power. It lets children make plans, decisions, and choices. It lets them create activities that lead to successful finales, to mastery. Have a car wash, make a pizza, build a hideaway.

> *A poor human environment* presents experiences where the adult has all the power and makes all the decisions. When children do not feel power and the ability to control, their behaviors may be out of control.

Good human environments view problem behaviors as opportunities for learning. This reinforces the idea to school-agers that learning is not based on fear of mistakes but on trial and error, new insights, and different ways to explore and resolve problems.

> *A poor human environment* confuses *discipline* (which involves teaching) and *punishment* (which inflicts pain) in dealing with misbehaviors. Discipline teaches; punishment continues to breed the resentment and hostility that leads to increasing misbehavior.

THE ART OF DISCIPLINE

Dictionaries tell us that *art* means skill; performance; and systematic application of knowledge, ideas, and skills to bring about a desired result; and *discipline* means instruction and learning.

The art of discipline, then, refers to the skill and application of knowledge to attain a desired result through instruction. This means teaching — skilled and knowledgeable teaching. Teaching requires imparting one's knowledge to another person and we cannot impart knowledge unless we have the knowledge to share. We need to know exactly what we are teaching and how it can best be taught. Good discipline is precise teaching. It is not impulsive action and it is not punishment.

The word *discipline* is also related to the word *disciples* — followers, students of a leader who teaches. The persons who want to follow the teacher do so not for fear of punishment but because they want to learn. People also follow the teachings if they respect the leader and also feel respected by that leader. Good relationships between adults and children, then, are crucial to good discipline. When children feel respect, they want to cooperate. The more children admire the caregiving persons, the more likely they are to respect them and respond to their values and ideas. The more they fear the adults, the more likely they are to respond negatively, and the potential for learning is thwarted.

Good discipline means not only that adults preserve the children's sense of their own importance, but also that adults, as helpers, remember the importance of their own identity as knowledgeable and patient leaders who care, teach, and discipline without dictating or punishing. They remember this role, choose their actions carefully, and think through possible solutions before they act.

Good discipline requires that staff are self-disciplined. They don't sink to struggles for power with the children. They do not allow themselves to be out of control in ways which frighten children.

The art of discipline requires that staff are secure about teaching without losing their self-control, without using the behaviors which they are trying to discourage among the school-agers — yelling (to tell everyone to be quiet), rudeness (to a child who is being rude), or physical aggression (to stop physically aggressive behavior). Because an adult's security stems from knowledge about children's behaviors, they do not feel personally threatened when a child shows disrespect. They do not respond in the same disrespectful manner. Whatever methods adults decide to use in responding to behaviors, one criterion is essential: does the adult's response meet the child's need for developing identity, good relationships, and power? [1]

Caregivers maintain good relationships. They champion the kinds of gentle human behaviors which foster trust and prevent violence. Yet this all takes time. It takes time for children to become self-disciplined and it takes time for caregivers to believe that good discipline is an art to practice until they feel they are on the right track.

Adults will find their own styles of good discipline. The ways may vary from child to child, from incident to incident. There are times when you must say, "No, you can't" or "Yes, you must." There are also times when you will say, "Hold on now. Let's work this out together."

All three of the following styles of discipline are perfectly valid for particular situations. The first two styles, however, can too easily become overused, permanent disciplinary styles which are neither art nor good teaching.

Style Number One: The Do-As-I-Say Relationship

This is the authoritarian approach to discipline. The problem with authoritarianism is the changed behavior may last only as long as the adult is present. You cannot turn your back and be sure the child has any kind of personal conviction that the behavior really needs to be changed. An overdose of bossy authoritarianism leads children and youth to believe they always need to be told what to do by someone in authority. They therefore become dependent on waiting for the commands of others. It says, "Your own judgments don't count for much; you can't trust your own reasoning." In the process of conforming to the rules of others, children may suppress their anger. Then the anger may become hostility and seep through, resulting in the negative behaviors which adults are trying to avoid. The anger may spill through in children's relations to the adult and in their relations with each other.

Style Number Two:
The Do-Whatever-You-Want Relationship

An overdose of this attitude toward discipline is observed in staff who literally turn their backs when trouble is brewing and walk away from children's conflicts without being sure that the problem is going to be resolved. This is usually the person who has paid little attention to environmental factors which may cause behavior problems and is uninterested in the reasons behind the behaviors. The do-whatever-you-want relationship may be appropriate as long as children are safe, have healthy and interesting tasks from which to choose, and are using good judgment. But there are many occasions when school-agers really do need help in preventing and working out problems. If the adult is not there to help, the children have the feeling no one really cares and self-esteem is endangered. When children and youth have the power to do whatever they want but don't know what to do to achieve their goals, this power does not help them develop personal control.

Style Number Three:
The Helping Relationship: Shared Solutions

Shared solutions means that good discipline comes from good teaching and good teaching is a two-way process. The adult learns from the children and the children learn from the adult. When there is a problem requiring discipline, helpers learn from the children just what the problem is (the cause). The helper then states the problem clearly so both children and helper understand it: "As I'm hearing it, you both want to use the typewriter." (If there is physical conflict, it must be stopped, of course, before shared solutions can begin; if a child is hurt, the adult must first attend to the injury.) Together the children and helper determine what feelings and needs are involved. This may include the feelings and needs of the helper as well as the children.

Children and adults together share ideas for all the possible solutions that might meet everyone's needs. If the children are allowed to present their ideas first, they gain a true feeling of being respected and having an active role in the decision-making process. Then consider everybody's solutions no matter how far out they may seem. Consider how things might turn out if certain ideas were tried ("If you tore up her paper, what might happen next?"). Of the proposed solutions, which ones are acceptable to everyone?

Decide on one or more solutions and try them. Talk about whether they work. Some may work well, others may not. School-agers will learn from the successful solutions as well as from the ideas that failed to solve the problem.

Together the children and helper determine what feelings and needs are involved in a conflict situation.

The process of mutual responsibility for solving behavior problems, then, involves the shared power of both adults and children. Shared solutions involve many immediate advantages. The shared-solutions process stops the conflict so that everyone can concentrate on the solution. It involves equal power between children and helper. It may involve humor to lighten the tension and can help boys and girls relax as they resume their activities. There are no labels of good guys and bad guys so the day can continue without resentments.

The shared-solutions process has many long-range advantages. Shared solutions enhance children's self-esteem and self-respect because they have become a part of the discipline process. Both children and caregiver have had a chance to express their own needs and resolve problems in positive ways. It maintains cooperative relationships among children and with the caregiver because there has been no scolding, shaming, or hurt feelings. It has encouraged the expression of personal convictions and a feeling of personal responsibility and power. Rules are more likely to be followed since children have helped create the rules.

Shared solutions also promote intellectual growth through creative thinking to solve problems. It helps develop proficiency of verbal expression. No one is threatened by making mistakes as the variety of ideas and plans are considered.

Shared control actually helps children and youth respect authority because the helping adult, the authority figure, is not directing, punishing, or ignoring but is involved along with the children in decisions which affect their lives.

School-agers are maturing as they develop self-reliance. They are learning how to get through a problem and see it to its solution. Shared solutions is a process which develops the traits essential for living in a democratic society.

THE TROUBLE WITH PUNISHMENT

Hurt feelings

"You hurt my feelings." Children express it this way, and it is true. Punishment can be hurtful. It can become too easy, too frequent. It has too many side effects: it sets the stage for sneakiness and lying, blaming others, hatred and distrust of authority, and aggression or withdrawal. It may make a child feel like a victim or a villain. It makes children want to get back at the adult who inflicted the punishment. Above all, punishment breeds anger, which in turn breeds negative behaviors. Children and youth who constantly behave in negative ways are often angry because they have already been punished many times and their feelings about themselves have been hurt.

Punishment implies hurt and pain and suffering for an act of wrongdoing. However, the process of hurting does not assure that persons understand how to behave better the next time or that they know what is the right thing to do. Many children are still learning the skill of seeing things from another person's point of view and understanding another person's feelings and reactions. They may not see punishment as the adult sees it — a logical consequence of their behavior — therefore, they frequently interpret punishment as a personal attack. The punishment promotes anger and pain rather than teaching.

Punishment may hurt our feelings, too. As we punish we may also be the victims of the side-effects. Rather than using more thoughtful, slower, kinder ways of teaching, we may begin to view ourselves as police-persons, checking for, silencing, and eliminating behaviors. We may begin to believe that children are "out to get us," spiteful, uncooperative. We are in real emotional trouble when we see children as "them against me." If we become the source of judgment and punishment and are expecting quick change, we must always wonder to ourselves how lasting the behavioral change will be. If we are not present will it occur again? Have we made a child feel powerless, shamed, disliked? Have we lost the respect for children which, in turn, helps them respect us? As aggressive, punishing adults have we become inappropriate models of aggressive, negative behavior?

Positive teaching requires positive feelings. It requires feelings of optimism. Better behaviors are better taught not through harsh punishment, but through our own examples of firm and gentle guidance and consistent respect.

Punishment does not cure

When adults punish, they believe they will cure, make the child well. Cures, however, are always individual prescriptions. There is no cure-all which works for every child. Well children may survive punishment. Troubled children, however, may be so threatened that they hurt more, and one too many punishments may be their breaking point. The problem is that it may be difficult to tell the stable children from the troubled children. Punishment tries to cure them all.

Children who really don't know what to do need to be taught what to do — not punished. Children who know what to do but persist in inappropriate behavior need to be helped — but not punished. We need to know what the problem is, why these children behave as they do. Children whose behaviors are simply a result of their stage of development need adult understanding and patience. We should be applying our knowledge and skills, not inflicting punishment.

Punishments which do not help

Throughout time adults have found the easiest ways to punish children. They are easy because they quickly satisfy the adult and may, for the moment, stop a behavior. They may put the adult solely in charge, solely in power. In so doing, however, they tend to make children so resentful and dependent on the control of others they fail to develop their own means of self-discipline, self-control, and ways to deal with their own behaviors.

The kinds of punishments most frequently used by adults have been *physical punishment*, *scolding* and *isolation*.

Physical Punishment

"All that kid needs is a good paddle!" When we strike children we are teaching that hitting others is an acceptable way to solve problems. Children model behavior, learn what they see. School-agers who grow up believing that hitting is acceptable will strike out at adults. They may hurt other children. When they become adults, they may be accused of assault. These children are in for a lot of problems.

Hitting children also teaches them to be afraid, and fear does not encourage confident, healthy development. In hitting kids we teach them to believe they are bad. If they are taught that they are bad, they will continue to display negative kinds of behaviors and believe that they are not worthy individuals who can do things well. They will not respect themselves, and the lack of self-respect will impact their later development. With nothing to lose, they can do what they choose. If they do not respect themselves, they will not respect others.

Most children do not hit back. Therefore, they will try to get back at adults through other ways such as disobedience, hostility, withdrawal, and delinquent behaviors. When we strike children we are teaching them the violent behavior that they can use now — or when they become parents, teachers or caregivers. Violent behavior breeds violent behavior.

Scolding

"I scold and I scold." "If I told him once I told him a thousand times!" That's just the trouble with scolding. The more we scold the more children feel, "Well, I survived, I can take it!" So they misbehave again or they feel so belittled that they tune us out in self-defense. Sometimes they are so used to the scolding that they even put on an act of bravado and declare "I'm glad I did it!" Repeated scolding becomes boring. Scolding may cause anger. It can breed resistance to real cooperation. Scolding is not teaching. It humiliates, attacks self-esteem, and emphasizes a sense of failure.

Scolding damages the children's perception of the adult as a kind and caring person. It may endanger children's need to trust adults for the kinds of help, advice, and teaching which will not dwell on past mistakes but will help them find ways to behave appropriately in the future. If school-agers expect to be scolded, they will cease to be honest or open. They will cease to view adults as a source of learning, growth, and understanding.

Scolding is closely related to shouting — high-pitched adult voices which scream and yell at groups or individuals. It is disruptive to children who are not involved in inappropriate behaviors, and it is embarrassing to the child who is involved. But we get impatient and angry. We may scream to get attention in a loud, noisy room or when we just don't know how else to handle a situation. Sometimes adults even scream and yell to tell children not to scream and yell!

Scolding usually means we are mad. If this is the case, let us say so: "I'm mad because..." Scolding sometimes is merely a habit. Habits can be broken.

Isolation

"Time-out!" It's quick, it's easy, and it's convenient for adults. It removes the child from the problem. Perhaps that is the real trouble with time-out: it *separates* the child from the problem. Do we really want separation or do we want interaction so that children are helped to work through problems and figure out ways of solving them?

Indeed children may need to be separated from a situation they cannot handle well in order to calm down and get a fresh start. But isolation, or removing them from the situation, will not promote the self-control which is needed unless the adult helps children deal with the problem rather than isolating them from it. These are usually the very school-agers who need the practice of interacting with others in appropriate ways, rather than being shamed and alone. "Now, just sit there and think about what you did!" You have heard this said to children. In the moment of being pointed out as guilty, however, children are not usually doing their best thinking. Nor could any one of us.

When children must be separated from a situation (such as fighting), it is clear a time-out may be appropriate if it can be used by the children as a time to resolve the problem. "Donnie and Matt, take some time together and try to figure out what happened and how you can work things out. Take five minutes and then, if you have trouble, I'll come over and see if I can help you."

Sometimes time-out can merely be a change in activity: to a calmer scene, a more relaxing part of the room, or outdoors to release energy. Then, "In about ten minutes come on over and let's discuss the problem." Staff need to share the time with the children as they think through together how to deal with the feelings which led to the conflict. This conversation should be in private. It should not be threatening, nor should it be viewed as punishment. Time-out may not be necessary at all if the children involved in the problem can work out solutions themselves, on-the-spot, as the problem occurs.

Another difficulty with isolation is that separation says to the rest of the group, "This kid has been bad." Remember the child who used to sit in the chair wearing the dunce cap? Remember the child who was placed in the corner in front of the other children? Is the time-out chair any different? It labels, it embarrasses, it shames. It is neither a way of learning better ways nor a way to achieve self-esteem. It leaves a child troubled and resentful, and it isolates and separates the very child who needs to have secure relationships with others. Finally, time-out can become so routine that it has no effect. Children perceive it merely as a nuisance routine.

Other Methods of Punishment

There are other less obvious styles of punishment which tear children down instead of building them up:

Criticism	"You're always so clumsy. Can't you do things right?"
Sarcasm	"Is that an 'antique' shirt you're wearing?"
Put-downs	"Don't be such a fraidy cat!"
Impatience	"Hurry up; I don't have all day."
Comparisons	"Can't you make yours as good as Joshua's?"
Threats	"If you don't clean that up, I'm going to tell your father! "
Shaming	"Look at you. You'll never learn."
Depriving of food	"No snack for you today!"

Name-calling	"Look, dummy..."
Making fun of children	"Poor Luke. He's so skinny his pants won't stay up."
Denying children's feelings	"Stop crying. He didn't hurt you!"

And even more subtle:

Ignoring when children desperately need attention.
Threatening with voices, actions, or facial expressions.
Being dishonest, which tells kids you can't be trusted.
Making children feel unacceptable because of behavior, language, age, intelligence, size, family, or any aspect about themselves.

"I punish and punish and nothing works." That's just it. Punishment doesn't work.[2]

HELPING CHILDREN WITH CONFLICT

"If we are to reach real peace in this world...
we shall have to begin with the children."
Mahatma Gandhi

We hear the adults:

"He's always hitting on the other kids, so I told them "Go hit back!""

"If she doesn't win, she just goes off and kicks someone."

"Don't you dare spit at him!" "Quit fighting!"

We hear the children:

"She punched me first!" "He took my pencil!"

"That boy has it in for me!"

"You think you know it all; well you don't!"

"Ouch!"

Conflict. Violence. Wars among school-agers.

Staff live with many kinds of problem behaviors when they live among school-agers. Some behaviors are trivial behaviors, the kinds which may distract or bother others but really don't hurt or injure (children who tease, tattle, show off, yell, or whine). Others are the defiant behaviors which often display children's needs for recognition (repeated breaking of rules, cursing, talking back). These kinds of behaviors usually can be tolerated and handled with humor, patience, or personal attention. The behaviors discussed in this section are behaviors that cause conflicts between children or between children and adults. These are conflicts which may be minor, or may become injurious and lead to violent action.

A conflict-free atmosphere is every caregiver's dream! But dreams are rarely realistic and conflicts are not always to be avoided. The important goal is helping children handle conflicts without hitting back or trying to prove who is most powerful, without involving injurious and violent behaviors. If children are helped to resolve conflicts without violence and harm to other people or to themselves, if they grow up in a culture of caring for others, with self-respect and nonviolent behaviors, perhaps as adults they will have the skills to achieve peaceful solutions to conflict and to avoid global conflicts.

A certain amount of conflict is inevitable because both children and adults see things from different points of view. Conflict of ideas can lead to progress and the growth of new perspectives. Conflict of ideas can also lead to cooperative methods of reaching solutions. Finding ways to resolve conflicts without being warlike and destructive is what is important.

What are some factors which lead to conflicts?

For staff to help children and youth deal with conflict in peaceful ways, it is useful to look at some of the reasons for conflicts, just as we look at the reasons for all behaviors.

We all see things differently

Individuals perceive the world from their own particular viewpoints, their understandings of what they have seen, heard, and experienced. Because the ways we view things are so varied, conflicts arise. This is especially true during the years of school-age development when the drive for personal identity is so intense. We need to keep this struggle in mind as we assist children and youth in resolving problems without violent action. *Conflicts arise due to differing opinions about the same thing and from children's needs to believe in and act on their own values.*

The need to be a winner

School-agers' lives are full of competition to be the best, the one who is always right. Arguments start, name-calling begins, fist-fights brew. This happens among children, adults, and nations. They all want to be winners. The need to be a winner, however, does not necessarily imply someone else will be a loser. When children feel like winners because they are comfortable with themselves and their relationships, they need not feel "winning" is so essential nor do they have to win at someone else's expense.

Competition is an integral part of much of school-agers' lives. Children face competition in school for grades, teacher approval, friends, to win games, make teams, get into plays or college. They are surrounded by it. We can make certain that a nurturing environment does not contribute to any competitive feelings which lead to conflict — winners and losers. Children get plenty of that everywhere else. *Conflicts arise when children's environments promote competition.*

Experiences with violence

Another factor which relates to violent behaviors in settling conflicts is what children and youth have observed from families, peers, neighborhoods, and the media. Frequently school-agers are the victims of violent behaviors and abuse or they may have witnessed violent abuse to family members — siblings, parents, older persons. Because some school-agers know first-hand the hurt and tragedy of physical violence, they may also view it as a method of resolving conflicts. It is challenging to teach peaceful solutions if violent action is all children know.

Play materials (guns, swords, war-lasers) with which school-agers have grown up have often encouraged violent and stressful kinds of play. Pretend, hostile, war-like play may be impossible to prevent, but it is good to take a firm stand that war-like toys, weapons which hurt other living beings, are not welcome. If we are teaching non-violent action, then violent props for play will surely contradict the teachings. Our guidance can also include information about the risks in the use of real weapons, both to the user and to all the possible victims. *Conflicts arise when only violence has been experienced as the way to solve problems.*

The physical environment and the school-age program

Some conflicts arise because of factors right in front of our eyes. These are the easiest to remedy. Look at your facilities. Programs must provide the resources which children and youth need to master skills, because developing competency and *feeling* competent are goals for school-agers. There must be enough materials of interest for everyone with enough to do and enough space to do it in. Materials should work well, be in good repair, and do the job they are supposed to do. There also must be sufficient and interesting activities geared to the development levels of the children enrolled, from the youngest to the oldest. Frustration and boredom lead to conflict. *Perhaps the greatest number of conflicts arise over sharing an inadequate amount of equipment and materials and participating in uninteresting or inappropriate activities.*

The drive to satisfy human needs

This drive relates to much of what has been discussed throughout this text and is relevant to situations which result in conflicts among individuals. *Many conflicts arise over the needs for personal attention (identity), affection (relationships), and control (power).*

The role of the staff

The peaceful settlement of conflict requires that adults play an active role and are alert to conflict situations in order to respond to them. Conflicts of ideas and opinions can be signs of healthy intellectual growth. Physical conflicts, when verbal resolutions of conflicts break down or are not resolved, are not signs of healthy growth.

Often we need not intervene, step in, or smooth things over because the children are already working out the solution. Sometimes we need to look at the specific incident and have techniques to help, or look at the particular children and know why they are so distressed, aggressive, or tightly strung. Many times we need to look at the school-age setting and say, "What is the atmosphere like?" or "What may be leading to any of the unhealthy war-like conflicts?"

Adults also look at their own roles and the roles of other persons who work with the children. The way adults interact with the children can itself be a source of conflict.

- Are the adults anticipating problems, looking for causes of conflict?

- Are the adults praising, using humor, giving smiles?

- Are the adults helping children discuss, negotiate?

- Are the adults tense, edgy, demanding, so youngsters behave the same way?

Have adults become such dictators that children feel a need to fight back? Imposing adult power does not work. Mature adults help resolve conflicts between people in ways which no person, including the child, comes out feeling shamed, cheated, or feeling like the loser. Staff act as mediators and negotiators, encouraging children as they work on solutions to conflicts by helping them brainstorm, think through and try out different options. Children are helped to see adults as a source of support, persons who are with them and not against them, persons who are trying to get them where they want to go, persons who are on their side.

We may be helping both children and youth resolve conflicts in different ways from those practiced in their homes. Keep families informed, then, about non-punitive and non-violent approaches to solving problems and conflicts. Invite families to observe your approaches and actions. Help them encourage their children to see the strong qualities in other human beings. Help them instill in their children the self-confidence which allows for acceptance of many points of view.

Fighting

School-agers do fight — a lot — at home, at school, and in out-of-school programs. This is a normal part of development. They fight for many different reasons. Sometimes it is fun and playful, involving the physical energy which abounds in both boys and girls. At other times it may be due to fatigue or hunger, when the brain is not in its usual state of control. It may be due to anger or to feeling worthless and not knowing how else to achieve importance. The reasons go on and on. It is wise to recognize the normalcy of fighting as a form of conflict in school-agers and try to understand the role of the adult in relation to it.

We are not in the business of being the referee, of making judgments, or taking sides. "You're right" and "You're wrong" are just what children may want to hear. They translate this into "You're good" and "You're not." This is no way to encourage good relationships. We are not participants; our own feelings need not be involved.

A recurring form of conflict among school-agers is what starts out as an argument (over breaking a game rule or sharing a material, over who said what to whom) and ends up with a physical fight. However, if we look closely, we see a variety of forms of physical fighting.

Children's spontaneous roughhousing may look like fighting, but is really something quite different.

Roughhousing

Children's spontaneous roughhousing may look like fighting but is really something quite different. School-agers wrestle, chase, tussle, roll around on the ground. They may use angry words, but roughhousing may also involve giggles and affection. Roughhousing is common behavior among school-agers. The difference between roughhousing and real fighting is that roughhousing is usually by mutual consent. It can be allowed as long as it continues as friendly and no one objects or is getting hurt. Adults will need to keep an eye on it and make sure it does not escalate into a real fight. It is good to find out from the children involved whether it is just a roughhouse fight or a real fight. When roughhousing is no longer fun, or someone is getting hurt, it is no longer roughhousing. School-agers understand that if someone gets hurt they are fighting and must stop.

Minor skirmishes

First a squabble, a shove, and then each child walks away or starts to talk things out. Hardly a real fight. These children are on the road to settling things themselves, toward stopping short of serious physical or violent action. An adult need not become involved.

Major battles

You may see a lot of these — the argument, then the shove, the punch, followed by the all-out, physical fight. Physical fighting is probably the most common violent method used by children and youth when they are really angry at each other. Some children will even physically strike out at adults when they feel backed against the wall and don't know what else to do. Both boys and girls who use physical force are often used to these kinds of behaviors. They have seen others use physical violence; physical violence may have been used on them. All-out fighting must be stopped and the problem must be settled. The adult helps children to a better, safer solution.

War!

When fighting has escalated to the point of danger, it must be stopped immediately. The children must know that it is not safe. If children's tempers are out-of-control, it may be hard to keep your own temper in control — hard not to blame or threaten. It may be wise to delay dealing with the matter, resolving the conflict, until angry feelings have subsided. At these times it is best for adults, as helpers, to be firm, calm, and patient in coming to grips with solutions. "Each of you go find something else to do. In a few minutes we'll all get together to talk about this problem." In a few minutes the adult begins the role of mediator, negotiator, the person who helps bring peace. The peacemaking process can begin.

Negotiating solutions to fighting and other forms of conflict

No matter how well staff have tried to prevent physical conflict through carefully considering all the aspects of the program, fighting may still occur when tempers flare. Many children cannot control themselves yet and are grateful to know that adults care enough to keep them from hurting others and from being hurt. You can focus on these children who become violent. Share some personal time with them. Give some extra attention and support. You can watch for opportunities to make them feel strong in their ideas and opinions so they need not strike out in frustration. Offer activities which encourage their assertiveness and strengths.

Above all, keep a sense of reason, siding neither with the victim nor the abuser. You will need to be sure the victim has not been harmed, but you also need to be sure children who have hurt others are not treated as bad persons. They may already be convinced by this label and may continue to live up to it. Punishment, as we have stated, may only add to their worries, fears, and anger. Sympathy for the victims must not blind us to the problems of children who hurt others.

Staff also cannot fall into the "easy-way-out" in trying to prevent future fighting:

Easy-way-out: "Apologize! Say you're sorry!"

Apologies usually are not helpful to either child when an adult demands them. Children who are forced to apologize may simply feel pressured to lie if their own angry feelings are still there; lying does not make angry feelings go away. The child who is forced to accept an apology is aware it is not sincere. Apologies may be in order at some future time when rational thinking has replaced the emotional heat, when friendship is ready to resume.

Easy-way-out: "Hit back! Tit for tat!"

In anger, adults may strike out at youngsters who are hurting others or they may encourage a child to fight back. Hitting back, or encouraging others to strike back, can only teach that it is an acceptable way to act. It only teaches that it is a violent world where people will hurt and be hurt. It promotes future conflict because of the anger it encourages.

The easy way out does not help children deal with the anger which leads to fighting.

Making peace

Angry feelings have led to angry actions. Now peaceful solutions can be taught in an atmosphere of peace. Adults assume the important role of helper in the process. Peacemaking skills begin. The fight or conflict is stopped. A non-threatening word, or hand, separates the children who are actually fighting and calms those who argue. A private place is chosen for conversation.

- Each child is allowed to express the anger verbally. ("The ball was over the line!"/"The ball was *not* over the line!") The adult recognizes these points of view: "You're mad at each other because you each think differently about where the ball landed."

- Recognize it if there seem to have been "misunderstandings." Many conflicts are simply mistakes in children's perceptions of how things happened (You can say, "You said... and Juan said... so it seems you see things differently.").

- Let the children know this may be a hard problem to solve. ("So from what you saw, each of you feel you're right. That's a tough one!")

- Assure the children that they will be able to settle this and think of a solution together which makes them both comfortable. They can use their brainstorming skills. You may offer a few sample solutions ("Any witnesses?" "You could play it again."). Older children may wish to write down possible solutions.

- Tell the children that you will return to them in about five minutes to see how they are doing. Then return as planned.

- Listen to each suggestion. If the children wish, or if they are unable to arrive at a satisfactory solution, you may suggest bringing the problem to a larger group for some more ideas. If you do so, be sure that others do not take sides but are genuinely interested in helping with solutions.

The problem is now the children's responsibility to solve in a peaceful way. Violent action is being settled with *non-violent* action.

Peer mediation

Peer mediation refers to children and youth who learn to help peers settle fights. Most children don't really want fights to continue, but don't know how to end them gracefully and without losing face. Children who act as mediators help the children involved in the dispute save face because they make it clear to them that there are no losers and that they will come up with their own solution. Peer mediators may be selected for training from volunteers or nominations. They need not be the model, well-behaved children. In fact, the skills and responsibilities are often helpful for at-risk, problem children, the usual trouble-makers. It helps them with a sense of self-importance, with relationship skills, and with a sense of having some control. Peer mediators can represent various ages, genders, and cultures.

"Cease fire!" What a relief this can be to the kids in conflict. They may then be asked if they want some help from a mediator. If so, they meet in a designated, private place with a trained peer who reminds them of the rules of mediation:

- No name-calling or interrupting each other

- Everyone gets a chance to tell their own side of the story (older children may write this down if they wish)

- The mediator will not take sides

- The children involved will then decide on a way to settle the conflict (this may also be written)

Major disputes involving weapons, drugs, or criminal behavior should not be handled by peers. These must be referred to adults and carefully handled in appropriate ways.

When there is only one solution

There are times when an adult must intervene quickly to resolve a problem. For example, Nathan gets ready to go home and Andrew hides Nathan's bat because he wants to continue to use it. Nathan curses and grabs for Andrew. The adult must intervene: "Nathan needs the bat right now because his father is waiting for him." The adult can still try to leave the power to solve the problem with the boys, "You two must work something out, right now, about the bat. Nathan has to go home." The adult is firm, states the problem, allows for some problem solving, but the solution is evident that the bat must be returned.

When the tattle-tale tells

Children who "tell" on other children's misbehaviors may have very different motivations. Frequently these are simply children in need of adult attention. They may be worriers. Often they are the very children who have been punished for their own misbehaviors, or they may think in good-bad or right-wrong terms of justice, a developmental characteristic of school-agers. In any case, as an adult, you can reassure tattlers that you realize *they* know the rules. Then calmly check out the situation without threatening either the tattle-tale (who may be in need of a more positive self-esteem) or the children in conflict (whom the tattle-tale may hope to get into trouble). You may acknowledge to the tattler that the children in conflict must be stopped. If the situation is dangerous, you may thank the person who alerted you.

It is generally best not to encourage tattling since it can lead to hostility among children. Encouraging children to be responsible for their own behaviors is better than encouraging watch-dog behaviors. As youngsters resolve their own conflicts in positive ways, neither the tattler nor the children in conflict become winners or losers and therefore have a chance to be friends rather than opponents.

Bring it to a vote?

Several children are involved in coming to a decision, perhaps even the whole group. Everyone's point of view has been heard. The discussion still has not settled the conflict of opinions and a decision must be made. Usually an open discussion will resolve a conflict but if action depends on one solution or another, voting is an option. Voting, however democratic it sounds, should be recognized as a method which says to the winners, "Wow, you won!" and the losers are naturally disappointed. In calling for a vote it can be stated that "If you want to vote, we'll go by the most votes, but we all understand that the side with the least votes may not be really happy with that solution. We can try to make them feel okay about it. Sometimes we win, sometimes we lose."

Let's just change the subject!

Macey and Donald, good friends, have been bickering all afternoon. Wherever one goes the other follows, teasing, name-calling, pushing. Trouble is on the way. Tina, Marie and Abby can't decide who has the best hairstyle. They pat, yank, then pull at each other's hair. Trouble brewing.

Neither of these conflict situations is dangerous yet, but they don't seem to be getting resolved. The situations are trivial but could end up with hurt and anger. Staff may wish to casually intervene, diffuse the situation, separate the children. This does not involve punishment or scolding. It merely involves giving the children other things to do and other places to go: "Macey, I need you to take these papers to Mrs. Johnson." "Marie, please check out the bird cage and see if it has been cleaned." It only takes an alternative activity and a few gentle words. It blames no one. It doesn't turn superficial squabbles into major battles. It simply stops the action and helps everyone on to other experiences.

Humor

Humor, so appealing to children of all ages, can often both prevent or stop tension. "If you two keep fighting, you'll be too beat up to enter the world championships!" If humor is used, be sure no one has hurt feelings, even if it was meant to be a joke. School-agers may feel hurt by what was meant to be funny, although they try to be good sports. Shared humor may be used beneficially but never at the expense of a child.

War or Peace: Building Foundations for Peace

To build a peaceful society we look to teachers of peace and depend on these persons as models for leadership and guidance. Adults, in living with children and youth, are truly peacemakers, teachers of peace. They believe that peace can be a reality for children only when it is a part of their own lives. They teach peace by modeling peaceful living.

We can help young persons in their desire to live in peaceful ways if we share with them the skills and experiences of peace. If we do not, we may be denying them the feelings and understandings which could prevent the violence in many of their lives.

We have already discussed many factors which can help children and adults live together in peaceful ways — basic ideas for thoughtful program planning. There are also many structured experiences which can be incorporated into daily plans. It is important that planned activities are suited to the ages and skills of the children so that each child is participating with comfort and it is fun for everyone.[3]

We offer here a few specific planned activities which relate to three topics previously discussed in this chapter:

- creating cooperative environments which encourage close relationships and a sense of group

- interacting with children in ways which will affirm each child's sense of importance

- specific experiences to teach conflict resolution skills

STRUCTURED EXPERIENCES TO CREATE COOPERATIVE ENVIRONMENTS WHICH ENCOURAGE A SENSE OF GROUP

The goal of these particular experiences is to help the staff and members of the group create a climate which encourages sharing and cooperation and a sense of community. The activities may be appropriate for the entire group, small groups, or even just two group members.

Group sharing times

Call this activity whatever you wish. The children can decide a name for it: group meeting, sharing time, talk circle, peace table. Everyone has a chance to talk without interruption. If the group is not large, each child may be invited to take a turn.

When:

- Right away at the start of the year — weekly, maybe daily, whenever there are things to be shared

- When new personnel are employed, so they are introduced and become familiar

- When new children arrive, to help them feel more comfortable

- When exciting things happen, as well as when simple problems need to be discussed

- When plans must be made or announcements shared

- When interesting guests visit

Why:

- To help group members and adults get to know each other and build feelings of friendship

- To help children feel good about their own importance

- To encourage the confidence to communicate ideas in group situations

Where:

- In a comfortable area for a circle, so every person, adult and child, has an equal role and can be seen easily

Sharing feelings

Recognize with the children that we all have the same kinds of feelings: happiness, sadness, anger, jealousy, fear, etc. Make it safe to talk about feelings anyone wants to share, whether positive or negative. Conversations may begin anywhere, but you might start with non-threatening or humorous topics: "How do you feel about our playground?" "Were you ever fooled on April Fools' Day?" Then try out other conversation openers:

- "Share something new that you're excited about: a new friend, pet, bike, idea."

- "Share a feeling about something that worries you."

- "Share a feeling about something that makes you happy."

- "Share something you appreciate about someone in the group."

- "What kinds of comments would make someone feel good? Feel angry? Sad? Have you ever made these comments to anyone?"

Try role play. Suggest a situation. For example, Matt is waiting on the corner for Jim to meet him after school. Jim's mother does not let him go. Assign or ask for volunteers to act it out. How does Jim feel? How does Matt feel? Talk about it.

Sharing projects

- Community service projects

- Interest clubs

- Productions — drama, dance, musical performances, videos, newsletters

- Student government

- Group trips

- Environmental responsibilities

- Food preparations

Solving problems

- Talk about the problem with everyone having a chance for comments and opinions.

- Brainstorm the various ways to approach and solve the problem.

- Speculate on what might happen if various solutions are tried.
- Assure the group they will find a solution and you will help if needed.
- Come to an agreement on which solutions to try.
- Meet again to discuss how things worked out.

Using the arts

- As children take a good look at paintings, photography, and sculpture, stop to talk about the ideas and feelings expressed by the artist. "How does it make you feel?"
- Literature, videos, dance, and drama can be used as starting points for group discussion. Freeze the action and discuss the ideas.

Current events and real life happenings

- Brainstorm solutions to problems about which children read, hear, or observe, such as floods, conflicts between nations, political issues.
- Help children identify with familiar feelings and situations such as sadness, fear, loneliness, divorce, death, joy, success, and cooperative ventures. Their common experiences help them see similarities with each other. Their diverse experiences help them learn about and appreciate how other persons may be feeling.

Cooperative creations

- Murals, group carpentry, cardboard box construction, block building, and   construction projects
- Group drawings, paintings, collage: "If you were stranded in a cave what would you like to have with you?" or "Draw your ideas for the perfect school, the perfect neighborhood, or the perfect party!" Participants contribute and discuss their ideas and can add to the ideas of others.
- Making monsters, robots, imaginary creatures, fantasy machinery, future human beings, etc. Participants contribute all the different parts, as they wish, using materials such as papers, cardboard, wood, glue, staples, tapes, markers, pipe cleaners, found objects.
- Cooperative storytelling. The story is developed as participants contribute one word, a sentence, or a story segment.

Cooperative games

There are many games which teach cooperative rather than competitive skills. In cooperative games the group members work together for common goals. Cooperative games need not replace the competitive games school-agers devise and so much enjoy. They are simply a different approach with an emphasis on the unity of the group. There are many examples of board games, paper-pencil games, and physical action games.

STRUCTURED EXPERIENCES TO AFFIRM EACH CHILD'S SENSE OF IMPORTANCE

These activities lead participants through experiences that help them feel good about themselves, without striving to be winners or thinking of others as adversaries. The closer children feel to each other, the less likely they are to have unsolvable conflicts with each other. Children and youth develop sensitivity as they share experiences, feelings, and ideas. Friendships can be encouraged through specific activities.

Getting to know each other

Paired introductions

Find out about each other and share information with the group.

Name tags

"Make your own and add something you like to do." "Make your own and pass it to the person next to you who adds something he likes about you."

Interviews

Pairs of children meet in a comfortable setting and interview each other. "What do you like to do best on weekends?" "What is your favorite sport?" Younger and older children can be paired in order to close age barriers.

Children interviewing each other can be a structured experience to affirm each child's sense of importance.

171

Quilt-making

Each child contributes a square depicting a scene from his life, something he is proud of, etc.

Getting to know oneself

Personal scrapbook

Keep a record of your life as the year progresses—photos, news, awards, etc.

Qualities I like in people

List. Do *I* have these qualities?

Stuffed cupcakes

Each child writes a positive wish and puts it in a cupcake. Bake. Children choose cakes at random and discuss how the wish might apply to them.

Storytelling or writing

Suggest ideas: What I will do when I get to Mars? This is my room after I have redesigned it the way I'd like it.

Wearable art

Make personalized T-shirts, badges, buttons, stickers, jeans, etc.

Personal photographs

Collect pictures of self, family, friends, pets, etc. for personal or group album.

Letter play

Use positive words to describe self or others (**M**ark is **M**iraculous! **B**arbara is **B**eautiful! ... My name is **C**hris **D**onner, I am **C**reative and **D**ashing!)

Birthday recognition

Group members dictate or write a friendship message and put it in a notebook or on a poster to present to the birthday child.

Bunch of balloons

Each child writes something which is important to him or her on a blown-up balloon (a person, an activity, a value). Bunch up everyone's balloons and display.

STRUCTURED EXPERIENCES TO CREATE CONFLICT RESOLUTION SKILLS

The goals are to help children practice the skill of discovering solutions to conflicts, recognizing different points of view, listening and clearly communicating in order to avoid misunderstandings, and being comfortable in sharing ideas and opinions without feeling threatened.

Brainstorming

This is a basic technique, previously mentioned in this text, which may be applied to many different situations whenever a group decision must be made. A problem is presented by adults or children and participants simply suggest as many kinds of solutions as possible. No ideas are censored or ruled out. Then the group decides which solutions are actually possible to try. The process helps everyone understand that there are often many solutions to problems and they are capable of finding answers. Discuss this.

Quick decisions

Present a problem to the group, then form pairs or small groups to think up an agreed-upon solution. Limit the decision-making time to only a minute or two. This helps the skill of making decisions quickly, under time pressure. Discuss how this feels.

Wishful thinking

Children present a conflict they have encountered in school, in out-of-school programs, or at home. Brainstorm "wishes" as to how the conflict could be resolved and what could prevent the wishes from coming true.

Role play or puppetry

Children act out an example of a conflict. For example, a person's jacket is missing and someone is suspected of taking it, but there is no proof. The action may be followed up in a variety of ways:

- Stop the role play before the conflict is resolved and let the audience suggest possible solutions. The actors can choose from the solutions and play it out.

- Stop the action before the conflict is resolved. Divide into small groups. Each group discusses solutions, rehearses, and then acts out its own solution.

- Reverse roles of the actors and discuss how it feels from another person's point of view.

- Reverse male and female roles, child and adult roles. Discuss the feelings of the players as the action progresses or after it is completed.

- Videotape an entire skit. Play it back, stopping the film whenever the audience has a comment about how the actors help or do not help resolve the conflict.

Always talk about role play when it is finished. For instance, how could the conflict have been prevented? How did the players feel during the action? Afterwards? Did the solution seem to work? What else might have worked?

Conflict stories

- Tell or read a story that presents a conflict situation. Stop before the conflict is resolved and brainstorm solutions. Finish telling or reading the story and discuss the final solution.

- Tell or read a familiar story but stop before the usual ending. Have children tell or write a new ending (*Cinderella*, *Wizard of Oz*, etc.).

- Let group members draw a comic strip leaving the conflict unresolved. Pass comic strips around or pick them from a common pile for another person to finish by creating a solution.

Conflict stories help children depersonalize a situation while giving them practice in thinking through conflict resolutions.

Pick a solution

Present examples of conflicts which affect the group. Have members think of various ways to solve them: the wackiest solution, the most awesome, the easiest, the worst ....

Misunderstandings

One child starts a story, skit, or puppet show. Stop after a few minutes and have another person tell what he believes is happening. If he is correct, the first child proceeds. If not, the first child explains what he meant to happen. Discuss why people see things in ways which cause misunderstandings to occur.

Jumping to conclusions

- Using a busy picture depicting an action scene, cover all but one part of the picture with paper. Ask group members to describe what is happening in the total picture.

- Create situations such as:

  Opal just pushed Latonda down the hill. Why?
  Mrs. Crain patted Joshua on the back. Why?
  My mother was really upset this morning. Why?

Discuss the importance of seeing the whole picture and knowing all the facts.

Seeing things in different ways

- Discuss a mutual experience, or a video, painting, etc. Have children contribute their opinions about what they liked best, what they thought was most important or interesting.

- Complete statements such as "When I think about school I think..." "The job of being a policeman is..." Note all of the different points of view.

The use of games

Many games (board games, chalk games, ball games) involve the kinds of strategies which are needed to solve conflicts: problem solving, cooperation, playing by rules, taking turns, predicting outcomes, evaluating decisions — all competition without violent confrontation. As adults participate in games they can point out some of the learnings: "Good cooperation," or "You really looked at all the choices!"

WAR VERSUS PEACE

What are the differences between arguments and discussions? Between bossiness and leadership? Where is the line between comparison and competition, between competitive play and hurtful play? How well can we tell people's feelings from their language, facial expressions, body movements? When do certain words have "loaded" meanings? Is there a difference between dislikes and prejudices?

As you become aware of both the positive and negative aspects of conflict and as you help promote peaceful living among school-agers, you will be helping develop persons who may eventually affect their families, communities, and nations. The experiences which help children deal with conflict now, in their personal lives, can make them feel confident that they have the understandings and skills to deal with future conflicts in their larger and less personal world.

Dealing with Behaviors Means Remembering Human Needs

THE NEED FOR IDENTITY

Children want to be important and wonderful. Usually they try their best in acceptable ways.

BUT

Sometimes a behavior is not acceptable and must be changed to preserve children's good feelings about themselves.

Think *positive*, *negative*, *positive*.

As an example, consider a group of children who are making model ships:

Positive: Things are going okay. No one is interfering with anyone else's work.

Negative: A disruption occurs. One child purposely breaks another child's ship.

Positive: Help children through the disruption (negative experience) and smoothly on to positive action. Check out the problem. Use your conflict resolution skills such as recognizing and discussing the hurt or angry feelings by exploring with the children various solutions as well as providing materials to help fix the ship.

School-agers will learn they can get through negative situations, come out on the other side, get moving in a good direction again, and feel okay about themselves. *Positive, negative, positive.*

THE NEED FOR GOOD RELATIONSHIPS

Children need close and dependable relationships with peers and adults. They will risk a lot for their friendships.

BUT

Sometimes a behavior is not acceptable, even though it may be an attempt for relationships (a fight, name calling), and must be changed to maintain the children's good relationships.

Find out the problem and encourage cooperative thinking about solutions that will satisfy each child's needs. Any methods that shame or separate children will not help. School-agers need guidance in learning acceptable behaviors to help them make and keep friendships and other relationships.

THE NEED FOR CONTROL AND POWER

Children need to feel they can be in control before they can have self-control. They give opinions, make decisions, feel a sense of power.

BUT

Sometimes a behavior is not acceptable and must be changed to encourage the children's ability to control and cope with situations.

Adults do not take over by controlling and assuming the power. Share the power to control with the school-ager. Recognize the feeling which caused a behavior problem, but help the child work toward better solutions ("That bothered you, I know. What else could you have done?"). Help with words. Give suggestions. With your support, children gain the confidence to control their own actions. Adults do not play super-power or make up children's minds for them. When that happens, children only fight back for their own control. And fighting back will not lead to the power of personal control.

> *Children have never been very good at listening to their elders,*
> *but they have never failed to imitate them.*
>
> James Baldwin

Things to Think About

Dealing with behaviors which trouble you, perplex you, make you wonder what to do

The following anecdotes are among those submitted by staff in school-age programs. In each case share what you think about the situation.

1. Think about how the child may be feeling.
2. What need is this child expressing?
3. What would be the *worst* way for you to help? Why?
4. What would be the *best* way to help? Why?

Six-year-old Melissa, wearing a dress, ankle socks, and sneakers, was directed to select a pair of slacks from the supply of extra clothes to put on under her dress before going outside to play in the snow. She began screaming that she would not wear any of the slacks and finally threw a tantrum.

During a football game, ten-year-old Derrick was tackled by a boy, began to fight him, and was assisted by his best friend who joined in the fight. When the fight was stopped by an adult, there were four boys involved.

Eight-year-old Timmy repeatedly refuses to participate in group activities such as art projects and games. During these activities he keeps to himself but yells at the other children, telling them to "shut up" and that they're "ugly."

Juliette, twelve, is usually calm and in good humor. Today she arrives fidgety and cranky. When asked if she feels okay, she says her 13-year-old brother was shot in a street fight last night.

Kevin is fourteen now and has been in child care since preschool. He arrives daily with a sulking face and slouching gait and resists when asked to join in activities, particularly those involving younger kids.

NOTES

[1]Steve Musson, in *School-Age Care: Theory and Practice*, Addison-Wesley, 1994, suggests additional criteria: Does the adult response communicate sympathy, respect, and caring? Does it help toward self-control and ability to clarify and recognize choices? Does it enhance self-esteem and strengthen the relationship between the child and adult? Does it build children's understanding of their behavior, help eliminate the behavior, and minimize future misbehaviors?

[2] For more on discipline issues with school-age programs see Dale Fink's *Discipline in School-Age Care: Control the Climate Not the Children*, available from School-Age NOTES.

[3]In the field of peace education there are excellent resources available which describe in detail specific structured experiences that contribute to building peace. Each has an extensive bibliography. Useful examples are:

> Cherry, C. *Please Don't Sit on the Kids*. 1983.
> Furlong, L. and Kreidler, W. *Adventures in Peacemaking: A Conflict Resolution Activity Guide for School-Age Programs*. 1996.
> Gibbs, J. *Tribes: A Process for Social Development and Cooperative Learning*. 1987.
> Kreidler, W. *Creative Conflict Resolution*. 1984.
> Levin, D. *Teaching Young Children in Violent Times, Building a Peaceable Classroom*. 1994.
> Prutzman, P. et al. *The Friendly Classroom for a Small Planet*. 1988.

RECOMMENDED READINGS

Carlsson-Paige, N. and D. Levin. *Who's Calling the Shots? How to Respond Effectively to Children's Fascination with War Play and War Toys*. Philadelphia: New Society, 1990.

Cherry, C. *Please Don't Sit on the Kids*. Belmont: David Slake, 1993.

Faber, A. and Mazlish, E. *How To Talk So Kids Will Listen and Listen So Kids Will Talk*. New York: Avon, 1982.

Fink, D. Borman. *Discipline in School-Age Care: Control the Climate, Not the Children*. Nashville: School-Age NOTES, 1995.

Gibbs, J. *Tribes, A New Way of Learning Together*. Santa Rosa: Center Source, 1994.

Ginott, H. G. *Teacher and Child*. New York: MacMillan, 1993.

Glasser, M.D. W. *Schools Without Failure*. New York: Harper and Row, 1969.

Gordon, Dr. T. *Discipline That Works: Promoting Self-Discipline in Children*. New York: Penguin, 1991.

Kreidler, W. *Creative Conflict Resolution*. Glenville: Scott Foresman, 1984.

— and L. Furlong. *Adventures in Peacemaking: A Conflict Resolution and Violence Prevention Curriculum for School-Age Programs*. Cambridge: Educators for Social Responsibility, 1996.

Levin, D. *Teaching Young Children in Violent Times*. Philadelphia: New Society, 1994.

Prutzman, P. et al. *The Friendly Classroom for a Small Planet: Children's Creative Response to Conflict Program*. Philadelphia: New Society, 1988.

Slaby, R. G., et al. *Early Violence Prevention: Tools for Teachers of Young Children*. Washington DC: NAEYC, 1995.

Smith, C. A. *The Peaceful Classroom*. Beltsville: Gryphon House, 1993.

Wilson, P. M. *When Sex is the Subject: Attitudes and Answers for Young Children*. Santa Cruz: ETR, 1991.

Five

What Do The Children Do?
Respecting Childhood With A Balanced Program

"We get to go to see movies, go bowling, skating, have picnics, go to the beach, to the zoo, sometimes to the teacher's home. Sometimes Mr. Rogers, the custodian, helps us to make toys. Sometimes he lets us help him make stuff.
I get to play with my friends. There are no friends my age at home. My friends live too far away.
In the summer we go to the snowball stand, run under the sprinklers, sunbathe on the black top and have summer fruit for snacks — watermelon and strawberries."

> Tom, age 8
> Brian, age 9
> Laura, age 8
> William, age 8

"Children…are the last candid audience left. They don't care what the critics say and they will let you know immediately what delights and what bores them."

> Gian Carlo Menotti

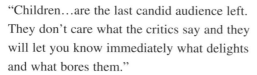

In this chapter...

➤ The Issue Is Quality
➤ Respecting Childhood
    — The Program Responds To Children's Human Needs
    — The Program Respects Each Particular Child
    — School-Age Interests Last A Lifetime
    — Creative Use Of Leisure Time
➤ Play: A Lifelong Business
➤ Creating A Program

The Issue Is Quality

Excellent quality depends on how well we respond to the needs common to all children and how well we respond to the needs of each individual child. Quality programming is more than a big room staffed to keep children safe. It is more than a home which welcomes in a neighbor's child or a friendly teen who comes over to keep a child company until a parent returns home. It is more than sleek gym equipment or filled-to-the-brim libraries, more than a tutor or a sports field or a series of activities, more than arts and crafts or kickball. Quality programming for school-age children and youth on a regular basis requires meeting the human needs and the total development of each child. Whatever the setting and wherever they meet, success depends on the way the children and adults mesh, complement, relate to one another.

There are many models of excellence, many examples of quality center, family, and in-home care, each with its own focus and flavor, its own philosophies, goals, beliefs, and values. Such a variety provides families with choices so they can choose what they believe to be right and comfortable for their children when they cannot be with them. Every care provider, however, must consider whether the arrangement a family has chosen remains right for each child. The elements of quality must be known and recognized by both families and providers of care. While out-of-school programs abound in a vast display of variety, there is also a vast display of varying quality.

DON'T LET QUALITY SLIP AWAY

Excellent quality, once implemented, must be maintained. When a program is new, staff enthusiasm is high, and both families and children are interested, hopeful, and full of anticipation. As staff, you have every good intention of implementing all of your knowledge and beliefs about children and youth. You know how to adhere to sound policies and procedures, in compliance with the laws and regulations for school-age care. You understand the importance of good relations with the children, families, other staff, and community persons. And you pay close attention to quality space, materials, and appropriate activities, and allow for children's own choices and ideas. The point is that when quality has been created it must be nurtured and upheld, with continuing and enriching training for staff. Time passing, staff or location changes, difficult children — none of these must interfere with sustaining the excellent care that each child deserves.

CREATING THE RIGHT FIT BETWEEN THE CHILD AND THE PROGRAM

Look closely at each child, different at five and six, eight, or ten, so different at twelve from fourteen. Different by age, skills, interests, personality, and development. Look closely, and then plan for excellence.

Looking closely requires time, time together to get to know each child through conversation and the exchange of ideas, time to listen and respond. Looking closely also requires small groups (the smaller the better so that relationships can be individual and personal), so that adults are not always managing, administering, dealing with too many children to be sensitive to each one of them.

Respect the differences. Not only is each child's personality different, but each child's day is different. Children wake up in different worlds, to different people and different demands. Friends may be plentiful and available or may not exist at all. The family and the neighborhood may be filled with fun and comfort, or filled with fears and uncertainties. School, camp, or child care present challenges to some youngsters, terror to others.

In relating to all of these children and planning for the hours they are out of school, we are responding not only to their total days but to their total lives. While we may not always be able to know each child's particular experiences or determine each child's individual feelings, we can remember the developmental similarities and basic needs as we plan a program.

RESPECTING CHILDHOOD

Childhood only comes around once. It deserves our interest, time, enjoyment, and respect. If we expect children and youth to become truly mature adults, then we must not cheat them of their childhood years, lest they cling to childhood behaviors for the rest of their lives. School-agers are often hurried to grow up, pushed into the values and problems and culture of adults. They are hurried right past their only time to be young.[1]

School-age programs can help youngsters to slow down by respecting what is interesting and challenging to boys and girls right now, whatever age they may be. Our programs are a relaxation time from often pressured lives of rushing to get up, finish breakfast, get to child care, make the bus, school, then child care again, before hurrying home to homework, dinner, and bed.

Time for childhood gets crowded out amidst the hurry. Well-planned programs respect childhood time and the relationship of childhood to the kind of adult a child may become.

Respecting Childhood:

THE PROGRAM RESPONDS TO CHILDREN'S HUMAN NEEDS

The program supports children's need for a personal identity

"What am I good at?" "What would I like to do better?" "What do other people think of me?" By the time children are in school-age programs they already have a perception of their individual identity. They have been developing this from birth. A child may feel, "I am a capable, smart, well-liked person." "I'm very good at soccer." "I'm needed in the band." Or the child may think, "I don't do anything good enough." "No one even knows I'm around." "No one needs me or likes me."

Every person wants the respect of other people. If we do not help children feel respected, they may make a desperate attempt at an identity that they think others will respect and admire. This attempt may result in acts of vandalism, aggression, involvement with drugs, sex, or other behaviors that result in a certain notoriety. Ultimately, however, these behaviors will not achieve self-respect and threaten to pull down the very children who wanted to be successful. As school-age experiences are developed, whatever the age of the children and wherever the service, each child needs to feel a sense of self-respect and success. Regardless of the negative feelings children may bring from home or school, we have a chance to prove to them that they have competencies and character and that we like and value each one of them very much.

The mastery of skills becomes increasingly related to the developing sense of identity. Adults will encourage the need for mastery and the personal achievement of skills by helping when needed, exposing each child to the variety of experiences which are possible. We should not pressure or compare children or have them compete with each other for mastery. The sense of mastery is the child's own sense of achievement, the feeling of enjoying and doing something well. Competence is valued but never to the point where children might believe that their skills are more important than they are.

As young school-agers reach out to increase their skills, they often reach in many directions at once — sports, music, reading, hobbies, art, writing — experimenting, dabbling, trying out what they enjoy. Even homework is looked at as an interesting task. As they get older, they may focus in on particular activities, excelling in those which interest them most.

Mastery of skills brings with it a sense of self-confidence. As children approach adolescence and seek strong peer approval, often with members of the opposite sex, they develop the mastery of skills in sports or acting or other activities. These particular skills are specific and recognized, even when a young adolescent may lack confidence in social skills such as dating or the intellectual tasks of schoolwork.

As their abilities develop, children find themselves teaching friends, and as they help others, they further increase their own skills. As they experience the feeling of being accomplished persons, they are better able to withstand group pressures. They even can dare to be different when they feel secure within themselves.

Variety of choice is particularly important. Because children seek to develop a unique sense of self, there need to be experiences from which to choose, from which to develop personal ideas, and from which to strengthen good feelings about one's own abilities.

Think of each child's need for a personal identity as you plan the program:

- How will each child gain a feeling of success?

- How will each child be able to build on skills and share them?

- How will familiar activities be used to build new interests so that there is a basis in comfortable, familiar experiences upon which to develop new ideas?

• Is there time to practice and get good at new skills?

• Is there a variety of activities to choose from?

Through appropriate, challenging, and understandable experiences, children and youth become more capable, thoughtful, and responsible.

The program supports children's needs for good relationships

To a great extent our sense of identity develops from all of our relationships with other people. From birth we come to feel a sense of connection. We imitate others, and we gain security from others. We learn from all sorts of human relationships, not only from those with family and teachers. We learn about ourselves in relation to our constantly expanding personal world, and we define ourselves through all of our relationships.

Children may need help in developing or maintaining relationships. When they don't get the help they need, they may behave in a manner that interferes with the very relationships they hope to develop. Their behaviors, then, frequently aimed at gaining a friend or being liked, may disrupt the best activities you have planned. Children may pick a fight, talk back, show off. They may concentrate on wrestling with or talking to friends while you are trying to get the attention of the group. As you see this, you can keep in mind their motivation and realize that their behavior may be a cry for recognition, a cry for closeness.

As you plan your program, think of each child's need for the kind of relationships that provide support, security, and friendship:

• Does this child have a specific need for positive relations with an adult? Who on the staff seems best matched to help?

• Does this child need a special friend? How will I help to make this happen?

As you plan your program, think of each child's need for the kind of relationships that provide support, security and friendship.

- What activities encourage friendships through the close collaboration of a small group?

- Is ample time provided for forming friendships among children and between children and adults?

- Are there private spaces where friends can talk and share?

- Are there responsibilities that can bring children close?

- Are activities cooperative rather than competitive?

- Are there opportunities for children to relate to the feelings of others?

As youngsters pursue their personal interests, share their ideas in an accepting environment, and help others in the group, they will develop friendships and a sense of personal value

The program supports children's needs for personal power

Just as a sure sense of self and of dependable relationships provides the basis for feelings of personal control, your program can also help assure children that they do have control over some aspects of their lives.

In mastering skills, school-agers demonstrate control. They are biking, reading, skating, catching ball, acting, cooking, verbalizing, calculating, and thinking in critical ways. These skills require control of both their thinking and their actions. In personal relationships they invent ways to solve problems. In sharing ideas, choosing between personalities, and selecting ways of communication, they are gaining the feeling of personal power and gaining confidence in those powers.

If youngsters do not believe that they are capable of making good decisions, or if they lack a healthy feeling of power, they may attempt to seize or create power. They may disrupt, interrupt, cause chaos. They may take extraordinary risks to cause others to look at and listen to them.

School-age programs give children legitimate opportunities for personal control so that they feel some power to make their own decisions and do not always feel under the power of others. They may come directly from school where many decisions are made for them. Even at home a busy family may provide little time for choices in the limited hours available between jobs, meals, and home chores. In school-age programs, however, there can be time to help children make their own determinations and feel good and wise and strong and in control.

Think of each child's need for personal power as you plan activities:

- How will you involve children in the planning?

- Are there chances to share their opinions?

- What experiences will you provide so that a child feels a sense of accomplishment, achievement, completion?

- How are children helped to solve their own social problems?

- Are there opportunities for children to help others, thereby rein-
forcing their own competencies and the feeling that they are able
to make a difference in the lives of other people?

The need for some personal power and control is very closely related to the
school-ager's sense of responsibility, industry, and the drive for mastery and completion. They like to carry through projects, reach goals, gain a sense of finality.
They like beginnings, middles, and endings. It helps them to find order in this very
complex world.

THE PROGRAM RESPECTS EACH PARTICULAR CHILD

No two programs look alike, whether in a home or a center, and no two programs are the same each day or month or year, because each program is responding to the particular children enrolled. Some of the factors which shape the personality of individual children and the nature of each individual program are:

- developmental levels

- personal life experiences

- family expectations

- desire to be at home

- cultural environments

Because of these factors programs cannot be mass produced and based on
fixed curricula. Such programs will not respect or be sensitive to the individual
child.

Developmental levels

Enjoying childhood, at each level of development, is the child's best preparation for growth into a trustworthy, happy, mature adult. With each aspect of a
school-age program we should meet each child at a particular point of childhood
and not push too early or hold back the maturing experiences.

Respecting each child's age and development applies to many aspects of
program planning from size of furniture (older school-agers should not be
demeaned by nursery-sized table and chairs) to activities (younger school-agers do
not yet cope well with highly competitive ball games). Five-year-olds, and even
six- and seven-year olds need very different experiences and nurturing than ten-,
twelve-, and fourteen-year-olds. Staff-child ratios and group size need to be considered closely in terms of children's developmental needs for attention and support.

Personal life experiences

Children each differ as a result of what has been happening in each of their
lives. They bring their knowledge, beliefs, fears, and hopes based on the home and
community environments in which they have grown. Their thinking, play, behaviors, and skills all reflect their very individual lives. Providers must be aware of

these many life experiences in order to plan how to help the children and where to lead them.

Family expectations

Families have a variety of expectations for their children and they may have different expectations for each of their children. They may select a certain kind of school-age program because of the way it meets these expectations with an emphasis on art, sports, music, or play. They have different expectations for behaviors, competencies, even future occupations. So programs are designed with family interests in mind and also with the awareness that each child may already reflect the expectations of the family.

The desire to be at home

There are many reasons for children to be in school-age programs as has been discussed earlier, but whatever the reason most children would rather be at home with their friends, in their own neighborhood, in their own house, with their own furniture, pets, and family. Staff, knowing this, help these girls and boys become as comfortable as possible, providing:

- a friendly, comfortable, homelike environment

- free time and choice of activities

- chances to be out in the community

- continuity of experiences so there is something to look forward to the following day

- opportunities to pursue personal interests

- encouragement of friendships

- personal attention and recognition.

Cultural environments

Some school-age groupings consist of children who have similar cultural, racial, religious, or economic backgrounds and other groups are quite diverse. Examples of diversity include mannerisms, eye contact when speaking, intergenerational respect, the concepts of guilt and shame, gestures, word uses, and body language. As adults, we can help children respect the uniqueness of one another and even celebrate the differences. As people become friends, they can go beyond the differences to the personal qualities. Because youngsters see adults as examples of ways in which to mature, the more variety of adults in their lives, the better. The more we offer children contacts with a rich variety of people, the more they feel secure and are comfortable with persons who are different from themselves.

School-agers, very aware of differences, are often quick to label and judge. The need for approval and peer acceptance often creates situations where there are insiders and outsiders, us and them. They judge others by their appearance, language, behaviors, beliefs, and ideas. Helping children believe in their own personal value and importance also leads them to an awareness of the similarities as well as the diversity in all human beings.

There are many resources to find ideas that relate to multicultural program planning. But, most important, consider the variety of living patterns in your particular group of children and youth and look at their communities. Include families in the planning so that they are aware of your activities reflecting cultural diversity. Find out what events are celebrated by families and how, and be sure not to emphasize any one celebration or culture more than another. It is essential to do your homework, know your facts, be accurate and respectful of each child's cultural life. Here are a few general guidelines to help children feel comfortable with cultural differences (many sources for specific experiences are cited in the bibliography at the end of this chapter):

- Activities that emphasize the uniqueness of every person, avoiding stereotypes.

- Materials—toys, books, pictures, games, tapes—which portray a wide diversity of images.

- Sharing a wide variety of languages, literature, music, dance, art, drama, and foods.

- Recognition of cultural differences in dress and hairstyles, verbal expression and ideas.

- Equal attention to the celebration of customs of children and families in the group.

The children who feel comfortable with themselves have less need to see differences or to use difference as a means of criticizing others. They are more open to curiosity, new information, and understanding. The children who shun certain people, or who tease and taunt them because of their differences, are usually crying out for more secure feelings about their own selves.

SCHOOL-AGE INTERESTS LAST A LIFETIME

We are each an extension of what we were in our school-age years, both in personality and in the things we like to do. Think about your own beginnings. Do you still enjoy some of the things which were important to you when you were growing up? Many adult pursuits, hobbies, and vocations were already beginning in the school-age years, and failure to acquire interests during this time may leave life-long gaps.

Children and youth already have special skills and interests. You can learn about them as you talk together and watch their play. Then you can introduce new ideas, new ways, new activities to try, because children need to grow into experiences they may not have known about. A child's ideas and abilities will grow from contact with play materials as well as from contact with caregivers, friends, visitors, and others in the community. School-age experiences help shape the direction which each child's life may take.

CREATIVE USE OF LEISURE TIME

How many times have you heard a child say, "There's nothing to do"? This lament is troubling because it is possible that there are few choices available to this child. Perhaps there have been so few experiences to draw on that the child feels that life is boring and uninteresting; or the child, unable to build on personal strengths and ideas to create a full life, is simply waiting to be entertained by someone.

Good use of leisure time is probably one of the best preventions for later occupation with substance abuse, premature sexual experiences, and other inappropriate activities that often occur when "there's nothing to do." Good use of leisure time includes an outreach toward many experiences and encourages an openness to the varied adventures the world can offer.

"I have an idea!" This, too, we hear from children. Then they begin to take action on their own ideas. This means that as we live with children, we try to expand their vision with ideas and activities that may take root and resurface throughout leisure hours.

Programs may have a single focus, such as sports, tutoring, or dance and these programs surely help toward the perfection of one skill. But a program that fills a great many of a child's hours, such as after-school care or summer camp, has the additional responsibility of showing children a wide variety of experiences so that later they can readily find "something to do."

PLAY: A LIFELONG BUSINESS

This business of play

Program quality can be measured, to a substantial extent, by the opportunities presented for rich, interesting play. Play, in the lives of children, is nourishment. It is learning, imagination, recreation, and enjoyment. It relaxes tension and makes up for defeats and disappointments. It is "research" because play is motivated by curiosity and a desire to learn about living. By trial and error, play discovers satisfactions through thinking and doing. It is what children like to do the most, and it is what children most need to do.

Play is a child's livelihood. To respect childhood is to respect play.

A profitable business

For every child at every age play is an enterprise where everyone gains confidence, social skills, and problem solving, because play is an experience where everyone can find joy in doing things well. When children play, they profit and thrive.

A universal business

Children at play the world over are learning about their culture and their roles within that culture. They develop their language skills and exchange ideas. They personalize small parts of their own society and make it a part of their own lives.

An essential business

Play is an experience which benefits every aspect of a child's development—social, intellectual, physical, emotional. When children play, they are using their minds and their bodies. What they think and what they do become related. They try out new ideas. They repeat ideas that work. They imitate the behavior of the adults in their world. They learn about their own feelings and become more sure of themselves as they judge what to do in each new situation.

Relation of play to human needs

The need for personal identity

When children play, they choose activities which they feel comfortable with and reinforce feelings about what they can do well. They remain absorbed in their own selected tasks until they are satisfied with the results. They work out solutions with their own imagination, trying out ideas and then accepting or rejecting the results. Play is building a person — play with objects, friends, and ideas. All of these meld together to help create a sense of autonomy and a belief in one's self.

The need for good relationships

When children play, they become aware of the identity of others. They distinguish between different behaviors, ways of thinking, personalities. They can become more sensitive to the feelings of others. They give and take, share, listen, make promises, argue, make up. These social skills take a lot of practice. Play is a wonderful setting in which to practice.

The need for personal power

Play probably prepares us better than anything else for the ability to develop a feeling of personal power and control. Play is spontaneous and unpredictable. (What might happen next?) As children play, they become used to making things change. They learn to be in charge of their own activities, actions, bodies, plans, decisions. This is self-discipline. Using their own powers, they come to believe in their own powers.

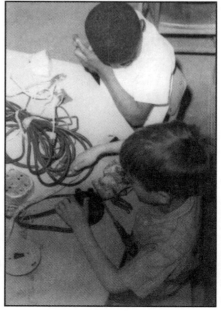

Just imagine!

Much of young school-age play is still "make-believe" — trying out ideas, trying out roles, replaying super-heroes and stories, pretending to be "grown up."

Make-believe is not solely part of a child's world because use of the imagination is essential at every age. Imagination is good practice in thinking and makes it possible to plan by imagin-

Program quality can be measured, to a substantial extent, by the opportunities presented for rich, interesting play.

ing the steps in achieving goals. One can imagine ways of behaving, and our imagination requires us to think about and weigh the consequences of our actions.

Just imagine how it would be if we could *not* day-dream, pretend or make-believe.

Fun and games

Play is many things for school-agers. It is informal, fun, and spontaneous. Play involves fantasy and imagination, physical activity, rough-housing — all open-ended experiences with no particular goals.

But to school-agers "play" also involves games, with rules, expectations, and definite goals. Spontaneous play may be pure pleasure and relaxation whereas games, though enjoyable, may also produce stresses and tensions, rules and penalties. When adults do not take over or interfere, the concepts of fun and games can merge because children will experiment freely with the joys of informal play (negotiation, problem-solving, give and take, laughter) as they become involved in the more structured world of games. They may offer varying points of view, rule changes, creation of new games, etc. If adults take over the control of games, or the games are too difficult, children, especially younger school-agers, may become confused or threatened. They may give up and prefer to return to spontaneous play activities, where they will not face defeat or shame. It requires sensitive adult leadership to preserve the fun of play and yet promote the skills of the games.

The ability to play is forever

Children at play are learning to create activities. They do not wait to be entertained. They are finding within themselves the capacity for enjoyment. When we help to nurture this capacity in childhood, we help to create happy, whole human beings in adulthood. How often have you heard, "Can I go out and play?" from a child? You can respond knowing full well that this request is an essential part of growing up.

Creating a Program

GET READY AND GET SET TO GO

Each day...new hopes and feelings

School is closed and the program begins. Staff think about their hopes and goals for the children.

- They hope it will be possible to keep warm relationships with so many different children.
- They hope they have prepared enough activities.
- They hope the children will be happy here, when they cannot be with their family.

Each day the children have some of the same hopes and concerns.

- They are eager to like the adults and be liked in return.

- They are hoping to have fun and want to be able to choose interesting things to do.

- They may be a little leery of unfamiliar adults and peers.

- They might wish that they were at home, that there were not so many other children, or that they could have some quiet time alone.

- They may hope that this will be a wonderful part of their day.

So, these hours need to be made special.

- School is out, and play is in.

- Classroom quiet is out, and conversation is in.

- Sitting at desks is out, and moving around is in.

- Gone are school pressures.

- Children and adults decide what they want to do in this time they spend with one another.

Some children may arrive with resentful feelings.

- Children and youth let adults know in a variety of ways that they no longer want to be taken care of. They may resent the fact that other classmates have gone home to family or are outside playing with neighborhood friends.

- They may not want to be in child care or any other program.

- They may be angry. They may be sad. They may have a lot on their minds that has nothing to do with the school-age program.

- All of these feelings may get in the way of enthusiasm and cooperative behavior.

What will this resentment look like?

- Children may be loners.

- They may be fighters. "I'm not going to do what you tell me to do."

- They may be spoilers who destroy materials, the schedule, or the friendships of others.

The staff pull all children in.

- They encourage the children to express their feelings in words. They accept these feelings.

- They develop trusting relationships with the children based on honesty, confidence, confidentiality.

- They help children build friendships so they won't miss other friends so much.

- They build activities on the children's interests so that there is much to look forward to each day.

And each day:

- Children and staff grow in friendship.

- They both are excited by challenging experiences.

- They become more skilled and more sure of themselves.

THE PROCESS OF PLANNING

The future well-being of children and youth depends on the quality of their experiences now. Even as they want and need more independence, they retain the need for support from adults. They still need help to plan for the richest use of their hours as their personal choices are made, their capabilities are further developed, and new interests are discovered.

Days are planned, but not rigidly, and so are the weeks and the months ahead, but not inflexibly. There must always be the openness that allows for spontaneity and welcomes the unexpected.[2]

Structure and schedules are useful tools in organizing the program. The choice of activities, however, and the time spent on them belong to the child. The job is to plan a program that ensures that each child knows and feels success.

Who helps to plan?

Staff

Every staff member has unique ideas. If you are planning, trust yourself. You remember what it was like to be a school-ager and what you liked to do. What can you share now? Be sure, also, that you are well tuned to each child and learn what each child needs, wants, likes. Don't be so busy writing your own script that you miss the clues from the children.

Children

They are thoughtful and verbal. They know how they would like to spend their time. As school-agers mature, their involvement in the planning process should increase. Many five- and six-year-olds, for instance, may not think of all the possible options, but when they are offered choices, they can easily decide what they wish to do. Later, older children and youth draw from their own interests and generate their own activities using the available materials and environment.

Planning with children is an ongoing process because they constantly change as they mature—physically, socially, emotionally, intellectually. Part of change is developmental, and part is a result of interactions within their environment. So adults must remain alert to be in touch.

Children can help you plan with one-to-one and group conversations, interviews, suggestion charts. Remember to ask for their help.

As school-agers mature, their involvement in the planning process should increase.

Families

Parents know about their children—what they enjoy, what they would like to try. Invite their input, and make it clear that their comments are truly welcomed.

Community

Individuals in the community—artists, business persons, entertainers, sports enthusiasts, writers—know what they are able to offer for various ages of children. Resources with expertise in many fields are available from museums, zoos, schools, recreation and park departments. Books, periodicals, consultants, and training opportunities will stock you well with new ideas.

Who decides if the plans are working?

These same people—staff, children, families, persons in the community—are all important contributors to the ongoing evaluation of the program. They can assess the problems and successes, the specific and general concerns. New ideas are added and successful experiences are continued. Activities that children do not seem to enjoy may be revised, tried again at a later time, or discarded.

The skill of planning a balanced program

Continually evaluating activities and experiences helps staff to develop a sensitivity to the need for a balanced program. A well-balanced program provides children and youth with the experiences that foster self-identity, good relationships, and a sense of power. A well-balanced program respects their childhood.

The Skill of Balanced Program Planning

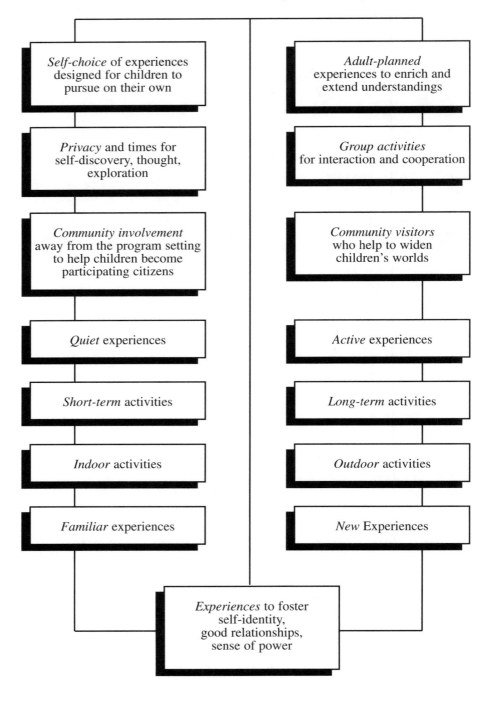

Self-choice of experiences designed for children to pursue on their own	*Adult-planned* experiences to enrich and extend understandings
Privacy and times for self-discovery, thought, exploration	*Group activities* for interaction and cooperation
Community involvement away from the program setting to help children become participating citizens	*Community visitors* who help to widen children's worlds
Quiet experiences	*Active* experiences
Short-term activities	*Long-term* activities
Indoor activities	*Outdoor* activities
Familiar experiences	*New* Experiences

Experiences to foster
self-identity,
good relationships,
sense of power

Activities make the day!

Activities may be planned in a variety of ways. Each activity meets many needs, has many purposes, and involves many experiences. In thinking about any activity, keep in mind the developmental appropriateness: age, health, physical, social, intellectual and emotional levels of functioning. Does the activity encourage creative thinking, self-awareness, self-esteem, or self-direction? How will it meet the need for friends and good relations with adults, for the strengthening of families, and for the use of the community?

Here are some examples that indicate various ways activities may be thoughtfully planned to benefit children.

A Plan for Photography

Photography may be the beginning of a hobby that carries over into home and school life, and it may influence career and adult leisure time. It also contributes to the spirit of the program as the photos of children and activities are displayed. With inexpensive still or video cameras, many kinds of learning are encouraged. Your plan may be based on encouraging the following skills.

Physical Skills

Eye-hand and muscle coordination are developed in the use of the photographic equipment, picture-taking, developing, and editing.

Social Skills

The prestige of mastering photographic skills provides real success for some children who do not achieve in academic or other areas of growth. For all children it can provide a means to friendships, helping relationships, and the social skills of presentation. It also encourages interaction with community resources as school-agers use the library or consultants for information, purchase needed equipment and film processing materials, and present their work to community audiences.

Self Skills

Photography implies expression of one's own ideas, feelings, and independent thinking through personal decisions. A sensitivity to subject matter leads to involvement in ideas about the world and the growth of personal discoveries. The sense of responsibility and usefulness encourages self-respect, leadership and confidence, and the desire to tackle tasks.

Intellectual Skills

Problem-solving skills are developed through using equipment, getting desired angles, sequence, lighting, and film development. Reading and writing skills are applied in using directions, titling, and applying narration and music.

A Plan for a Hike

Many activities on a hike can be directed toward personal growth, both creative and intellectual. A hike can be planned to meet the special needs and expanding interests of each child. A hike may be in the city, suburbs, or country. It may be short, extensive, spontaneous, or planned. A variety of experiences may be included.

Plan where to go, what to take, how to get there, what to wear.

Note the various plants along the route. Are some edible? Are some poisonous? Collect the edible for preparation.

Make sketches along the way. Keep a log.

Note the different kinds of trees.

Collect seeds from plants and trees.

Collect materials for art projects.

Look under some large stones or wood and observe insect life with a magnifying glass.

Make a note of the different birds. Make a bird call tape.

List all the animals.

Notice the different types of soil and rocks.

Take a tour of your neighborhood, town, or city.

Notice environmental hazards such as signs of pollution and erosion. Notify appropriate authorities or take personal action.

Plot a route map from a commercial map. Measure the distance on the map.

Make an original map of the route.

Use a pedometer to see how far you have traveled.

Use a compass to find directions.

Estimate distance and time for the hike.

Compose a hiking song.

Make new friends, cement old friendships, and become personally close to adults.

Include a treasure hunt.

Get physical exercise.

Enjoy the outdoors. What else?

A Plan for an Outdoor Stage

The skills of construction are combined with the skills of performance and the many other uses that children make of a defined-space structure. A planning outline can help assure you are satisfying these particular human needs.

Self-Identity

Mastering such skills as planning, measuring, and carpentry. The glory of being on stage. What else happens?

Good Relationships

Working closely with others for a common idea. Negotiating differences of opinion. What else?

Power

Presenting personal contributions. Assuming responsibility. The pride that comes with completion. What else?

Play is a child's response to life — almost where life begins, play begins.
Play ... is the way the child learns what no one can teach him.

Lawrence K. Frank
1890-1958

Sample Activity Chart

Activity	Materials Needed	Purposes of Activity	Length of Activity	Ages	Number of Participants and Extent of Supervision
<u>Community Trips</u> Court House Butcher Shop Construction sites Garage and repair shops Local newspaper office Hospital etc.	Depending on proximity—feet, cars, buses, bikes	To acquaint students with strengths of the community; to help them feel comfortable with many environments; to promote interests in vocations and professions; to help make new friends	1-3 hours	All ages, but gear to interest	One adult to every 10 children; two adults recommended
<u>Community Visitors</u> College professor Author Politician Artist Plumber Homemaker Folk Singer etc.	Children can prepare refreshments; any equipment requested by the visitor	To promote interests in vocations and professions; to learn about complexion of the community; to be able to ask questions of specialists first-hand; to meet new people and feel comfortable with many types of people	1-1 1/2 hours (preparation of refreshments may require additional time)	All	The smaller the better. Eight to ten desirable in order to maintain an atmosphere and allow for questions and conversation with the visitor. Larger groups possible if presentation geared to all ages present.
<u>Neighborhood Newspaper</u>	Paper, pencils, typewriter or word processor; duplicating machine	To provide opportunities for intellectual stimulation, vocabulary growth, and facility with written expression; to learn to clarify positions and opinions; to learn how to influence others; to discover the importance of getting along with people on any cooperative undertaking	Ongoing, daily, weekly, monthly	All can participate using various levels of skills	Unlimited with certain defined roles and responsibilities (editing, reporting, layout, distribution, etc.)

Activity	Materials Needed	Purposes of Activity	Length of Activity	Ages	Number of Participants and Extent of Supervision
Puppet Show	Popsicle sticks or other base for body; scraps of fabric, construction paper, scissors, glue, tape, buttons. Carton, board or plank and large piece of cloth (optional) for stage	To foster creative thinking; to encourage communication; to encourage expression of feelings; to develop cooperative problem solving.	Brief and spontaneous or planned and extended over days.	All	This may involve only a few interested children, or maybe more
Rock Art	Rocks, pebbles, slate, paint, markers, glue, collage materials, etc.	To develop imaginative thinking; to become familiar with and aware of natural materials as sources of construction, art or useful objects	1/2 to 1 hour depending on age and interest	All	Individual participation or maximum 10-15; one adult, assistants when needed
Dancing, Square Dancing, Body Movement	Records, tapes, piano, guitar, drums, etc.	To encourage expression through many musical media; to foster self-confidence; to appreciate many dance forms; to give a comfortable feeling about free body movements	1/2 to 1 hour depending on age and interest	All	Individual participation or maximum of 25

This Sample Activity Chart may be reproduced for training purposes only, with appropriate credit given to the source: *Half A Childhood: Quality Programs for Out-of-School Hours.* (Copyright 2000) by Judith Bender, Charles H. Flatter, and Jeanette M. Sorrentino, published by School-Age NOTES, Nashville, Tennessee.

NOTES

[1] Eda LeShan expresses so well the pressures on children in *Conspiracy Against Childhood*, and so does David Elkind in *The Hurried Child* and *All Grown Up And No Place To Go*.

[2] Steve Musson, *School-Age Care: Theory and Practice*, presents an integration of what he refers to as the "Four Program Flows: daily, weekly, seasonal, and developmental." He provides a detailed description of many different planning models and includes formats for structuring activities in relation to organizing the children.

RECOMMENDED READINGS

Allen, J., E. McNeill, V. Schmidt. *Cultural Awareness for Children*. New York: Addison-Wesley, 1992.

Bergstrom, J. *School's Out, It's Summer*. Berkeley: Ten Speed Press, 1992.

—. *School's Out — Now What?* Berkeley: Ten Speed Press, 1984.

Bredekamp, S. *Developmentally Appropriate Practices in Early Childhood Programs Serving Children Birth Through Age 8*. Washington DC: NAEYC, 1987.

California Department of Education. *Kids' Time: A School-Age Care Program Guide*. Sacramento: CA Dept. of Education, 1994.

Hartley, R. E. and R. M. Goldenson. *The Complete Book of Children's Play*. New York: Thomas Crowell Collier, 1963.

Hopkins, S. and J. Winters, editors. *Discover the World: Empowering Children to Value Themselves, Others and the Earth*. Philadelphia: New Society, 1990.

Katz, L. and S. C. Chard. *Engaging Children's Minds: The Project Approach*. Norwood: Albex, 1989.

Klugman, E. and S. Smilansky. *Children's Play and Learning: Perspective and Policy Implications*. New York: Teachers College Press, 1990.

Lewis, B. *The Kids' Guide to Social Action*. Minneapolis: Free Spirit, 1991.

—. *The Kids' Guide to Service Projects*. Minneapolis: Free Spirit, 1995.

Milford, S. *Hands Around the World: 365 Creative Ways to Build Cultural Awareness and Global Respect*. Charlotte: Williamson, 1992.

Six
What Do The Children Do?
The Physical Environment Says "Welcome"

"After school I say like Hey! Just put out the games 'til the end of the day and let's play!"

Damon, age 10

"Children should be able to come into a room each day and say 'wow, look at that!' And head for it!"

Dr. James Hymes, Jr.

In this chapter...

What is the physical environment?

The physical environment is the framework in which activities take place—the places and the spaces—in the home, center, or the surrounding community. The use and the quality of these areas reflect the planning and sensitive thinking of the staff and the particular goals and interests of children and families. The physical environment makes a big impression as we welcome children. How the space is designed and organized says something to children—what to do, how to behave, how much adults care. Space also contributes to how staff function, how well they can comfortably share their skills and interact with the children.

Setting it up

Materials and equipment determine the kinds of experiences that take place within the space, so they become an essential part of physical environment. The nature of the surrounding community will also affect the experiences.

This chapter recommends some considerations for organizing and designing a welcoming physical setting. A suggested list for equipment and materials is included at the end of this text as supplement #3. Some spaces go well together and can be designed near to each other: areas for role play and construction, music and movement, and art, cooking, and sources for water. Certain activities should be separated, such as reading and quiet games, which clash with carpentry or sports. The amount and shape of the physical environment, both indoors and outdoors, as well as any considerations related to shared space, will determine exact design. Space design is not static. It changes as children and adults wish it to change and help it to change.

INDOOR SETTINGS

"What's there to do today?" Children arrive and look around, and what they see gives them answers. What they see, however, is not a standard room design that can be prescribed for all school-age settings. Every indoor space is different because every space responds to individual boys and girls and to their ages, interests, needs. Every indoor space is different because school-age programs take place in so many different settings—homes, classrooms, multipurpose areas. Wherever the program, however, the room becomes a comfortable place, an attractive place, a space for both children and adults to feel at home.

Wherever the space, whatever the size or shape, the following factors should be included in designing the indoor play environment:

✦ a special or separate entrance with a name and decoration created by school-agers and symbolizing a personal welcome

✦ a place where children can find a friendly hello upon arrival

✦ spaces for children's personal belongings (coats, books, and treasures)

✧ spaces for accessible play materials, defined for each choice of activity and divided by shelving, screens, floor levels, hangings, carpeting, etc.

✧ spaces of adequate size for specific experiences such as block building, box or cardboard construction, group gatherings, or games

✧ places for messy activities like painting, sculpting, and food preparation

✧ space for large-muscle activities

✧ spaces enclosed for privacy

✧ spaces for clear pathways between activity areas

✧ places for just sitting around with good friends

✧ places that are soft for comfort and relaxation (pillows, bean chairs, rugs, and soft furniture)

✧ places for touches of color, pleasant lighting, and decorative items such as art, flowers, and wall hangings

✧ spaces that are high or low for a variety of children's groupings (platforms, wells, and lofts)

✧ places to display children's art and sculpture, or pin up notices, photographs, and news items

✧ places to keep unfinished work and long-term projects

✧ spaces to store materials and equipment when not in use

✧ spaces with easy access to outdoors, bathrooms, and drinking water

✧ places for staff work responsibilities—tables, desk, storage areas, etc.

OUTDOOR SETTINGS

"Can I go out and play?" Remember what children need to do, then open up the doors. You are the planner, the builder, the supervisor, the companion. You may have a wonderful outdoor environment, thoughtfully designed and equipped, or you may be starting from scratch. Outdoor play areas can be exciting or deadly dull. They can be safe or dangerous. The same children may be using the area for five, six, or seven years, so the outdoor space should be designed for modification and change.

What do school-agers need in an outdoor environment?

Change, choice, challenge, and complexity. What do they do? Climb, leap, run, hang, swing, bounce, create, take apart, take risks, and make decisions. Wherever school-agers are, indoors or outside, they need to think, try out new ideas, arrange and rearrange, work and rework materials, discover and rediscover.

Usually outdoor areas are sparsely equipped, yet there is little connection between spending a whole lot of money and successful outdoor settings. The effectiveness of your outdoors will be obvious in the children's play, their cooperative ventures, and their enthusiasm. You will see the results of effective planning in their faces and bodies and actions. Sometimes what they actually do with the equipment on hand is more intriguing than what the finest designer had in mind. Sometimes the richest play emerges from the least expected improvised materials. Whether the outdoor environment is lavishly equipped or discouragingly bare, you can take the lead from children's needs and continually enhance whatever exists. In developing outdoor spaces keep some basic concepts in mind:

✧ spaces that are small, spaces that are large, spaces that are functional for both active and quiet activities

✧ spaces for different interests (active sports, quiet games, imaginative play, reading, art, carpentry, club meetings, building, and nature and science)

✧ spaces for storage of materials (sheds, chests, huts, and portable carriers)

✧ spaces where materials can be moved around in order to change the shape, size, and challenges of existing structures and play areas (spaces for scrap lumber, crates, logs, ropes, cargo netting, bales of straw, ladders, poles, large building blocks, blankets, sheets, and fabric pieces)

✧ places for privacy, under a tree, in a tree, hammock, carton, cement pipe or pit, and on a bench, hill, or platform

✧ places for group activities (a stage, covered pavilion, platform, amphitheater) for performances, rehearsals, games, and meetings

✧ places on different levels, for climbing high, hiding down low (pits, mounds, climbers, and slopes)

✧ spaces with different surfaces (grass, sand, blacktop, rocks, cobblestone, and brick)

✧ places to experience natural materials (water, earth, woods, fields, gardens, campfires, and boulders)

✧ places that attract birds, insects, and small animals

✧ places with protection against sun, wind, rain (tarps, porches, roofing, shrubs, and trees)

✧ places for pathway choices (down steps or a slide or a pole or through a jumping pit or over a hill)

Regardless of the number and variety of spaces and places, the total physical environment should be safeguarded against hazards such as automobile traffic, slippery surfaces, deep water, wiring, suspended hazards, machinery, sharp edges and protrusions, pinch or crush points, entrapment or strangulation areas, hot surfaces, debris, poisonous plants, and toxic materials.[1]

IN THE COMMUNITY

Consider the surrounding community as an integral part of the physical environment to be explored and to expand children's lives out from confining walls. The choices in the community serve much the same purpose as choices in the program setting. Boys and girls are exposed to the kinds of community activities that invite them to make choices and participate, and from this involvement lifetime interests develop about people, places, and experiences. Community experiences may include:

- ◇ walks to discover people, parks, nature areas, play areas, bike paths, stores, and services

- ◇ interviews with community workers and residents

- ◇ adopting playgrounds, gardens, streets, preschool programs

- ◇ community travel clubs — exploring architecture and historic features, communication centers, recreation areas, foreign specialty stores, and animal habitats

- ◇ relationships with other school-age programs (visits, game challenges, debates, performances, parties, and "twinning" – pairing with another family or center setting)

- ◇ environmental activities (farming, erosion control, insect and weed control, recycling, and litter removal)

- ◇ participation in established community programs (first-aid classes, fitness and health programs, Scouts, 4H Clubs, sports, recreation, and enrichment programs)

- ◇ visits to malls to observe marketing techniques, fashions, and the multiple functions of the mall

- ◇ exploring community resources (museums, theaters, libraries, historical societies, food and clothing distribution centers, and health and safety services)

- ◇ interpreting the community through snapshots, videos, sketches, dance, drama, stories, and poetry

- ◇ performing in the community (mime, clowning, puppetry, plays, music, dance, readings, gymnastics, and juggling) for such audiences as senior centers, preschool centers, family child care homes, hospitals, and street audiences

- ◇ raising money for community causes (car wash, yard work, yard sales, selling home-grown vegetables, baked goods, jellies, and toys)

- ◇ sharing with the homeless and other needy persons (food, clothing, blankets, toys, and books)

- ◇ volunteering: Ask "Where could we help? What do we do well that could be of help to others?"

⬧ community-planning projects: How is this community planned to meet the needs of the people who live in it? What could be changed to make it a better place? How could changes be brought about? What could we do?

As children become familiar with and at ease in the community, they are building an understanding of the importance of jobs, services, resources, and comfortable living for all persons. These basic understandings are the foundation for mature judgment about thoughtful planning for people's lives in neighborhoods, cities, and countries. As children and youth participate in communities, they become more confident in their own powers as agents of change and as agents for community enrichment and improvement.

EQUIPMENT AND MATERIALS

Activity materials are available in a rich variety to appeal to each child's interests, clearly arranged, in good repair, and accessible for individual choice. It is clear where they are stored and to where they can be returned. There may be no real distinction between many indoor and outdoor materials; most can be used in either place, space and weather permitting. Older children have usually mastered the standard playground equipment. They are eager now for flexible portable building materials for creative structures and for real sports equipment. Most materials fall into the following categories:

⬧ *Materials for vigorous play*: climbing, balancing, exercise, and active sports (balls, racquets, hoops, chalk, ropes), construction activities (lumber, tools, crates, blocks, logs, and cartons), hot and cold weather activities (hoses, sleds, and snow shovels), movement (bikes, skates, and wagons)

⬧ *Materials for daily living and homelike activities*: making believe (props, dress-ups, and mirror), reaching into the adult world (cooking, woodworking, and tinkering with machinery), using and respecting natural resources (plants, earth, and water), and caring for pets

⬧ *Materials for expressive activities*: art, writing, music, song and dance production, plays, puppet and talent shows

⬧ *Media materials*: to keep in touch with ideas, literature, the outside world (books, magazines, newspapers, radio, television, and tapes), coordination of interests with training tapes (soccer, tennis, football techniques, chess strategies, music, dance, art and self-improvement tapes)

⬧ *Materials for media arts productions*: computer art, filmmaking, photography, photo processing, sound recording and synthesizing, lighting, and stage techniques

Materials and equipment determine the kind of experiences that take place within the space, so they become an essential part of the physical environment.

◇ *Materials for enrichment, discovery, cooperative problem solving*: science, nature, and reference (things to open, take apart, measuring devices)

◇ *Materials for quiet activities, cooperative decision-making, and manipulative skills*: board games, puzzles, magic tricks, pencils, markers, papers, table constructions, computer games, and calculators

◇ *Materials for special events*: celebrations, trips, hikes, parties, and performances

PLANNING FOR THE EXPANSION OF IDEAS

Healthy, growing persons are constantly adding new concepts to those that are already familiar. It follows that the more experiences school-agers are exposed to, the more ideas can be generated. Since new materials cannot always be provided for each emerging new idea, it is especially useful to plan an environment that is both flexible and adaptable. In addition, as children get older, their play matures and becomes more complex. They should not be held back by the repetition of stale activities.

Select activities that can be used in different ways with maturing interests, skills, and developmental levels (art and construction, sports, dancing, drama, debating, swimming, hiking, shopping, and cooking). Supply games that can be played in different ways at varying levels (board games, cards, chalk, and ball games). Provide natural, open-ended materials (clays, wood, found objects, sand, and rocks).

Solving Some Special Environmental Problems

SHARED SPACE

The best efforts at creative environments may need to be stored away at the end of the day or the end of the week. The need to share physical space is probably the most common problem for staff, in center care when other programs use the same room during the school day, evenings, or weekends or in family or in-home care when family members use the child care area for personal living activities before and after the child care hours. Sharing space is often a major barrier in developing high quality programming. To help children feel a sense of ownership of their personal environment, they need space that is designed and decorated to reflect their interests and personalities.

When designating shared space, consider the compatibility of the various programs sharing the space. When space is shared at a school, church, or other facility, it is wise to keep in close contact with the maintenance personnel and the persons with whom the space is shared, so that they understand the design and purpose of the school-age program. When space is shared in a home, all the family members need to be agreeable and comfortable with the double use of family space.

School-age programs require certain space considerations, and it is essential that this is understood when any program is established. It may be useful to say, "There are certain things which are required, such as an activity area, storage areas, etc. Tell us what we need to do to successfully share this space with you."

It is also useful for each person involved in sharing the environment to be invited to visit and observe each other's activities in order to know the nature of their respective needs. School or church personnel can then understand the need for items such as homelike furniture, storage units, clubhouses, or occasional space for unfinished or large sculpture projects. Family members will be aware of how and why the home areas are used by school-agers. It also must be clearly agreed upon as to which equipment, materials, or physical areas are necessary and must be available, and which are off-limits to persons sharing space. For instance, in a center, can the school's multipurpose-room stage be used? Which sports or gymnastics equipment can be shared? What display space is available? In a home, are there certain rooms exclusively for the family belongings? Which toys may or may not be used by child care children? When these kinds of issues are decided, everyone should be aware of any limitations.

Although children's need for ownership of space is very important, it is not always possible to assure a sameness and familiarity of room design. In this case, focus can be shifted from the importance of the environment to the strength of the group; friends, after all, are certainly more important than furniture. The emphasis can be on the feeling of "we," "We're going skating. We want to have our pet show on Monday. We want the games over here today."

Children, with one another's help, can give life to their environment by setting it up afresh and maybe with a new twist.

The following suggestions may help in easing transitions when space is shared:

✧ *Time:* Time can be scheduled to allow for both setting up and putting away furniture, activities, storage units, and wall displays. Shared areas are more quickly cleaned when newspapers or throw-cloths have been placed under messy work areas.

✧ *Movable equipment:* Furniture, including cabinets, shelving, cubbies, and easy chairs, can be put on wheels for easy rearrangement.

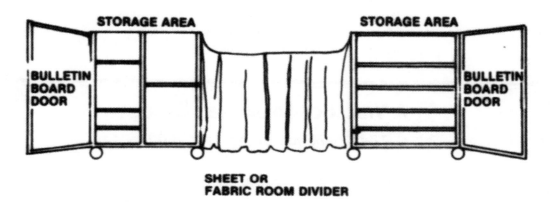

STORAGE AREA   **STORAGE AREA**

BULLETIN BOARD DOOR   **BULLETIN BOARD DOOR**

SHEET OR FABRIC ROOM DIVIDER

✧ *Functionally designed equipment:* Cabinets can be designed to serve as combination storage areas, room dividers, and bulletin boards. These can be folded, closed, locked, and wheeled aside as needed. When closed, the cabinets double as screens to separate and protect program materials.

✧ *Flexible equipment:* Equipment can be designed to be dismantled easily and reconstructed as desired. Crates and boxes provide movable and flexible storage areas.

Tri-Wall™, a sturdy plywood-like cardboard, can be cut and designed with interlocking sections to create privacy, dramatic play props, temporary tables, benches, and room dividers.

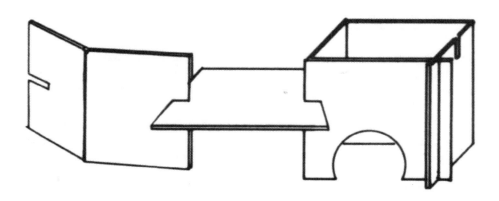

◇ *Mobile units:* Mobile units, on wheels, provide movable storage space, as well as a way to organize play materials.

◇ *Making a plan:* A detailed sketch may be kept on hand so that staff, substitutes, and children know where and how to set up and store away materials.

◇ *Emergency evacuations*: Emergencies may arise when the usual space must be used by other persons. Plan in advance. What other spaces are available? Are there storage units that can be taken elsewhere? Perhaps some special new activities can be stored in special containers for easy transport. This situation may require using the outdoors or places in the community.

A VISION OF DEDICATED SPACE

The Challenge of the Year 2000

by Rich Scofield

(School-Age NOTES, November 1993, reprinted with permission)

The challenge for the future of quality school-age care will be obtaining dedicated space in schools instead of using barren cafeterias and gyms or using shared space in classrooms and libraries.

Shared space in schools (most often cafeterias or gyms) is the most difficult space to use.

NOISE

They almost seem as if they were made to create noise. In a sense cafeterias and gyms with high ceilings, smooth floors and unadorned walls are perfect for bouncing sounds.

I have walked into a cafeteria in which each child was appropriately engaged. Children were at tables participating in activities, playing board games and the older kids were sitting on a rug socializing. None of the behavior individually was too noisy, inappropriate or out-of-control and yet the din pulsated in my ears. It was too loud.

We know that noise can be a stress factor in the workplace. One can only wonder at the stress for a child in a noisy gym or cafeteria for 2-3 hours a day all week long. And what about the stress on the caregiver who has inside duty all of the time?

No one has looked at the issue of noise as a stress factor in school-age care.

LACK OF PERSONAL SPACE

Each set of standards or indicators of quality school-age care points to the importance of making the program feel like home including having a place for children's belongings. Programs have been extremely creative in providing portable bins, putting markings on the floor, and designing personalized rolled-out mats for belongings. However, these do not replace the need for one's own permanent space where one can leave belongings from day to day without feeling like a nomad.

The clearest image for me of what we don't want is the school where the children carried their book bags and coats with them as they trudged to the different spaces in the school the program had access to-many different spaces and rooms, but none they could call their own.

LACK OF WARM, HOME-LIKE ENVIRONMENT

Another key to quality that we always hear about is to provide a warm, home-like environment. Usually rugs, plants, soft lighting, bean-bag chairs, stuffed chairs and sofas, and creating divided, cozy spaces are given as examples of changing the environment. Gyms and cafeterias by their nature don't feel warm and home-like.

SPACE FOR PROJECTS

Finally, having space for leaving projects out to dry over night, leaving forts up for several days, or leaving marathon board games out undisturbed, is not usually available in shared school space.

OBTAINING DEDICATED SPACE

When schools are overflowing, how can you get dedicated space?

- Ideally: a school system would appreciate the importance of dedicated space and let the SAC program have a classroom inside the building and just add another portable classroom to the row of existing portables. (Of course, the new teacher would get assigned to the portable.) The program might offer to "share" its space with itinerant teachers, speech pathologists, or counselors or with other adults needing a place to work with individual or small groups of children. Making double use of the space is an obvious selling point for this concept.

- Second choice: the school places a portable classroom on the school grounds for the SAC program to use. Less desirable because of lack of water availability and going to restrooms in the building presents security issues in the late afternoon when the building is not occupied. Similar security issues might exist when using school gyms or libraries.

  In some communities programs have raised funds and bought portable buildings to be placed on the school property. Again, best use would be to trade for a classroom inside.

- In Wisconsin, a non-profit, youth agency raised $250,000 to build an addition to the school building for the SAC program.

- In Seattle a city bond issue was passed to have separate SAC space built into all new school buildings.

- Some programs have sought nearby houses to renovate and use as a center in order to have their own space.

DEDICATED SPACE WITHIN A CAFETERIA

SAY, Inc. of San Diego runs more than a dozen SAC programs in school buildings. I finally saw a program in a cafeteria that made me feel as though there was hope for shared space situations.

They made their own dedicated space by using a corner of the cafeteria about the size of a classroom and by placing low bookshelves (about three feet high) as the other two "walls." The corner created by the two walls of shelves meeting was left open to create an entrance way. A board acted as a gate during the day to keep kids out. Their security system was all the kids who attended the program watching during the school hours to make sure no one "messed" with their program.

Inside, their "room" was carpeted and had bean-bag chairs and a sofa and cubbies for each child's possessions and the other fixtures of dedicated space. The children also had access to the cafeteria's tables for messy projects or just to spread out. The playground and access to it was right there and allowed for a flow back and forth according to the children's interests.

SETTING A GOAL

Getting dedicated space doesn't happen by accident. Even in the ideal situation of being given your own classroom it doesn't come about unless you ask for it. Documents such as the principals' Standards for Quality School-Age Child Care obviously can be used to back your case for dedicated space.

Often in the child care field we are too accommodating and too willing to settle for the "scraps." (Our knack for being good scroungers and being innovative in recycling things can get in our way.) We may have to learn to say, "No, we can't do a quality program in this cafeteria. We need dedicated space to provide a quality program that these children may end up using every afternoon for four, five, or six years."

So the first step to obtaining dedicated space is to make it a goal. Put your goal in writing and set a date-two, three, ten years from now.

Without setting a goal of obtaining dedicated space, programs by default are doomed to inadequate and inappropriate space for quality school-age care. Every program in shared space should have a vision of being in its own space some day.

THE NEXT STEP

The next step to obtaining dedicated space is to let parents, school administrators, and the community know about your goal and then bring them into the process of brainstorming ways to get dedicated space. (Remember dedicated space can even mean moving out of the school building. It should not be viewed as a win-lose situation with teachers and principals.)

FOOTNOTE

Yes, there are some great programs working in incredibly difficult space. But those are extremely creative school-age care professionals. Our education system has not been able to replicate Marva Collins' success in teaching. She is unique. We cannot replicate the talented SAC professionals who can "run a program under a tree." Our school-age care space must be such that the average caregiver can run a quality program in it. And our very creative SAC professionals certainly should not be expending their talents compensating for inadequate space rather than focusing on the program and the children. The vision and its goal always has to be dedicated space.

References used were:

Standards for Quality School-Age Child Care by the National Association of Elementary School Principals.

Assessing School-Age Child Care Quality by the Wellesley School-Age Child Care Project.

Developmentally Appropriate Practice in School-Age Child Care Program, 2nd Edition by Kay M. Albrecht and Margaret C. Plantz of Project Home Safe.

MULTIPURPOSE ROOMS AND SCHOOL CAFETERIAS

In these large areas there is usually too much or too little space – too much space in large gyms or multipurpose rooms yet too little space when cafeteria tables and chairs are set up. Both situations require inventive thinking.

✧ *Dividing the space*

Each situation requires subdividing space for specific groups, as well as for presentations of activities and materials. When there is too much or too little space, children tend to lose focus and in the confusion cannot ascertain or concentrate on what is available and of interest to them.

Large gym areas may be divided by area rugs, bulletin boards, screens, furniture, or storage units. The cafeteria furniture may be rearranged to define space for each group and to present materials for each interest area. In both cases the goal will be a well-designed balance between open space and chances for privacy.

✧ *Dividing the children*

Groups of school-agers need not all be in the room at the same time. Some may be outdoors, others on short trips, still others in various parts of the facility. The fewer the children, the less competition for materials, intrusion into the space of others, confusion, and noise.

✧ *Reducing noise*

Noise becomes a significant factor in large areas, but the following ideas may help:

• A reminder to all staff to keep their own voices quiet and friendly and to approach individual children rather than yelling across space.

• Subdivision into small group areas.

• Soft materials that absorb noise.

• Limited number of children in the room at any one time.

✧ *Creating comfort*

These large spaces may also feel cold and institutional. How can they become homelike, attractive, and comfortable?

- Soften with rugs, mats, bean chairs, pillows, comforters, lawn chairs, and soft furniture.

- Beautify by adding color, plants, fabrics, and pictures.

- Personalize by displaying art work, photographs, and personal items.

- Keep the groups as small and family-like as you can.

✧ *Providing display areas*

These large areas often tend to create problems of little display space because there are few walls and often these walls must be shared. Determine which walls, doors, or screens can be used for children's work, news, notices, etc. Which can be permanent display areas? Which can be portable?

TOO LITTLE SPACE

Licensing requirements should determine the maximum number of children allowed in the available space, in both family and center care. But even so, space may often seem limited, cramped, cluttered. Look around for room for growth. Can the floor itself be used for many activities, so that some furniture can be eliminated? Can some materials be rotated, so everything need not be out at the same time? Can other areas in the home or center be used as activity space—a porch, deck, basement area, or hallway? Can groups of children be separately scheduled for indoor, outdoor, and community experiences? Can nooks be created for individual and small-group privacy in order to prevent interference?

NOT ENOUGH EQUIPMENT

There are two somewhat related problems with limited equipment. The first is that with a limited variety of materials the school-agers become bored. As a result, their behavior may deteriorate. The second problem is that with a limited quantity of any one kind of equipment, the children have to wait their turns. Only two board games to play? The same dozen books? Only two puppets? Not enough blocks to build anything? As the children work, deficiencies quickly become obvious. To supplement equipment, ask the children for ideas, and trade with other staff. Keep an eye on budget requirements but realize that constructive play requires enough tools to make it happen.

WIDE AGE RANGE

It is common to have school-agers ranging from five or six to twelve or fourteen years of age in one environment, but in such cases the environment must be

Community experiences may include volunteering. Ask "Where can we help? What do we do well that could be of help to others?"

adapted. Both younger and older children should have appropriate tasks, which they need not share unless they wish to do so. If materials are appropriate for all ages, there should be assurance that there will be no interference. For instance, dollhouses, cooking utensils, carpentry tools, easels, or outdoor equipment may be appropriate for all ages, but they may work well with only one age group at a time. Older children certainly deserve materials that encourage their increasingly sophisticated skills and interest in a final product (art, board and card games, and computer activities), while younger children still need time and space to learn, explore, and experiment at their own level. Older school-agers may need a separate space for homework, projects, being with friends, and reading. They may need space for active team sports and large-muscle skills without the interference of younger children. Even the furniture is a consideration so that each child has comfortable chairs and efficient work surfaces.

WHEN SCHOOL-AGERS ARE PART OF A PRESCHOOL GROUP

It requires careful planning when school-agers and preschoolers are combined so that each age group can develop its own capabilities.

Sometimes it's necessary to have a mixed-age group, especially in a home setting, and sometimes it's fun to be together for parts of a day, even in a large center. But when school-agers are combined with younger children, it takes some effort to make it work.

Making it work

School-agers should have some space of their own:

- for vigorous play (climbing, running, and games)

- for indoor activities (block construction, art projects, board games, and play productions)

- for supplies, treasures, and personal belongings

- for doing homework or reading, for making something, or being with a friend

- for privacy and clubs

School-agers need to have their own materials and furnishings:

- which do not have to be shared (special games, special paints, special balls, or science equipment)

- which are geared to their new and expanding interests

- with furniture their own size

School-agers should have their own time with certain activities and equipment:

- building blocks

- a dollhouse

- the swimming pool

- the outdoor play yard

- the kitchen for cooking

But everyone can go walking or shopping or picnicking together. And everyone likes to swing, sing, dig in the sand, and play in the snow. When the environment fits the children, they know they are welcome.

Good Environments Meet the Needs of Everyone

Environment and the Needs of Staff

What are the benefits to adults when space is well designed, materials are accessible for choice, and children are busy? The greatest benefit is that adults also have freedom of choice: to talk with a child who has had a rough day, to try out a new art technique, and to see which activities seem to be working and which need a new prop to extend ideas. Leaders have time now to respond to individual youngsters, to circulate as consultants, to step back and observe what is going well and what needs attention.

Because space is well planned, equipped, and prepared, staff need not spend their time seeking and delivering materials upon request, ignoring children as they seek missing pieces or lost parts, or hurry to mix the paints. Adults now need not be policemen or guidance counselors, because when there are plenty of activities, children display fewer behavior problems. Adults need not be constantly leading, bossing, giving orders, and thinking up activities in which resisting children must follow specific, preconceived directions.

Staff are not so busy handling problems and emergencies that they cannot make their own choices about where they are needed. They are free to be real professionals who have planned thoughtfully and can now act thoughtfully. The stage is well set.

ENVIRONMENT AND THE NEEDS OF CHILDREN

Mastery of skills and the discovery of self

Children are free to select things to do in an organized environment where space is sufficient and materials are plentiful and in good repair. Then tasks can be completed successfully: one cannot achieve mastery with insufficient tools, when parts and pieces are missing, or when equipment is broken. The environment offers activities that school-agers are comfortable with or wish to try out, activities they can practice, repeat, and master. Mastery in using school skills in a noncompetitive environment helps children, whether or not they excel in school. They may write songs, enjoy leisurely reading, practice skills such as dance, gymnastics, and musical instruments.

The environment offers activities that school-agers are comfortable with or wish to try out, activities they can practice, repeat, and master.

Places for privacy allow for chances to think, contemplate, and digest ideas, so one can confidently move on to a next step. Materials for the imagination add to a sense of capability for thinking up one's own unique ideas. Open-ended materials, where there is no right or wrong use reinforce feelings of success. Areas for personal collections and materials that reflect one's own culture and interests keep the environment personal.

Friendship and good human relationships

Cooperative relationships require cooperative environments. Out-of-school environments offer small-group activities so that children relate and work together to attain common goals. Rooms are designed to consider both the ages and the sizes of groups in order to encourage close relationships. There are spaces for two or three persons to be together.

Since school-agers are likely to take physical risks to make, impress, and keep friends, equipment is kept challenging, always in safe condition, and within the view of adults. Part of risk-taking means new discoveries, so the environment requires ever-changing and fresh experiences.

As children and youth become a part of the surrounding community, they gain feelings of familiarity and companionship with the people whom they meet and with whom they work, thus broadening their relationships.

Independence, self-direction, and power

Here are some simple questions to ask in designing and redesigning an environment: Does this environment create an atmosphere where children and youth can choose what they wish to do and pursue their choices? Are materials categorized and presented so that they can be independently retrieved and returned? Is there a rich variety of experiences from which to choose?

It is not simple to provide positive answers, because of age and interest range, budgetary matters, and availability of appropriate space. However, children can exert independence, self-direction, and power as they help to design and set up activity areas and as they make their decisions between indoor, outdoor, and community experiences.

Suggested Plans For Physical Environments

Some environments are limited to one area; others may reach from room to room or spread over outdoor spaces. Each setting is different. The following illustrations shows general arrangements that are applicable for both home and center care, suggesting the experiences to be included.

SUGGESTED INDOOR ROOM PLAN

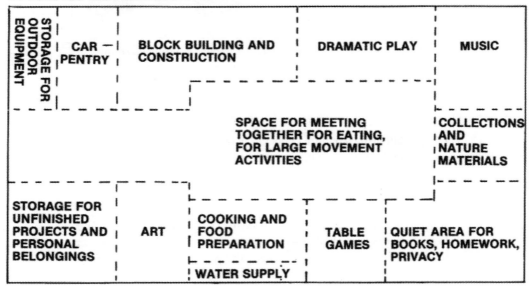

SUGGESTED OUTDOOR PLAN

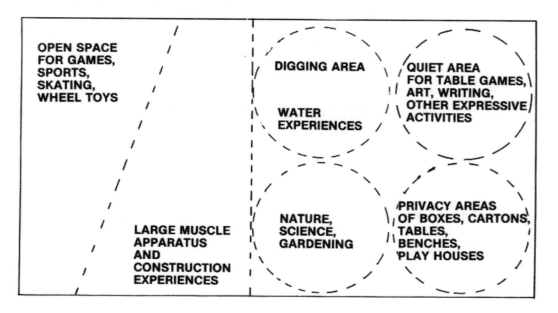

Children seek access to ... a place where they can dig in the earth, build huts and dens with timber, use real toys, experiment ... take really great risks and learn to overcome them.

Lady Allen of Hartwood
1897-1976

NOTES

[1] Joe L. Frost, *Play and Playscapes*, presents a comprehensive look at playground design as it relates to safety and the prevention of injuries, and to child development and concepts of play.

RECOMMENDED READINGS

Frost, J. *Play and Play Spaces*. New York: Delmar, 1992.

Heseltine, P. and J. Holborn. *Playgrounds: The Planning and Construction of Play Environments*. New York: Nichols, 1987.

Kosanke, N. and N. Warner. *Creative Play Areas*. Nephi: Innovation Station, 1990.

Rivkin, M. S. *The Great Outdoors: Restoring Children's Right to Play Outside*. Washington DC: NAEYC, 1995.

Seven
What Do The Children Do?
Scheduling, Grouping and 1,000 Things To Do!

"I love to just chill! And do whatever!
To hang with friends and talk about big,
important topics for hours and hours,
in person or on the phone. Maybe I'm
weird but when I'm really bored I like
to organize things like doll houses and
stuff – always find something to do."

Patrice, age 14

"Youth is the time to go flashing from one end
of the world to the other both in mind and body;
to try the manners of different nations, to hear
the chimes at midnight, to see sunrise in town
and country…write halting verses, run a mile
to see a fire…"

Robert Louis Stevenson
1850-1894

In this chapter…

➢ Designing For The Flow Of Time
  — Daily Schedules; Self-Directed Activities
  — Getting Together: Group Times
  — Transitions: Changes in Place, Time, and Experience
  — Food: The Way To A Child's Heart!
  — The Media: So Simple To Use, So Easy To Abuse
  — Is There Time For Homework?
  — Private Times
➢ Children And Groups
  — The Strength Of The Group
  — Creating Groups
  — Mixed-Age Versus Same-Age Groupings
  — Five-Year-Olds In School-Age Groups
  — School-Age Children in Preschool Groups
  — Hanging Out: The Older Kids

Designing the Flow of Time

DAILY SCHEDULES

The following suggested schedules are appropriate for both home and center care. They relate general time frames to both the needs of the children and the responsibilities of the adults. As a schedule is created, the following questions should be addressed:

- ✧ Is the schedule flexible enough to allow for the unexpected — a weather change, a visitor, a community activity, a current event that needs discussion and understanding?

- ✧ What changes may need to be made for a school holiday? an emergency school closing?

- ✧ Is it appropriate for each child in the group — the youngest as well as the oldest, the child with special interests, the child who needs lots of rest, the child who comes infrequently?

- ✧ Does it alternate active and quiet activities?

- ✧ Does it include indoor and outdoor experiences?

- ✧ Has time been allotted for routines such as snack and meal times, bathroom breaks, transitions?

- ✧ Is there time for children to plan for their own daily activities, for future experiences, for special occasions?

- ✧ Is there time for children to choose what to do and for how long to do it?

- ✧ Is there sufficient time for children to talk with adults and with one another?

SUGGESTED DAILY SCHEDULES

The following schedules suggest plans for before-school, after-school, and full-day school-age programs. They relate staff responsibilities to the needs of the children. They may be applied to in-home care, family child care, or center-based programs.

Before-School Schedule
Opening of program until departure for school

Children	Staff
May still be sleepy.	Provide chance for rest or sleep with couches, cots, floormats, pillows, and blankets.
May be hungry.	Provide breakfast or a light snack.

May need some "warm-up" time.	Allow time for slowly getting into the day.
May have homework to complete.	Provide a comfortable, quiet space to work; keep useful materials accessible such as pencils, scissors, and paper.
May have forgotten school supplies in rush to get to program.	Keep on hand extra supplies such as pencils, pens, erasers, crayons, and paper
May be wide awake and need to run off some energy before school.	Allow for some time indoor or out doors with large-muscle equipment.
May want to complete a project left unfinished the previous afternoon.	Provide space and time for completion of projects.
May enjoy using expressive and creative materials before the more directed school activities.	Offer choices such as art, block building, cooking, small construction materials, and carpentry.
May just want to sit around and talk with friends.	Need not schedule every moment, so that children may enjoy just being together to chat, play games, or listen to music.
May want to plan for something special to do when the school day is over.	Plan for this with children if adult ideas are requested.
May need some close adult company.	Are available for listening, for questions, for comfort.
May be anxious or concerned about going to school.	Are understanding about these feelings, provide pleasant and positive experiences before the children leave for school, and send them off with a warm goodbye.

After-School Schedule

*Program begins midday, when kindergarten children arrive
from school, or midafternoon, when older children arrive.*

Children	**Staff**
May be hungry.	Serve food or allow children to prepare food in a buffet or sit-down style.
May be tired.	Provide a time for rest, quiet activity, or maybe even a nap.
May be so upset about a certain school incident that anger or disappointment spills over to the after school situation.	Take a few minutes to chat, accept the feelings, reassure, and listen to the complaints.
May be full of chatter after a full day of school.	Build in ways for children to talk with each other and with adults.
May need to use large-body muscles after a day of sitting.	Have activities and active equipment available indoors and outdoors or in neighborhood play areas.
Will need fresh air, having probably been inside much of the day.	Provide time outdoors with appropriate supervision.
May want individual attention after being in a large group all day.	Spend time with each child talking, working on a project, or helping with homework.
May want to play with just one or two friends rather than deal with a large group.	Encourage activities in which children participate in small groups.
May want to spend time alone.	Respect this by designing areas for privacy and activity where children can be on their own.

Will want to make personal choices rather than being told what to do.	Have designed indoor and outdoor experiences for self-directed choices.
Will enjoy community experiences in order to be with neighborhood friends, pursue their own interests, and feel a part of the larger world.	Plan for experiences away from the school-age setting: special classes, trips, walks, errands, and special events.

5:00 - 6:30 p.m. or closing time

Enjoy an individual pursuit, reading, art, games, or homework.	Present a variety of materials and provide space and opportunity for homework with resources such as reference books, extra pens, and paper.
May be in the middle of an unfinished project or activity when the day is over.	Provide space for unfinished projects until they can be completed.
May need some time to gather up belongings or finish projects before leaving.	Provide time and warning for activities to be brought to a smooth close. Families are often in a hurry, and this rush can be inconvenient for a child who is involved in a project.
May want to show family something or have them meet a new friend or staff member.	Encourage the family to come into the setting so they will be familiar with the child's interests, skills, and friendships.

Full-Day Schedule
Morning opening of program.

Children	**Staff**
May be sleepy or still asleep if this is an in-home program.	Provide soft areas and quiet activities so children can continue to sleep or return to sleep.

Children	Staff
May be slow or fast starters, may need breakfast, may just want to be on-lookers for a while.	Set up activities for the day in advance and can focus now on each child gearing to his or her pace, providing for the hungry, nurturing the slow starter, motivating the active to choose from the array of materials in the setting.

8:00 - 9:00 a.m.

Children	**Staff**
May have ideas for the day's activities and can help in the planning.	Meet with individuals, a small group, or the entire group of children to decide plans for the day, share information, and have discussions.
May be looking forward to continuing an activity previously started.	Provide opportunities to carry out long-range plans and experiences.
May be anticipating an activity away from the center.	Plan a community experience and discuss preparation and details with the children.
May already be busy with friends or materials.	Supervise play and enrich the children's ideas.
May seem at a loss for direction.	Bring out a new game or piece of equipment; present new ideas or instructions for independent activities.

9:00 - 11:30 a.m.

Children	Staff
Are probably at the peak of interest and vitality, indoors and outdoors, eager to choose experiences and be exposed to new activities.	Use the time to interact with the children, extend their thinking, and introduce new props for play. This peak activity time can be used for both self-directed and adult-directed activities, community projects, short trips, visits around the neighborhood, errands with a few children, and rehearsals for performances.

Will get hungry again.

Provide snacks or let the children prepare their own. They may take food and drink on trips as well.

Will want to go outside and play.

Schedule outdoor activities. The length of time will depend on weather, shared play areas, interests, and the activities involved.

11:30 - 12:00 noon

May be ready to wind down.

Plan a quiet transition time before lunch: story telling, mime show, reading, science experience, dance, or soft music.

12:00 - 1:00 p.m.

Wash hands, may help in lunch preparation, serving and cleaning up, relax and sit with friends, and enjoy eating lunch in different styles—picnicking, lunch buffet, cook-out, or brown bag.

Consider the involvement of the children in menu planning and lunch preparation and serving; provide food for any child who forgot lunch, arrange for variety of ways to serve lunch, and recognize that small groupings allow social conversation and less chance for out-of-bounds behavior

1:00 - 2:00 p.m.

May need some quiet time after eating. Some school-age children still like to nap when given the opportunity, but others do not sleep and have no need for this.

Offer a rest choice of cot, mat or sleeping bag, perhaps next to a friend. Other choices may include board games, card games, quiet activities, arts and crafts materials, story reading.

2:00 - 5:00 p.m.

May enjoy going someplace or doing "something different."

Understand there is a need to plan for this long span of afternoon time. Activities may include swimming, sports, hiking, working on a tree house, talent show, gardening, building snow castles, going shopping, and interest clubs. The span of time allows for spontaneity and unhurried ventures.

Are hungry again by midafternoon.	Get out the snack!
May want to continue an activity started earlier in the day. Children like a feeling of completion.	Encourage this. Children now have a sense of continuity and industry.

5:00 - 6:30 p.m. or closing time

May be restless, anxious, or want to go home. Or some may not want to go home because it is often hard to break away from friends. They may be exhausted after such a long day.	Recognize these behaviors and help a child to verbalize feelings, as well as offering a variety of quiet, comfortable activities to choose from for a happy day's end.
Show varied reactions to family members when they arrive.	Recognize these mixed feelings, which are sometimes joy, sometimes resentment, sometimes anger, often love.

SUMMERTIME IS TRULY DIFFERENT

Summertime planning:

Longer hours, many days, hotter weather!
- More staff (this may be a twelve-hour day)
- Ways to keep cool
- Enough activities to hold interests

- Age groupings that are compatible
- Trips away from the program setting
- A flexible full-day schedule (see full-day schedule)

But now there is time at last:

- for all the activities that could not be included in before-school or after-school programs or on the occasional full-day school holidays;
- for friends to have leisurely time together;
- to plan for long-range activities that can be carried over from day to day.

Let the school-agers:

- draw up plans for their day, their week, their summer;
- name their summer program: "Holiday Paradise," "Our Club," "Camp Midtown";
- plant a garden for summer salads;
- plan for long-range projects: musical production, puppet show, motion picture production, dance festival, playhouse construction;
- create a sports fair, swim ballet;
- plan for overnight camping, picnics, and bike trips;
- dream up theme weeks: Neanderthal Man, Futuristic Fantasy, Alaskan Adventure, African Village.

Remember to make plans for a variety of activities:

- Centers of interest to provide materials for learning, experimenting, and practicing.
- Growth of personal skills. Now there is plenty of time for hobbies, collections, music, sports, art, playwriting, swimming, and typing.
- Group experiences in conflict resolution and cooperation in the form of projects and small group games.
- Community involvement: volunteer work, fairs, theater, sports, and classes in special skills.

FREE TIME: SELF-DIRECTED ACTIVITIES

Free time and a free choice of activities can be the life of the school-age program, especially during summer hours. These large blocks of time may start the day, end the day, or be scheduled for an entire morning or afternoon. Free time is a chance for self-initiative as well as cooperation, a time for growth, learning, and play. The physical environment and human environment blend and the children's feelings of personal freedom connect with the rights and welfare of everyone else. Self-assertion can operate within the cohesiveness of the group.

The environment invites the self-selection of experiences. The staff has planned for this in both the indoor and outdoor settings with a variety of available activities and materials. The activity selections change, develop, and evolve as school-agers and staff work together and expand their respective interests. There are choices of familiar experiences which consolidate existing skills and develop expertise and there are chances for related experiences into the less familiar. There are clearly defined zones for quiet activities, active play, or privacy. Depending on space and supervision, there may be a free flow of choice between indoors and outdoors or between a main room and special activity areas (spaces for music, carpentry, gym, etc.).

Self-directed activities are the essential core of an effective school-age program.

During free choice time, some children will know just what they want to do and who they want to play with. Other children may wander for a while, observing activities or sampling from several interest areas. The children will group and regroup. There will be ongoing projects such as pet care, tending a garden, or rehearsing a play, and there will be special projects such as preparing for a party or a cooking activity. Some children will opt for spontaneous play or just hanging out with their friends.

The staff have created the free-time environment before the children arrive at the program. The space is ready, the choices are clear. The goals of self-direction are evident: self-sufficiency, success, opportunities for friendships, decision-making, problem solving, and mastery of skills. Staff act as consultants, circulating among the activities, choosing when and how to nurture a child by determining what is needed, building on interests, and helping develop skills. The staff work alongside the children, talking with them, supplying information, interacting with groups or individuals. They comfort, befriend, and encourage. Self-directed activities are the essential core of an effective school-age program.

GETTING TOGETHER: GROUP TIMES

We have talked about children coming together for planning and to solve common problems, but there are many reasons to meet with small groups or with an entire group. Sometimes it is most successful for children of similar ages or interests to meet; at other times a mixture of ages works well. Get-togethers may be indoors or outdoors. They may be planned or spontaneous, very brief or as long as enthusiasm is high. They may be at the start, in the middle, or at the end of the day. When get-togethers are interesting and varied, kids look forward to them. Sometimes, in the case of announcements, a group time may be essential for everyone. At other times, if persons in the group are restless or uninvolved, alternative activities can be on hand so that the interested children are not disrupted.

These get-togethers succeed when everyone can see and hear everyone else and the adult is an integral member of the group, especially when everyone meets in a circle. The adults vary their place in the circle, sharing their own ideas and helping the less verbal children express their thoughts. Visitors are encouraged to join the circle. Adults or children may open up the meeting.[1]

Occasions which bring children together may include: announcements, discussions, demonstrations, problem solving, games, gripe sessions, introduction to new activities or materials, planning, singing, visitors, dance or drama presentations, letter writing, storytelling or reading, watching videos, listening to recordings, greetings and goodbyes to new or departing children or adults.

TRANSITIONS: CHANGES IN PLACE, TIME, AND EXPERIENCE

A transition is simply the change from one experience to another. The ease with which children handle transitions may vary, depending on the ways that experiences of change have been approached throughout their lives—ranging from harsh commands to gentle introductions, from threats to appeals to the sense of adventure. Reactions to changes in experiences may result in confusion, resentment, or resistance, but if transitions are handled well, they can result in cooperative, easy-going behaviors. School-age programs generally include transitions such as the initial enrollment in the program (a big change in routine), the daily arrival from home or school, the return after absence or illness, movement from indoors to outdoors or to another group, or simply the time between one activity and the next activity.

Transition times can be thoughtfully planned by reviewing the activity schedule, room arrangement, traffic flow, and the manner in which adults give directions to children. All of these factors relate to the prevention of transition problems. Since the goal for children is self-control and self-direction, the fewer adult commands and gimmicks (e.g. bells, whistles, flashing lights), the better.

Minimize waiting time. If some children must wait for others, provide something to do, with books, tapes, videos, songs, etc.

Encourage an activity if there's nothing to do. On long transportation rides or at the end of a day when a parent has not arrived, children can pass the waiting time with travel games, books, tapes, a new board game, or a snack.

Provide ongoing projects. Some activities that children can start and stop while waiting are weaving, large puzzles, knitting, construction materials, and ongoing chess games.

Specific transition times include:

Welcoming new children. Even older children may need help in entering a new out-of-school program. A personal interview, introductions to staff, and visits before starting are important. One or two children can show newcomers around, or children might enjoy a buddy system. New children can also bridge their personal lives with the program by borrowing records, tapes, and books from the program or by sharing personal materials with new friends.

Daily arrivals. Each boy or girl likes to be genuinely recognized by a familiar adult, warmly greeting them by name, giving a smile, offering a compliment. Staff members pick up on a conversation started the day before or inquire about school, family, or a pet. This is not a time for staff to talk to other adults or to become involved with setting up activities. As children arrive, they need their own places for their belongings. In the early morning they may be slow in getting started, so quiet activities or breakfast may be appropriate. But after school most youngsters are boisterous and want to talk and move.

At arrival, suggestions might be made about special experiences that are available, and some children can help set up materials. Food is certainly a welcoming offer. Often school-agers are so eager to get to their friends that they bypass adults completely. That's fine. In any case, a good start to the day pays off in many ways as the day proceeds.

When a child has been absent or ill. The transition back to a program is often eased if staff or peers have written or called the child at home. When the child returns, a special greeting is appreciated.

Getting started. Adults sometimes worry about wild dashes and grand chaos as children begin to choose activities. Effective transitions into free-choice periods will vary according to factors such as available materials, room design, scheduling, and the size and age of the group. The transition may be approached in different ways:

- Activities are clearly set up and accessible, and children choose what they wish to do and with whom they wish to play. Some children may wander around and observe before settling into a choice.

- A planning time precedes children's choices as they are briefed on any daily plans and availability of experiences. Choices are made before approaching activities, but there must not be so much emphasis on this planning stage that children lose enthusiasm or are not clear about what each choice entails.

Each approach has advantages and disadvantages and will depend on the program. When children are assured that they will have plenty of time for their play, the mad dashes can be avoided.

Clean-up times. School-agers generally can be responsible for putting away their materials as they finish with them. Sharing clean-up responsibilities may be appropriate for materials such as art, carpentry, or sports supplies which have been used by many children during a free-choice time. Planning adequate time for clean-up is as essential as planning the time for any other activity, and children need to know when to start the process.

Daily Departures. Just as when school-agers arrive, this is a time for a good-bye and the personal touch: "Hope I'll see you tomorrow," a handshake, a pat on the back. It is a time for greeting families but not for discussing their child or family problems. If a parent needs to talk with staff, a better time can be arranged. Since children go home at varying times, the end of the day may include new and familiar activities that a child enjoys alone or with two or three friends.

When children leave a program. Sometimes this may be sudden, without warning. If this happens, the group, a staff member, or a special friend might call or send a letter of goodbye. If the family has notified you of the last day, you might consider a goodbye get-together or a small gift, but in any case let the other children know in advance, so they can say their goodbyes.

FOOD: THE WAY TO A CHILD'S HEART!

From the very beginning of each child's life, comfort, warmth, trust, acceptance, and satisfaction are associated with food. Food carries emotional significance all through our lives. The giving and receiving of food is a symbol of caring and love. Since habits and attitudes about food are deeply rooted in past experience and become a lasting part of our way of life, children bring their own memories and feelings about food based on experiences of hunger, deprivation, nagging, arguments, or relaxed, happy gatherings.

Food makes strong impressions! When you ask children what they did on a field trip, they will usually tell you first what they ate or drank. Since emotional impressions and lasting memories contribute to both learning and the quality of living, the provision of food is an important and natural way of making children feel welcome when they arrive, and it is certainly an integral part of celebrations.

Program planning includes provision for appealing, nutritious snacks and meals, foods for special occasions, activity projects, field trips, and sharing with others. School-agers can participate in planning, purchasing (or growing), preparing, serving, and cleaning up. This may be done by school-age volunteers, by committee, or by everyone taking turns. Through this process each child becomes fully involved, not only in satisfying eating experiences but also in activities such as:

   ◇ *Working with friends*: planning, preparing, cooking, and eating.

   ◇ *Community involvement*: shopping, visiting restaurants, stores, or food processing plants; meeting culinary experts, farmers, cookbook authors, or persons who cook foods from diverse cultures; and cooking for or donating food to the hungry.

   ◇ *Decision making*: creating menus, selecting recipes, shopping, and serving the foods, as well as considering options for leftovers.

   ◇ *Mastery of skills*: using nutrition information, utensils, and appliances, as well as applying skills in writing, reading and math as prices and quantities are considered and recipes become realities.

❖ *Completion of tasks*: choosing and preparing each food, eating, and cleaning up.

All of these activities foster a sense of responsibility, usefulness, success, security, and belonging.

THE MEDIA: SO SIMPLE TO USE, SO EASY TO ABUSE

There are few influences in our lives greater than the media — television, recordings, newspapers — and children's experiences with media may be either enriching or destructive.

Ask yourself why, when, and how you present media experiences. Are you using it in thoughtful ways? The media can be catalysts for discussion, predictors for what might occur, and the basis for character studies. Use it to stimulate children's own thinking. Make up a better ending! Children can create their own media presentations to counteract media messages: messages for peace and against violence, drugs, and crime. Think of other ideas. Staff should be ready to discuss, interpret, and respond to questions.

The media are never a substitute for real-life experiences but are certainly resources for news, drama, music, language, and visual images. Through discussions staff can help youngsters in understanding the difference between reality and fantasy, living and play-acting, and can help children consider the use of media – its possibilities, reporting methods, recording styles, and advertising techniques.

TV or no TV?

Children learn from television. What do they learn? Are they lulled into believing that all learning is action packed and should be brought to them in jazzy images, living color, and one-minute segments? Are they taught what life is truly like? Do they learn that the language, dress, and actions that they observe on television are accepted in real life? Is there an adult with time to help them understand the ideas presented, build on these ideas, clarify concepts? Which teachings on television are appropriate for school-agers?

Children are interested in humor. What kind of humor is displayed? Whether cartoon or drama, is the humor at the child's level? Is humor presented as ridicule, teasing, sarcasm, or violence? Is an adult available to help children distinguish what is genuinely funny from what is not funny?

Children are learning to solve personal problems. Does television give children valid ideas on how to solve their problems? Does some television lead them to believe that problems are simply and quickly solved by new purchases, force, cruelty, trickery, or aggression? Can staff help school-agers see the actual complexities of problems and the different and useful ways to solve them?

Children are trying to figure out the components of human relationships. What does television teach about human feelings, behaviors, friendships, and sexual relations? Can an adult translate the words and actions of television into the realities of sensitive, successful relationships?

Children are emotionally affected by what they view on television. Is someone close by and tuned in to their feelings, ready to cope with their aggression, fears, and other behaviors that may result from watching television?

Children want to master skills. Does television take time away from real-life experiences, or can television provide information that is useful in developing skills? Does the school-age program create a balance between active involvement and passive entertainment, between actual experience and secondhand media experience?

Music and its messages

Children enjoy music. How can music be used with school-agers: for dance, listening, singing, composition, performance, exercising, or relaxing? All are valid uses. Are school-age staff introducing a wide range of appropriate and creative musical experiences which expand children's choices and knowledge of music?

Children listen to lyrics, the words of music. What messages are the children receiving through much of today's song lyrics? How confusing are the words to school-agers' developing values? How adult is content? Who is helping children sort out the messages and think about the meanings: the racial and religious slurs, the invitations to sex, violence against others, drugs, and suicide? Can staff help children behave in accordance with their increasingly maturing values, judgment, and sensitivity to the feelings of others?

Children are influenced by the emotional aspect of music: the pace (relaxing or frantic), the volume (soothing or blaring), and the plea of the words (optimistic and joyful or an invitation to hate and anger). Can staff help school-agers enjoy the many moods and varieties of music by presenting musical experiences that encourage self-esteem, cooperation, and happy living?

What about the ads?

Children often believe what they are told. Commercial advertisements tell them what to do and what to buy. School-agers may become confused about what a person needs to be happy and successful. They may feel dissatisfied with their own lives if they do not resemble what is in the ad. Commercials may cause confusion about whether the child's race, gender, ethnic group, or family structure is okay.

Children are learning to make personal decisions. Advertisements frequently give the impression that personal problems are solved fast, and easily, through a quick purchase — a drug, cosmetic, drink, diet, or new car. Ads tell children not only what to buy but also how to behave and how to achieve. Can school-agers still trust the adult world when they learn that actors and writers are paid to promote the often questionable products?

IS THERE TIME FOR HOMEWORK?

Today there is a debate about the value of homework and the question of whether homework should be drill, problem solving, research, self-expression, or any or all of these. Whether or not homework is advisable after regular school hours, the fact remains that many children are assigned schoolwork to do at home.

What is the role of a staff person who is neither teacher, parent, nor tutor? Whatever their own priorities and plans for space, time, and activities, staff are drawn into the homework issue and have to deal with it because the issue involves the needs of the children and their families.

Some thoughts to consider about homework:

Time, space, and student responsibility

Both younger and older students probably have been sedentary and quiet all day in school. They usually emerge from that environment needing time to make their own choices, move around, and talk. Homework probably is not an immediate priority for student or staff except in very special circumstances. If homework opportunities are included in out-of-school programs, it is wise to include these *after* children have had a chance to make independent choices, socialize, and be physically active.

Since homework generally should be respected as the student's responsibility, all students should be provided with appropriate space, time, and materials. Sometimes it is fun to do homework along with the companionship of friends, more fun than alone at home. But sometimes a student needs privacy to think through the more difficult homework assignments.

Family involvement

The role of the family must be respected in supporting children's completion of homework. Parents need to be involved with homework enough to be aware of what students are doing in school, so they can share ideas and note their children's strengths and skills, problems, and study needs. Even if parents are not available while the student does the work, they should be in close contact with their child's work, especially in the earlier years. Staff in out-of-school programs need not assume total responsibility.

Parents may request that homework be completed before they return for their child. This may be requested on a regular or a once-in-a-while basis. If it is on a daily basis, parents should be informed of the program's homework policy

Whatever their own priorities and plans for space, time and activities, staff are drawn into the homework issue and have to deal with it because the issue involves the needs of the children and families.

and should be assured that an effort will be made to provide time for the home-work as the daily schedule permits. In the case of a once-in-a-while request, the request certainly should be honored.

As you make clear to families just what children and youth are learning in your program and how they are using their developing skills, parental pressures for homework may decrease. Families will recognize that you are providing many other important contributions to their children's growth.

Can you help me?

Some students need assistance with homework. They may not understand the instructions or the subject matter, and they may need someone to get them started. Whenever possible, staff can help or, if unable, should suggest other sources: parent, teacher, friends, reference books, libraries, community resources, etc. Some school-age programs employ tutors for children who request or need help. Often a friend or classmate can come to the rescue.

PRIVATE TIMES

"I don't like to be alone very much. I'd rather be out playing with my friends. But sometimes I'm purposely alone. Sometimes I want my own space and my own things to do and for no one to bother me at all." (Ryan — age 7)

Maturing school-agers are social beings who want to be with other children their age and to be like other children their age. But their quest for self is never lost as they struggle to find and define their identity through others and as they struggle for acceptance and approval.

Privacy and the maturing sense of self

The process of growing up as a unique individual requires a certain amount of privacy. It requires solitude to think one's own thoughts, enjoy one's own com-pany, and entertain oneself without interruption or the need to share. It requires privacy to develop one's own resources (creative thinking, reading, music, and art) and to improve performance without fear of ridicule. Many such nonsocial activi-ties help build the child's capacity to become a self-sufficient human being. Private time and private space may be needed by children to define themselves, become more interesting persons, so that ultimately they can reach out to others with something to offer.

If given the privacy they wish, children become unique persons with an enhanced capacity for developing friendships. As they enrich themselves, they enrich others. They combine, then, the striving for friendship with the developing self. For this to occur, we need to give children time for themselves. As adults who control their time and space, staff need to understand the importance of privacy in the process of growing up and learn to recognize privacy-seeking behaviors.

Privacy and relaxation

Privacy allows children time to get away from constant social stimulation. It allows a way to withdraw from activities with expected standards of behavior, to take a break from responding to directions from adults, conversations with peers, and the constant need to share materials. It may be a time to sulk if youngsters are unhappy, to pull themselves together if they have been hurt physically or emotionally, to renew energy so they can merge back with others, strengthened and refreshed. Privacy can allow children an unpressured way to assess their past actions — to recall what they've said or done and figure out whether it worked the way they wished. Privacy can allow time for deciding what to do next. It is sometimes easier to think through a social encounter when one is not still in the midst of it.

The amount and type of solitude a child wishes is quite an individual matter. A child without siblings and living in a spacious home may have enough private opportunities in the home setting, so they may relish the continuous companionship of the many other children in a program. Yet another child from a similar home, used to private moments and private places, may continue to need such solitude. A child from a crowded family setting may find the program's additional stimulation too much and may become disruptive or retreat with privacy-seeking behaviors. Yet another child, used to groups of people, may be perfectly comfortable with constant group interactions.

Privacy is *not* to be equated with discipline methods that remove a child from a situation. If an adult uses privacy areas as solitary-confinement areas for punishment, then the positive aspects of individual or small-group privacy are destroyed. The child's own needs for privacy must not be confused with isolation mandated because of inappropriate behavior. The issue of dealing with behavior by removal from a group has been discussed in Chapter Four.

Creating privacy

Private spaces may be created by both adults and children. They may be permanent or temporary. Private places may be for one child or a small group. They may contain activities, or they may be empty areas into which children bring an activity or simply bring themselves. Here are a few ideas for creating privacy places in both home and center care, areas that are easy to create, rearrange, dismantle, and use in a variety of ways as children wish:

- sheet or bedspread over a table to create a tent
- real pup tent or teepee
- large blocks and boards to create temporary spaces
- refrigerator boxes that can be made into a playhouse
- arranging furniture such as book shelves or sofas to create private areas
- bean bag chairs or large easy chairs in a corner of the room
- tree houses
- platform spaces clildren can climb up into
- cardboard partitions
- individual mats or rugs, cots, or sleeping bags

Children And Groups

THE STRENGTH OF THE GROUP: WHAT IS THE RELATIONSHIP BETWEEN THE GROUP AND THE INDIVIDUAL?

Since school-agers are most comfortable when they feel that they are part of a group, the way the group meets the needs of the individual child is important. Children value their own *self*. Their concept of self is reinforced by the way they relate to other individuals in the group and by their sense of what other group members think of them. They never lose the growing sense of self. They build on it and refine it as they cherish best friends, share private secrets with a chosen few, and learn from the group — the behavior, the dos and don'ts of living with others. The group becomes a setting for developing the individual human being.

CREATING GROUPS: BY WHAT CRITERIA?

The group, however it is formed, provides a framework for the happy, healthy development of each individual. Groups should be small enough for close, personal interaction with staff as well as with the other children, and yet large enough for opportunities for making friends.

Groups may be created according to such criteria as common interests, personal friendships, level of maturity, age, or grade in school. Groups may be homogeneous or heterogeneous. Groups may also include preschoolers, particularly in a home-care situation. Children create their own groups-within-groups: bands of special friends or same-sex groups (but don't mistake this for lack of interest in the opposite sex — "I love Eric, but don't tell!").

MIXED-AGE VERSUS SAME-AGE GROUPINGS: WHICH IS BEST?

There are negative and positive aspects of each kind of grouping. Whatever the decision, however, there should be some opportunities for same-age relationships whenever possible.

The Upside and Downside of Combining Ages

A family affair

The mixed group presents some of the same challenges that exist in any mixed-age family. In fact, siblings may be together in an out-of-school group. Mixed-age relationships are real life, where each age has differing needs and all needs can be met.

The upside

Children are enriched by what each age has to offer. Leadership is developed in the older children, and new skills are learned by the younger children. Older kids may acquire the nurturing skills needed for successful relations with young children.

The downside

School-agers often resent sharing their time with "little kids." Older children take over the play, for they are bigger, stronger, more verbal, and full of ideas. They "get their way" through these new, developing powers. Also, adult time with younger children may deprive older school-agers of needed attention.

Neither babies nor baby-sitters

School-agers, however, do not want to be treated as "babies," nor do they want to be used as hired hands to keep younger children under control. The younger children, in turn, do not wish to assume the role of "baby" or be bossed around by older children.

The upside

Older children learn skills by helping younger children. Younger children learn by imitating older children. All ages learn the give and take of living with children of varying ages, interests, and skills.

The downside

Older children may limit their own development of increasingly complex skills when younger children demand their time, space, or materials. Young children, who cannot keep up with the pace, ideas, and abilities of the ten-, twelve-, or fourteen -year-olds, become overwhelmed and lose their confidence. They cannot compete and become merely watchers.

Materials, the stuff of learning

Many early-learning materials are still fine for older children. They will start from where they left off and continue to use the materials in more imaginative ways. But older school-agers also need to progress to new forms of materials, new techniques. It is an ongoing challenge to provide the time, the space, and the variety of materials and equipment for all of the ages in the group.

The upside

Children learn to include one another in their activities, recognizing the differences in the use of materials. Older children stretch their imaginations using the familiar materials, and younger children explore the possibilities of the more advanced materials.

The downside

Older school-agers use materials differently and need more of them, leaving, for example, little room for the five-year-olds when the nine-year-olds are block-building. The younger children may not have access to materials, and the older children, in sharing,may not fully develop their own powers.

The pursuit of ideas

Intellectual inquiries differ by age and interests, and the need for counsel and information changes as children mature. Such topics as gender relationships, drug abuse, and personal development are relevant to all ages, but they need to be approached in different ways for different ages.

The upside	**The downside**
Younger children can have a taste of the "world to come." If topics are carefully and sensitively discussed, they may pick up new data to think about. Older boys and girls may clarify their own thoughts as they converse with the younger ones.	Younger children may be exposed to conversations and discussions that they cannot understand, or to statements that may be confusing, inappropriate, and even false. Older school-agers may not have the opportunity to explore their concerns fully.

Managing competition

Mixed-age grouping may reduce both competition and conflict among children, but planning for normal, healthy competitive activities is complex when there are so many maturational differences.

The upside	**The downside**
There is a give and take in mixed-age groups similar to the interactions of the mixed-age world. Competition is seen as less threatening to all ages in mixed-age situations.	The older children may not be adequately challenged, and the younger ones cannot match their pace. For the older children it can become all take and for the younger children it can become all give.

FIVE-YEAR-OLDS IN SCHOOL-AGE GROUPS: CAN THEY SURVIVE?

Five-year-olds are still so close to preschool activities and preschool thinking that they cannot always live easily with older school-agers. In a school-age group five-year-olds are generally overwhelmed by their older and more skillful playmates. Appropriate activities should be offered so that five-year-olds can function and succeed at their own level. Five-year-olds may also need rest, especially after a day in kindergarten. While the school-age program must not be simply a repetition of their kindergarten day, they still need opportunities for make-believe, understandable stories, and close attachments to adults. Although they want a close friend, they are not yet forming cliques. They need hands-on experiences, not abstract discussions. They may be confused by organized games with competition and rules, and their attention span is relatively short. They are conformist, and they want to do the right thing. While they enjoy a good laugh, they cannot yet understand sophisticated school-age humor.

All of this means that when five-year-olds are included in school-age groups, they must not get lost in the shuffle.

SCHOOL-AGE CHILDREN IN PRESCHOOL GROUPS: HOW WELL WILL THEY GROW?

Programs designed for preschool children will need much careful modification to include the older child, both in designing the curriculum and in considering interpersonal relationships. There must be enough interesting, challenging, age-appropriate activities planned by people who understand the older child's social and emotional needs.

Will they feel fenced in? They might. School-agers are explorers reaching out into the larger world to know how they fit into it and how it works. They may feel captive in the younger child's more restrictive environment. While they certainly need protection for health, safety, and a feeling of security, the confines of the preschool setting may make them feel small and perhaps bored.

Will they act their age? Well, usually but not always. School-age children in a mixed-age group usually choose to be their real age. But what a temptation to slip back and act like a four-year-old again! As long as there are school-age activities and a school-age friend or two, however, by tomorrow, the next day or maybe next week they will once again be six or seven, ten or eleven.

HANGING OUT: THE OLDER KIDS

It looks as if they're doing nothing at all. In fact, they may be doing nothing at all, but they are doing it together. Twelve-, thirteen-, and fourteen-year-olds like to hang out together, and they enjoy organized programs mainly because they're with friends.

In addition, research suggests that:

> While a particular activity or flashy person may be the "hook" that draws teen-agers in, their loyalty to the program is dependent on an adult who understands them, upon the quiet sensitivity of an adult who has time to listen and to care. The nature of the activity may not be as important as the special relationships that these programs promote. (Lefstein & Lipsitz, 9)[2]

Although the older children may challenge your acceptance and optimism, your knowledge of their interests and development will help and even protect them. Increasing numbers of young adolescents have few out-of-school experiences with positive outcomes. The Carnegie Council on Adolescent Development reports that:

> Instead of safety in their neighborhoods, [adolescents] face chronic physical danger; instead of intellectual stim-

ulation, they face boredom and stagnation; in place of respect, they are neglected; lacking clear and consistent adult expectations for them, many youth feel deeply alienated from mainstream American society. The damage to individual young lives is staggering. American society pays heavily for such outcomes."[3]

Current statistics on pregnancy, heavy drinking, crime, and violence during out-of-school hours are frightening, but parents, aware of this, may be unable to find or afford a comprehensive out-of-school program that can successfully attract these older school-agers. All of the discussion in this text has been applicable to these early adolescents (and the activity list in this chapter will keep group leaders on their toes).

Some special issues relevant to older school-agers deserve consideration for smooth and effective programming:

◇ Responsibility and accountability for the children's whereabouts when they are not under direct supervision

◇ Parent and licensing approval for activities outside of the supervising home or center, as well as for any transportation arrangements

◇ Designated, comfortable, well-equipped space—a room, partitioned area, clubhouse, or trailer

◇ Trained staff members with clearly assigned supervisory responsibilities

◇ Contact with specialists who can teach advanced skills such as cycle repair, wood carving, rope climbing, computer literacy, mechanics, and ham radio

◇ Guided opportunities to discuss such relevant issues as health and physical well-being, boy-girl relationships, family relationships, divorce, drugs, sexuality, and personal problem-solving

◇ Encouragement to separate personal emotions and prejudice while debating varying points of view

◇ Experiences in leadership development and community service

◇ Awareness of opportunities for careers, training, employment, internships,

School-age programs need to support older kids in their pursuit of outside hobbies and interests.

volunteer work, youth advisory councils, resources for mentoring, preparation for parenthood, and personal counseling

◇ Skilled support in setting desirable and reachable goals and in taking control of their own lives, in order to reach goals that are short-range and easily attained (to make a swim team or learn to type) and long-range and more difficult (to curb one's anger or deal with a frightening environment)[4]

◇ Chances to develop helping skills with younger children, neighborhood residents, and community programs

◇ A nutritional program that meets the older child's needs for quantity as well as nutritional quality

◇ Creation of strong group feeling— a head start on the gang

◇ Time and opportunities to just hang out

Play And Other Activities

There's no end to the number and variety of activities that can be considered for school-age care. Check Supplement #4 at the end of this book for an alphabetical listing of more than 1,000 activity ideas. For additional ideas about play and activities, check with:

◆ the children

◆ community publications and newspapers

◆ families

◆ friends and neighbors

◆ schools and libraries

◆ licensing and supervising agencies

◆ training institutions

◆ literature related to children and youth

The child will have as an adult the imprint of his culture upon him whether his society hands him the tradition with a shrug, throws it to him like the bone to a dog, teaches him each item with care and anxiety, or leads him towards manhood as if he were on a sight-seeing tour.

Margaret Mead
1901-1978

Things To Think About

This is a program checklist for Chapters Five, Six, and Seven: *What Do The Children Do?* The observations relate to respecting childhood, the physical environment, and the program activities. Observe a school-age program or evaluate your own. Observe for at least three hours, or over an extended period of time.

Program Checklist

Respecting Childhood	Yes	No	*What I Observed*	*What I Would Change*
Does the program help every child to feel important? Are the children attaining success through a variety of experiences? Does the program help children to expand skills, knowledge, ideas?				
Does the program encourage good relationships? Are there cooperative ventures among children which encourage friendships? Are there supportive relationships with adults?				

Respecting Childhood	Yes	No	*What I Observed*	*What I Would Change*
Does the program provide for each child's need for personal power? Do activities build a sense of mastery, of completion? Are there opportunities for children to grow in independence through making their own choices, decisions, and expressing their own opinions?				
Are play activities a major focus of the program? Is there sufficient time for play? Do staff seem to value play?				
Does the program respect the differences within the group? Is it appropriate for each age level? Does it recognize varied cultural backgrounds? Does it provide for health and developmental differences?				

Physical Environment	Yes	No	*What I Observed*	*What I Would Change*
Is the general atmosphere attractive, comfortable, friendly?				
Are there both indoor and outdoor environments appropriate for the ages and abilities of the children involved?				
Are there large spaces as well as small group interest areas?				
Are materials complete and in good repair?				
Are there spaces for privacy?				
Is there easy access to bathrooms, water fountains, outdoor areas?				
If ages are mixed, do the older children have some space for their own activities?				
Is the community used as an extended environment?				
Are there clearly defined areas for activities?				

Physical Environment	Yes	No	*What I Observed*	*What I Would Change*
Is there sufficient space for each activity?				
Is space designed for easy traffic flow?				
Are indoor furnishings flexible enough so that change is possible?				
Are there soft places for rest and relaxation?				
Are needs met for children with special needs, who need special care or who become ill?				
Is furniture scaled to the size of the children enrolled?				
Are there spaces for children's personal belongings?				
Is there space to display children's art work, projects, interests?				
Is there space for storage of unused materials and unfinished work?				

Physical Environment	Yes	No	What I Observed	What I Would Change
Do adults have a place for belongings and work-related materials?				
Is the outdoor area sufficiently equipped for the number of children?				
Is some outdoor equipment moveable, open to change?				
Is there storage for outdoor equipment?				
Are there shaded as well as sunny areas?				
Are there contacts with the natural environment (trees, sand, plants...)?				
If you were a school-ager, would you want to spend your out-of-school hours in this environment?				

Activities	Yes	No	*What I Observed*	*What I Would Change*
Are the children part of the planning process?				
Does the schedule include time frames and activities that meet the needs of all of the children?				
Does the schedule include a good balance of activities?				
Is there a balance between children and adult-planned activities?				
Are both indoor and outdoor experiences included daily ?				
Are there opportunities for personal choices of activities?				
Is there a sufficient variety of choices for the number of children?				
Is there a sufficient variety of activities for ages and skill levels?				

Activities	Yes	No	What I Observed	What I Would Change
Are there a variety of activities attractively set up and accessible for children to use: large muscle and vigorous play, home-like experiences, expressive activities, enrichment activities, cooperative decision-making opportunities, manipulative and quiet experiences?				
Is there evidence of special events and celebrations?				
Is there evidence of experiences which can be carried over from one day to the next?				
Are there times to discuss issues which are of personal interest?				
Do transitions flow smoothly without abrupt changes, unnecessary waiting, or "militariza-tion?"				
Are meal and snack times pleasant, social experiences?				

Activities	Yes	No	*What I Observed*	*What I Would Change*
Do activities reflect respect for many cultures and human differences?				
Are all activities available to both girls and boys?				
Is there evidence, where applicable, that the needs of the following children are met? 1. The youngest children 2. The oldest children 3. Children who are ill 4. Children who have special needs				

NOTES

[1] One of the classic introductions to the dynamics of group meetings can be found in William Glasser's *Schools Without Failure*.

[2]Lefstein, Leah M. and Lipsitz, Joan. *3:00 to 6:00 PM: Programs for Young Adolescents*. Chapel Hill: University of North Carolina.1986.

This book was originally published by the Center for Early Adolescence at the University of North Carolina at Chapel Hill, however the Center for Early Adolescence closed in June, 1995. The Search Institute, an organization in Minneapolis, Minn., acquired the distribution rights to all of the Center's publications. The Search Institute is a non-profit organization dedicated to research, resources, and services on positive youth development. For more information call 800-888-7828 or write to the Search Institute at 700 South Third St., Suite 201, Minneapolis, MN 55414.

[3] "A Matter of Time: Risk and Opportunity in the Out-Of-School Hours." Report prepared by the Carnegie Council on Adolescent Devlopment's Task Force on Youth Development and Community Programs. The Carnegie Council is an operating program of Carnegie Corporation of New York.

[4] In *New Youth Challenge*, Steve Musson effectively discusses challenges and methods for helping youth develop and meet goals.

RECOMMENDED READINGS

Buhai-Haas, C. and A.C. Friedman. *My Own Fun: Creative Learning Activities for Home and School – Ages Seven to Twelve*. Chicago: Chicago Review, 1990.

Coles, R. *Their Eyes Meeting the World: The Drawings and Paintings of Children*. Boston: Houghton Mifflin, 1992.

Haas-Folletta, K. and M. Cogley. *School-Age Ideas and Activities for After School Programs*. Nashville: School-Age NOTES, 1990.

Hirsch, E., Ed. *The Block Book*. Washington DC: NAEYC, 1984.

Skeen, P., A. P. Garner and S. Cartwright. *Woodworking for Young Children*. Washington DC: NAEYC, 1984.

Therrell, J. *How To Play With Kids*. Austin: Play Today Press, 1992.

Wallace, E. *Summer Sizzlers & Magic Mondays: School-Age Theme Activities*. Nashville: School-Age NOTES, 1995.

Whitaker, D. L. *Games, Games, Games: Creating Hundreds of Group Games and Sports*. Nashville: School-Age NOTES. 1996.

RESEARCH AND OTHER ARTICLES RELATED TO SCHOOL-AGE CARE

Adler, P.A., & Adler, P. (1994). Social reproduction and the corporate other: The institutionalization of afterschool activities. *Sociological Quarterly* 35(2), 309-328.

Alexander, N. P. (1986). School-age child care: Concerns and challenges. *Young Children* 42(1), 3-10.

Belle, D. (1997). Varieties of self-care: A qualitative look at children's experiences in the after-school hours. *Merrill-Palmer Quarterly* 43, 478-96.

Bergin, D. A., L.M. Hudson, C.F. Chryst, & M. Resetar. (1992). An afterschool intervention program for educationally disadvantaged young children. *Urban Review* 24(3), 203-217.

Coleman, M., B. E. Robinson, & B. H. Rowland. (1991). School-age child care: A review of five common arguments. *Day Care and Early Education* 18(4), 13-17.

Coleman, M., B. E. Robinson, & B. H. Rowland. (1993). A typology of families with children in self-care: Implications for school-age child care programming. *Child and Youth Services Forum* 22(1), 43-53.

Coleman, M., C. Wallinga, & C. Toledo, (1999). School-age child care: An examination of philosophical priorities. *Early Childhood Education Journal* 27(2), 123-128.

Cutforth, N. J. (1997). What's worth doing: reflections on an after-school program in a Denver elementary school. *Quest 49*(1), 130-139.

Czerniak, J. (1993). After school: Probing production. *Landscape Architecture 83*(12), 54.

Halpern, R. (1992) The role of after-school programs in the lives of inner-city children: A study of the urban youth network. *Child Welfare 71*(3), 215-230.

Hellison, D. R. & N. J. Cutforth. (1997). Extended day programs for urban children and youth: From theory to practice. In *Children and youth: Interdisciplinary perspectives*, eds. H. J. Walbert, O. Reyes, & R. P. Weissberg, 223-49. Thousand Oaks, CA: Sage.

Howes, C., M. Olenick, & T. Der-Kiureghian. (1987). After school child care in an elementary school: Social development and continuity and complementarity of programs. *The Elementary School Journal 88*, 93-103.

Laird, R. D., G. S. Pettit, K. A. Dodge, & J. E Bates. (1998). The social ecology of school-age child care. *Journal of Applied Developmental Psychology 19*, 341-60.

Marshall, N. L., C. G. Coll, F. Marx, K. McCartney, N. Keefe, & J. Ruh. (1997). After-school time and children's behavioral adjustment. *Merrill-Palmer Quarterly 43*, 497-514.

Miller, B. M., S. O'Connor, & S. W. Sirignono. (1995). Out of school time: A study of children in three low-income neighborhoods. *Child Welfare 74*, 1249-80.

Morris, D., B. Shaw, & J. Perney. (1990). Helping low readers in grades 2 and 3: An after-school volunteer tutoring program. *The Elementary School Journal 91*(2), 133-150.

Nieting, P. L. (1983). School-age child care: In support of development and learning. *Childhood Education 60*(1), 6-11.

Pettine, A., & L A. Rosen. (1998). Self-care and deviance in elementary school-age children. *Journal of Clinical Psychology 54*, 629-43.

Pettit, G. S., R. D. Laird, J. E. Bates, & K. A. Dodge. (1997). Patterns of after-school care in middle childhood: Risk factors and developmental outcomes. *Merrill-Palmer Quarterly 43*, 515-38.

Pierce, K. M., Hamm, J. V., & D. L. Vandell. (1999) Experiences in after-school programs and children's adjustment in first-grade classrooms. *Child Development 70*, 756-67.

Posner, J. K., & D. L. Vandell. (1999). After-school activities and the development of low-income urban children: A longitudinal study. *Developmental Psychology 35*, 868-79.

Posner, J. K., & D. L. Vandell. (1994). Low-income children's after-school care: Are there beneficial effects of after-school programs? *Child Development 65*, 440-456.

Powell, D. R. (1987). Research in Review: After-school child care. *Young Children 42*(3), 62-66.

Roche, S. E., & M. J. Camasso. (1993). Parental preferences and considerations of cost in the selection of school-age child care. *Children and Youth Services Review, 15*(1), 53-70.

Rosenthal, R., & D. L. Vandell. (1996). Quality of care at school-age child care programs: Regulatable features, observed experiences, child perspectives, and parent perspectives. *Child Development 67*, 2434-45.

Ross, J. G., P. J. Saavedra, G. H. Shur, F. Winters, & R. D. Felner. (1992). The effectiveness of an after-school program for primary grade latchkey students on precursors of substance abuse. *Journal of Community Psychology 20*(1), 22-38.

Seligson, M. (1991). Models of school-age child care: A review of current research on implications for women and their children. *Women Studies International Forum 14*, 577-84.

Thiel, K. S., J. McCroskey, & D. J. Marquart. (1988). Program and policy considerations for school age child care: The California experience. *Child and Youth Care Quarterly 17*(1), 24-35.

Vandell, D. L., & M. A. Corasaniti. (1988). The relation between third graders' after-school care and social, academic, and emotional functioning. *Child Development 59*, 868-875.

Vandell, D. L., & J. Posner. (1999). Conceptualization and measurement of children's after-school environments. In *Assessment of the environment across the lifespan*, eds. S. L. Friedman & T. D. Wachs. Washington DC: American Psychological Association Press.

Vandell, D. L., L. Shumow, & J. K. Posner. (In press). Children's after-school programs: Promoting resiliency or vulnerability. In *Resiliency in families and children at risk: Interdisciplinary perspectives*, ed. McCubbin, H. Thousand Oaks, CA: Sage.

Vandell, D. L., & H. Su. (1999). Research in Review: Child care and school-age children. *Young Children 54*(6), 62-71.

SCHOOL-AGE RESOURCES AND ORGANIZATIONS

Listed below are other resources and organizations that offer more information and resources on issues of after-school care:

National School-Age Care Alliance (NSACA)
1137 Washington Street
Boston MA 02124
PH: 617-298-5012/FAX: 617-298-5022
www.nsaca.org

NSACA is the national membership organization for the profession and is made up of state affiliates. Founded in 1987, NSACA offers school-age care specialist training; hosts a national conference each year; provides materials on setting up school-age programs; and oversees an accreditation process for school-age care programs.

The National Institute on Out-of-School Time (NIOST)
Center for Research on Women
Wellesley College
106 Central Street
Wellesley MA 02181
PH: 781-283-2547/FAX: 781-283-3657
www.wellesley.edu/WCW/CRW/SAC

Originally known as at the SACCProject, NIOST was one of the first organizations formed to address the needs of school-age children. Operating out of the Center for Research on Women at Wellesley College, NIOST conducts research on various school-age related issues; works closely with other school-age care organizations to develop best practices criteria; conducts workshops and training on school-age care, including advanced summer seminars; and publishes resources for use in the field.

School-Age NOTES
P.O. Box 40205
Nashville TN 37204-0205
PH: 1-800-410-8780 or 615-279-0700/FAX: 615-279-0800
www.schoolagenotes.com

Publisher of the monthly School-Age NOTES newsletter since 1980 and provider of over 100 resources for after-school and summer programs. Publishes several books specifically on school-age care, including this text. Resources are available through the School-Age NOTES online catalog or from a semi-annual After-School Catalog.

California School-Age Consortium (CalSAC)
111 New Montgomery Street, #302A
San Francisco CA 94105
PH: 415-957-9775/FAX: 415-957-9776

One of the largest state coalitions that offers training workshops and conferences for its members as well as publications on school-age care issues.

Georgia School-Age Care Alliance (GSACA)
246 Sycamore Street, Suite 252
Decatur GA 30030
PH: 404-373-7414
www.gsaca.com

A state school-age care organization with resources and technical assistance guides for beginning and improving school-age programs.

WEBSITES OF INTEREST

www.schoolagenotes.com - online ordering of over 100 resource materials for running a quality school-age program. Activity ideas, excerpts from newsletter articles, links to other school-age sites.

www.nsaca.org - the website for the National School-Age Care Alliance with professional development topics, links to other related sites and a link to the SAC-L, an online discussion list ("listserve") for school-age care providers (click on "Professional Development" icon on home page).

www.afterschool.gov - a website sponsored by the federal government, designed to help families find safe, high quality after school programs, plus offers information on existing federal resources and ways to find other resources, including information on grant funding and federal publications.

www.ed.gov/21stcclc - the U.S. Department of Education (DOE) website for finding out about 21st Century Community Learning Center grants and how to apply for them. The site features a database of all the current grantees and their features, new examples of successful applications, new publications and related links. Some publications of interest that can be found at the site include:

> *Bringing Education into the Afterschool Hours* (1999) - helps local after school providers understand how to integrate content such as reading, math, college preparation, technology, and the arts into their programs to enhance children's learning and build on the regular school program.

> *Safe and Smart: Making After-School Hours Work for Kids* (1998) - a report, jointly authored by the U.S. Depts. of Education and Justice, that highlights research evidence on the potential of after school programs to increase the safety of children, reduce their risk-taking, and improve learning.

> *Keeping Schools Open as Community Learning Centers: Extending Learning in a Safe, Drug-Free Environment Before and After School* (1997) - designed to help schools and community-based organizations begin the process of keeping neighborhood schools open for children and families.

www.gse.uci.edu/schoolage - an Online Center called After-School Training and Resources Center dedicated to promoting high quality after school programs in California, but also has national information and resources. Very complete website on after school programs and good information on starting, funding, and programming school-age programs. Has links to other national school-age groups.

www.financeproject.org/osthome.htm - developed by the Finance Project of the DeWitt Wallace-Reader's Digest Fund. Offers tools for finding funding resources for starting after school programs.

www.nydic.org - National Youth Development Information Center, an online resource and excellent site for those interested in programs for young adolescents and adolescents. Also has good links to other sites.

Supplement 1

Training: What is the best kind of training for the best kind of staff?

Who needs training?

If school-age care is to be a profession, then training needs to be comprehensively developed. Training is probably the best predictor of good quality programming. It should be required and there should be some national consistency in the requirements. There would be many levels of training. It should be developed for beginning as well as experienced staff, for the high school graduate as well as the college graduate. Training is essential for administrators and multi-site directors, for program directors and group leaders, for assistants and substitutes. It is recommended for school personnel — principals, teachers, counselors and maintenance staff.

Persons who work with school-agers come from all directions, not only in experience and background, but also in personality, style, talent. They are young, old, parents, grandparents. They come from unrelated professions or from related fields such as education, recreation, human services, child and youth development, and early childhood education. Above all, they come with their own memories of childhood and with their own personal interests and competencies. The one thing most persons have in common is they are not specifically trained in the field of school-age care.

The unique field

School-age programs emerge as a unique entity with a distinct character, quality and spirit requiring a special body of knowledge; persons in the field are developing a common framework for their thinking. We know what quality programs look like. Training, then, helps to assure this quality.

Training is defined here as an integration of the philosophy, knowledge and skills which are required for all personnel regardless of their role or their background. The recognized content may be presented in the form of specific course work, workshops and seminars focused on school-age care and out-of-school programs or it may be mainstreamed into such existing academic curricula as child, youth or human development, recreation, education or human service. While training resources will be diverse, specific and appropriate content can be universally required and should be related to the developmental levels of the children in the programs.

This profession draws from many professions. It integrates the components of many disciplines. How many other professions require such a variety of knowledge and skills on the part of both trainers and caregivers?

From the field of *education*: opportunities for children to
– develop interests and learnings, work in groups,
– develop problem-solving, imagination, and skills

From the field of *recreation*: creative uses of developmental skills and leisure time

From the fields of *social work*, *psychology* and *sociology*: helping children with their concerns, behaviors, and values in relation to their often fragmented or frail family life and struggling communities

From the fields of *early childhood* and *child, youth* and *human development*: the importance of nurturing the individual person and the relationship of programs and activities to each child's developmental level

And finally, from all the *fields upon which activities are based* such as music, art, drama, science, sports, human relations and, above all, encompassing the concept of play. No field stands alone. They must all be related to children's thinking, feelings, abilities and development.

The training which prepares persons for such a comprehensive service is necessarily complex and must be on-going. It plays a major role. It educates, inspires, and rejuvenates. The quality of care depends on the quality of each caregiver.

The Basics for All

There is a philosophy, a body of knowledge and a set of skills to be acquired by everyone working with children and youth — the administrators, teachers, youth, recreation or scout leaders, camp counselors, religious school instructors, caregivers.

A PHILOSOPHY

A philosophy for school-age programs recognizes that there is a relationship between children and youth and the kind of adults which they become. It recognizes that there is a relationship between the school-age years and the kind of society we develop. The philosophy encompasses the view that children's behaviors and actions are perceived by them to be the best they can do at the moment, because of their personal field of reality and perception of self. It acknowledges the importance of individual care with the provision of close, positive and trusting contact between children, youth and adults. It encourages children's friendships, enthusiasm, curiosity, and self-confidence. It respects individual differences among cultures, genders, personalities, experiences, health, and development, and it endorses the relationship between children and their families as crucial for each child's well-being.

A BODY OF KNOWLEDGE

✧ What is happening, developmentally, during school-age years and what activities and experiences promote healthy development

✧ What guidance techniques allow for the development of self-identity and self-esteem, good human relationships, and self-direction

✧ What social forces influence children's thinking and feelings

✧ What community resources are accessible for children, youth, and their families

✧ What personal qualities, responsibilities and ethical conduct are required of staff

✧ What regulatory laws and policies are applicable

A SET OF SKILLS

✧ To plan with and for children, to communicate, organize, support

✧ To work well with a group of children and yet see and respond to each child as an individual

✧ To help all children and youth stretch to their potential

✧ To offer experiences through which children master familiar activities, enjoy new activities, and extend their interests

✧ To help children and youth solve problems and resolve conflicts

✧ To work with other adults on behalf of a child—families, teachers, agencies, and other staff members

MORE FOR STAFF IN SCHOOL-AGE PROGRAMS

✧ The nurturing skills which supplement a parent's role when children cannot be with their families

✧ The skills to implement the very special and comprehensive programming required for the out-of-school hours

✧ The methods to work with a wide age and developmental range of youngsters and with children with very special needs

STILL MORE FOR ADMINISTRATORS

All of the components above, plus:

✧ Administration of the total program — single or multi-site

✧ Development and implementation of appropriate budgets, business management procedures

✧ Provision of all supplies — equipment, materials, food, etc.

✧ Maintenance of safety standards

✧ Supervision of staff and effective on-going staff training

✧ Observation and evaluation of all program components

✧ Coordination with supervisory and regulatory agencies

✧ Maintenance of contacts with community resources

WHAT KIND OF TRAINING?

Since styles of teaching relate to styles of learning and to the content of the material, many different training methods may be effective:

✧ *Hands-on workshops* to develop skills for working with children in activities such as carpentry, pottery, drama, photography, dance, art, games, sports

✧ *Role play* to get the feel of how others react and behave

✧ *Discussions, seminars, lectures, films* to obtain and digest information

✧ *Small groups and committees* to work on projects, solve problems, create ideas

✧ *Observation* of children and programs to become sensitive to children and to evaluate effectiveness of care

✧ *Team coaching and peer supervision*

✧ *Video-taping* to provide personal feedback

✧ *Internships, practice teaching, mentors and personal advisors*

WHAT DO YOU THINK ABOUT TRAINING?

✧ What do you think is important?

✧ What kind of training do you enjoy?

✧ What methods do you prefer? suggest? would you like to try?

A SUGGESTED TRAINING CURRICULUM

We include here a suggested training outline for an introduction to school-age care. It basically follows the outline of this text. Instructors will, of course, personalize their own training designs.

The outline is meant to be the first course in a total training program. Topics introduced in the basic course warrant further study: child and youth psychology and guidance, curriculum development, environmental design, family dynamics, child and adolescent health and wellness, skill-building in art, music, drama, sports, conflict resolution, and other specific activities. Further course work may also include field practicums and case studies, program supervision, assessment and management, and building communities to respond to the needs of children and youth.

The Out-of-School Hours: An Introduction to School-Age Care

I. *School-Age Care: A Family Resource*

    Why programs are needed

    Risks of self and sibling care

    Some characteristics of families and their children

    School-age care:

        What it is and what it is not

        When it is needed

        Types of programs—in-home, family care, centers

        Advantages and concerns of various types of programs

    Quality control

        The role of regulatory agencies

        The role of parents

        The role of staff

II. *Who Are the Children?*

    Basic human needs of children and youth

        The need for a sense of identity

        The need for good relationships

        The need for power

    Basic human growth and development

        Overall view of ages from birth to five

        Developmental needs of the five- to fourteen-year-old

            Physical needs

            Social needs

            Self needs

            Intellectual needs

        Meeting Developmental Needs

        Children Who Need Special Care

Worries and concerns: What's on children's minds?
> Family, school, friends, loneliness, messages from
> the media, gender roles, sex and sexuality, violence
> and crime, drugs, death, etc.

When things go well and when things go wrong in the
> lives of children and youth

III. *Who are the Staff?*

The nurturing caregiver

Personal qualities for staff in relation to meeting the needs of
children and youth

Essential interests of staff

Ethical conduct in school-age programs

The right match between program and staff

Roles and responsibilities of staff members

Dealing with individual and cultural diversity

Bringing yourself to your job
> interests, skills, philosophy, personal qualities, and
> personal goals

The family connection
> communication skills with families, parents as policy-
> makers, family involvement, family as helpers, family
> and social events

IV. *Children's Behaviors and Helping Relationships*

Staff as helpers

Why children and youth behave as they do

Guiding behaviors
> Getting to know the children
> Preventing behavior problems: creating cooperative
> environments
>> The program and the physical environment
>> The program and the human environment
> The art of discipline
> The trouble with punishment
> Helping children with conflict

Dealing with behaviors means remembering the human needs

V. *Program: What Do the Children Do?*

The issue of quality programming

Respecting childhood in program planning
> Responding to children's basic human needs

Respect for the individual child

Importance of leisure-time and life-time skills

Significance of play

Creating the Program

    Planning

        The process of planning

        Balanced program planning

        Approaches to planning

    Environmental Design

        Indoor

        Outdoor

        Community

        Special environmental challenges

        Safety issues

        Selection, accessibility and maintenance of
         materials

        Environment and the human needs of children and
         youth

    Activities

        Things to do indoors, outdoors, in the community:
        Vigorous play activities, daily living activities,
           expressive activities, science and nature, games,
           community participation

        Group times

        Transitions

        Nutrition

        Using the media

        Homework

        Importance of privacy

        Workshops for skills in: art, music, construction and
        carpentry, environmental studies and outdoor
        education, photography, sewing and weaving,
        games, sports, mechanics, food preparation,
        language and computer skills, etc.

    Children and groupings

        Same age, mixed age, the youngest, the oldest

Suggested activities

Suggested equipment

Supplement 2

The NSACA Standards for Quality School-Age Care

The NSACA (National School-Age Care Alliance) Standards describe the practices that lead to stimulating, safe, and supportive programs for young people ages 5 to 14 in their out-of-school time.

These "Standards at a Glance" give you an overview of the standards which are organized into 36 "keys" to quality. The first 20 keys are things that you can see happening in a program. The other 16 "Administration" keys describe the policies and "behind the scenes" practices that are the foundation of a quality program.

Human Relationships

1. Staff relate to all children and youth in positive ways.
   a) Staff treat children with respect and listen to what they say.
   b) Staff make children feel welcome and comfortable.
   c) Staff respond to children with acceptance and appreciation.
   d) Staff are engaged with children.

2. Staff respond appropriately to the individual needs of children and youth.
   a) Staff know that each child has special interests and talents.
   b) Staff recognize the range of children's abilities.
   c) Staff can relate to a child's culture and home language.
   d) Staff respond to the range of children's feelings and temperaments.

3. Staff encourage children and youth to make choices and to become more responsible.
   a) Staff offer assistance in a way that supports a child's initiative.
   b) Staff assist children without taking control, and they encourage children to take leadership roles.
   c) Staff give children many chances to choose what they will do, how they will do it, and with whom.
   d) Staff help children make informed and responsible choices.

4. Staff interact with children and youth to help them learn.
   a) Staff ask questions that encourage children to think for themselves.
   b) Staff share skills and resources to help children gain information and solve problems.
   c) Staff vary the approaches they use to help children learn.

  d) Staff help children use language skills through frequent conversations.

5. Staff use positive techniques to guide the behavior of children and youth.
   a) Staff give attention to children when they cooperate, share, care for materials, or join in activities.
   b) Staff set appropriate limits for children.
   c) Staff use no harsh discipline methods.
   d) Staff encourage children to resolve their own conflicts. Staff step in only if needed to discuss the issues and work out a solution.

6. Children and youth generally interact with one another in positive ways.
   a) Children appear relaxed and involved with each other.
   b) Children show respect for each other.
   c) Children usually cooperate and work well together.
   d) When problems occur, children often try to discuss their differences and work out a solution.

7. Staff and families interact with each other in positive ways.
   a) Staff make families feel welcome and comfortable.
   b) Staff and families treat each other with respect.
   c) Staff share the languages and cultures of the families they serve, and the communities they live in.
   d) Staff and families work together to make arrivals and departures between home and child care go smoothly.

8. Staff work well together to meet the needs of children and youth.
   a) Staff communicate with each other while the program is in session to ensure that the program flows smoothly.
   b) Staff are cooperative with each other.
   c) Staff are respectful of each other.
   d) Staff provide role models of positive adult relationships.

Indoor Environment

9. The program's indoor space meets the needs of children and youth.
   a) There is enough room for all program activities.
   b) The space is arranged well for a range of activities: physical games and sports, creative arts, dramatic play, quiet games, enrichment offerings, eating, and socializing.
   c) The space is arranged so that various activities can go on at the same time without much disruption.

d) There is adequate and convenient storage space for equipment, materials, and personal possessions of children and staff.

10. The indoor space allows children and youth to take initiative and explore their interests.

   a) Children can get materials out and put them away by themselves with ease.

   b) Children can arrange materials and equipment to suit their activities.

   c) The indoor space reflects the work and interests of the children.

   d) Some areas have soft, comfortable furniture on which children can relax.

Outdoor Environment

11. The outdoor play area meets the needs of children and youth, and the equipment allows them to be independent and creative.

   a) Each child has a chance to play outdoors for at least 30 minutes out of every three-hour block of time at the program.

   b) Children can use a variety of outdoor equipment and games for both active and quiet play.

   c) Permanent playground equipment is suitable for the sizes and abilities of all children.

   d) The outdoor space is suitable for a wide variety of activities.

Activities

12. The daily schedule is flexible, and it offers enough security, independence, and stimulation to meet the needs of all children and youth.

   a) The routine provides stability without being rigid.

   b) Children meet their physical needs in a relaxed way.

   c) Individual children move smoothly from one activity to another, usually at their own pace.

   d) When it is necessary for children to move as a group, the transition is smooth.

13. Children and youth can choose from a wide variety of activities.

   a) There are regular opportunities for active, physical play.

   b) There are regular opportunities for creative arts and dramatic play.

   c) There are regular opportunities for quiet activities and socializing.

   d) Children have a chance to join enrichment activities that promote basic skills and higher-level thinking.

14. Activities reflect the mission of the program and promote the development of all the children and youth in the program.
    a) Activities are in line with the styles, abilities, and interests of the individuals in the program.
    b) Activities are well suited to the age range of children in the program.
    c) Activities reflect the languages and cultures of the families served.
    d) Activities reflect and support the program's mission.

15. There are sufficient materials to support program activities.
    a) Materials are complete and in good repair.
    b) There are enough materials for the number of children in the program.
    c) Materials are developmentally appropriate for the age ranges of the children in the program.
    d) Materials promote the program's mission.

Safety, Health, & Nutrition

16. The safety and security of the children and youth are protected.
    a) There are no observable safety hazards in the program space.
    b) Systems are in place to protect the children from harm, especially when they move from one place to another or use the rest rooms.
    c) Equipment for active play is safe.
    d) A system is in place to keep unauthorized people from taking children from the program.

17. The program provides an environment that protects and enhances the health of the children.
    a) The indoor and outdoor facilities are clean.
    b) There are no observable health hazards in the indoor or outdoor space.
    c) There are adequate supplies and facilities for handwashing.
    d) The heat, ventilation, noise level, and light space in the indoor space are comfortable.

18. The program staff try to protect and enhance the health of children and youth.
    a) Staff are responsive to the individual health of the children.
    b) Staff protect children from communicable disease by separating children who become ill during the program.
    c) Staff protect children from potential hazards such as the following: caustic or toxic art materials and cleaning agents, medications, and hot liquids; overexposure to heat or cold.
    d) Staff and children wash hands frequently, especially after using the toilet or before preparing food.

19. Children and youth are carefully supervised to maintain safety.
    a) Staff note when children arrive, when they leave, and with whom they leave.
    b) Staff know where the children are and what they are doing.
    c) Staff supervise children appropriately according to children's ages, abilities, and needs.
    d) Staff closely supervise activities that are potentially harmful.

20. The program serves foods and drinks that meet the needs of children and youth.
    a) The program serves healthy foods.
    b) Drinking water is readily available at all times.
    c) The amount and type of food offered is appropriate for the ages and sizes of children.
    d) Snacks and meals are timed appropriately for children.

Administration

21. Staff/child ratios and group sizes permit the staff to meet the needs of children and youth.
    a) Staff/child ratios vary according to the ages and abilities of children. The ratio is between 1:10 and 1:15 for groups of children age six and older. The ratio is between 1:8 and 1:12 for groups that include children under age six.
    b) Staff/child ratios and group sizes vary according to the type and complexity of the activity, but group sizes do not exceed 30.
    c) There is a plan to provide adequate staff coverage in case of emergencies.
    d) Substitute staff are used to maintain ratios when regular staff are absent.

22. Children and youth are supervised at all times.
    a) Children's arrivals are supervised.
    b) Children's departures are supervised.
    c) Staff have a system for knowing where the children are at all times.
    d) Staff plan for different levels of supervision according to the level of risk involved in an activity.

23. Staff support families' involvement in the program.
    a) There is a policy that allows family members to visit any time throughout the day.

    b) Staff offer orientation sessions for new families.

    c) Staff keep families informed about the program.

    d) Staff encourage families to give input and to get involved in program events.

24. Staff, families, and schools share important information to support the well-being of children and youth.

    a) Program policies require that staff and family members communicate about the child's well-being.

    b) Staff, families, and schools work together as a team to set goals for each child; they work with outside specialists when necessary.

    c) Staff and families share information about how to support children's development.

    d) Staff and families join together to communicate and work with the schools.

25. The program builds links to the community.

    a) Staff provide information about community resources to meet the needs of children and their families.

    b) The program develops a list of community resources. The staff draw from these resources to expand program offerings.

    c) The staff plan activities to help children get to know the larger community.

    d) The program offers community-service options, especially for older children.

26. The program's indoor space meets the needs of the staff.

    a) There is enough room in the indoor space for staff to plan various program activities.

    b) Staff have access to adequate and convenient storage.

    c) The indoor space meets or exceeds local health and safety codes.

    d) Written guidelines are in place regarding the use and maintenance of the program facility.

27. The outdoor space is large enough to meet the needs of children, youth, and staff.

    a) There is enough room in the outdoor space for all program activities.

    b) The outdoor space meets or exceeds local health and safety codes.

    c) Staff use outdoor areas to provide new outdoor play experiences.

    d) There is a procedure in place for regularly checking the safety and maintenance of the outdoor play space.

28. Staff, children, and youth work together to plan and implement suitable activities, which are consistent with the program's philosophy.
    a) Staff ask children to share their ideas for planning so that activities reflect children's interests.
    b) The program's daily activities are in line with its mission and philosophy.
    c) Staff keep on file their records of activity planning.
    d) Staff plan activities that will reflect the cultures of the families in the program and the broad diversity of human experience.

29. Program policies and procedures are in place to protect the safety of the children and youth.
    a) Staff and children know what to do in case of general emergency.
    b) The program has established procedures to prevent accidents and manage emergencies.
    c) The program has established policies to transport children safely; it complies with legal requirements for vehicles and drivers.
    d) A system is in place to prevent unauthorized people from taking children from the program.

30. Program policies exist to protect and enhance the health of all children and youth.
    a) There is current documentation showing that the program has met the state and/or local health and safety guidelines and/or regulations.
    b) There are written policies and procedures to ensure the health and safety of children.
    c) No smoking is allowed in the program.
    d) The staff are always prepared to respond to accidents and emergencies.

31. All staff are professionally qualified to work with children and youth.
    a) Staff meet the requirements for experience with school-age children in recreational settings.
    b) Staff have received the recommended type and amount of preparation. They meet the requirements that are specific to school-age child care and relevant to their particular jobs.
    c) Staff meet minimum age requirements.
    d) Enough qualified staff are in place to meet all levels of responsibility. Qualified staff are hired in all areas: to administer the program, to oversee its daily operations, and to supervise children.

32. Staff (paid, volunteer, and substitute) are given an orientation to the job before working with children and youth.

a) A written job description that outlines responsibilities to children, families, and the program is reviewed with each staff member.

b) Written personnel policies are reviewed with staff.

c) Written program policies and procedures, including emergency procedures and confidentiality policies, are reviewed with staff.

d) New staff are given a comprehensive orientation to the program philosophy, routines, and practices. They are personally introduced to the people with whom they will be working.

33. The training needs of the staff are assessed, and training is relevant to the responsibilities of each job. Assistant Group Leaders receive at least 15 hours of training annually. Group Leaders receive at least 18 hours of training annually. Senior Group Leaders receive at least 21 hours of training annually. Site Directors receive at least 24 hours of training annually. Program Administrators receive at least 30 hours of training annually.

a) Staff receive training in how to work with families and how to relate to children in ways that promote their development.

b) Program directors and administrators receive training in program management and staff supervision.

c) Staff receive training in how to set up program space and design activities to support program goals.

d) Staff receive training in how to promote the safety, health, and nutrition of children.

34. Staff receive appropriate support to make their work experience positive.

a) The program has a plan in place to offer the best possible wages and working conditions in an effort to reduce staff turnover.

b) Full-time staff receive benefits, including health insurance and paid leaves of absence. Staff are also given paid breaks and paid preparation time.

c) Staff are given ample time to discuss their own concerns regarding the program.

d) Staff receive continuous supervision and feedback. This includes written performance reviews on a timely basis.

35. The administration provides sound management of the program.

a) The financial management of the program supports the program's goals.

b) The administration oversees the recruitment and retention of program staff.

c) The director involves staff, board, families, and children in both long-term planning and daily decision-making.

d) Administration assists with ongoing evaluation. They aim for improvement in all areas of the program.

36. Program policies and procedures are responsive to the needs of children, youth, and families in the community.

   a) A written mission statement sets forth the program's philosophy and goals.

   b) The program makes itself affordable to all families by using all possible community resources and sources of subsidy.

   c) The program's hours of operation are based on families' needs.

   d) It is the program's policy to enroll children with special needs.

Note:

The NSACA Standards have been developed through a collaboration with the National Institute on Out-of-School Time and are based on their publication, *Assessing School-Age Child Care Quality.*

Reprinted with permission from the National School-Age Care Alliance, 1137 Washington Square, Boston, MA 02124.

The complete publication, *NSACA Standards of Quality School-Age Care*, also has concrete examples, guiding questions for staff discussion, a glossary, and an appendix.

Supplement 3

Suggested Equipment and Materials for School-Age Care

The following categories of materials can be considered for in-home, family, or center-based care. It is desirable to have a variety of materials from each of the following groups available and accessible to the children. Some materials may be rotated or used on special occasions; others should be available at all times. Most may be used both indoors or outdoors with the provision of portable storage arrangements.

This is a list of basic materials recommended for a well-balanced program. Certain activities may need additional supplies.

Program staff are responsible for the appropriate supervision of all suggested materials and activities mentioned throughout this book.

Vigorous Play

Because of their rapid growth, muscle development, and abundant energy, school-age children need opportunities for vigorous play.

CONSTRUCTION

large cartons, crates, boxes
large blocks
boards to extend structures
saw horses
large cable spools, drums, pipes
sheets of fabric, wood, or cardboard for "roofing"
plastic milk carriers
tires and inner tubes
sand and digging equipment
logs and tree limbs
wheels
old vehicles with hazardous parts removed (boats, cars, planes, motorcycles)

CLIMBING AND BALANCING

climbers
beams
boulders
trees
fallen trees
play sculptures
ropes
lumber
ladders
man-made hills and pits
see-saws

ACTIVE GAMES

balls (baseball, basketball, rugby, soccer, football, tennis, hockey)
racquets and bats, hockey sticks
nets
chalk for "sidewalk" games
balloons
beanbags
juggling balls
croquet set
bowling equipment
gliders
air pumps for balls

275

hoops
yo-yos
batons
jump ropes
high-jump pits
horseshoes
ring toss
tumbling mats
miniature golf equipment
obstacle course
ping pong
paddleball

MOVEMENT

wagons and carts
hula hoops
bicycles
roller skates
ice skates
scooters
trampoline
springboards
stilts, pogo sticks

cardboard slabs and boxes for hill sliding
swinging equipment

HOT WEATHER

hoses
water containers
sponges and paint brushes
sprinklers
approved pools

SNOW

shovels
mallets for ice breaking
sleds
skates
snow saucers, boxes, and plastic sheets for
    sliding

Daily Living

Homelike activities help to develop daily living skills and provide a familiar home-like atmosphere.

CARPENTRY AND REPAIR

tools (hammers, screwdrivers, planes, saws,
    vise, or clamps)
tool storage container
soft lumber
tapes, glue
sandpaper
cloth, string, wire, jar tops, dowels, knobs
paints and brushes
nails, screws
tape measure, rulers
stapler
workbench

GARDENING

tools (rake, hoe, shovel, mower, trowels)
seeds, plants, bulbs

soil, pebbles
containers (planters, jars, cartons)
garden catalogs
hose, sprinkling cans
lawn mower

COOKING

cookware (pots, pans, cooking sheets, muffin
    tins)
bowls, serving plates
measuring cups and spoons
pitchers
can and bottle openers
utensils (egg beater, mixing spoons, spatula,
    knives, rolling pin, eating utensils)
cookbooks and recipes
hot plate or stove
electric frying pan

aprons
pot holders
refrigerator
cleaning supplies
water supply
safe, clean work areas
fire extinguisher
timer
food ingredients

SEWING AND STITCHERY

frames
hoops and looms for stitching and weaving
sewing needles, threads, fabrics
sewing machines
crochet hooks, knitting needles, yarn

a variety of colors and textures of cloth
  (cotton, wool, flannel, felt)
pins and pin cushion
ropes for macramé
basket-weaving hemp
velcro
scissors
buttons, hooks, snaps
ribbons, rickrack
tape measures
fabric crayons, paints

Expressive Materials

The use of expressive materials related to art, music and movement, dramatic play, creative dramatics, and language encourages creative thinking, problem-solving, individual experimentation, and decision-making as well as a personal statement of feelings.

ART

General Use

papers, cardboards
display space
places for unfinished work
glues, paste
adhesive tapes
staples
paper punch
paper fasteners, paper clips, thumb tacks
pliers, metal snips
scissors
rubber bands
rulers
found objects and safe "junk"
tote bags, containers
paper bags

Drawing and Painting

paints (tempera, acrylic, oil, water color, finger paints)
body paints
chalks

chalkboards
charcoal, pastels
felt pens, calligraphy pens
pencils, colored pencils
crayons
brushes

Sculpture and Pottery

moist clays
oil-based clays
origami paper
papier maché
foil
dough art
sawdust
soft wood
soap cakes
soap stone
plaster of Paris
styrofoam
driftwood
cardboard tubing, boxes
wire, pipe cleaners, toothpicks, straws

wood scraps
wood tools
glues
metal scraps
plastic lids
newspaper
balloons
sand
wax
kiln
glazes

Collage, Weaving, Stitchery, Jewelry
papers, backings
needles, yarns, threads
frames
burlap
beads
gimp
fabric scraps
felt
cellophane
cotton
ribbon, strings, rickrack, buttons, sequins
tissue paper
plastic, leather, and other scraps
macramé rope
toothpicks
natural materials (pods, seeds, weeds and grasses, twigs, mosses, leaves, bark, feathers)

Printing
inks
stamps
wood blocks
gadgets
natural materials
cardboards
silkscreen
papers, fabrics

Batik and Tie-Dye
fabrics
dyes
paraffin
basins

Photography
still camera
video camera
film, video tape
developing materials

MUSIC AND MOVEMENT
Dance Props
fancy dress-ups
scarves, capes, tutus
dance shoes, clogs
streamers
hoops
pompoms
ribbons, ropes
balloons

Sound Instruments
bells
drums
castanets
tambourines
cymbals
clappers

Musical Instruments
harmonica
guitar
piano
autoharp
banjo
xylophones
recorders
kazoos

Improvised Instruments
gourds
sticks
cans
rocks
wood and spoons
washboard

Sources for Music
records and record player
tapes and tape recorders
synthesizers

ethnic

classical

jazz

contemporary and old music

folk and children's music

Composing

paper

pencils

notation paper

DRAMATIC PLAY AND CREATIVE DRAMATICS

Blocks and Accessories

block storage shelves or movable crates

unit blocks

large hollow blocks

crates or cardboard cartons with giant paper fasteners

boards

blankets, sheets, tarps, tents

slabs of cardboard

rug samples and fabrics for roofing, caves, etc.

human and animal figures

transportation vehicles

material for writing signs

Settings and Roles

pieces of fabric, lace

scarves

old curtains

jewelry

old costumes

mirrors

plastic flowers

paper dolls

men's and women's dress ups

Life Experiences

medical

stethoscope

doctor's coat

gauze

splints

watch

get-well cards

mechanical

old automobile parts

tools

old shirts

hats

flashlight

theatrical

old Halloween costumes

dance shoes

wigs

microphone

stage props

clowning materials

family life

dolls, animals, accessories

food containers

furniture

money

dishes

utensils, cookware

dress-ups

puppets

puppet-size props, stages

materials for scenery and costuming

Prop Boxes

circus

wedding

camping

space travel

fast food

veterinarian

disc jockey

florist

LANGUAGE DEVELOPMENT

books

pictures

posters

magazines

newspapers

encyclopedias

dictionary

paper and pencils for recording ideas; writing letters, stories, poetry; sign-making

envelopes

flannel boards, felt, or velcro cut-outs for composing picture stories

earphones

tape recorders

typewriters

telephones

duplicating and printing materials

Enrichment Activities

The school-age child is an explorer: asking questions, seeking answers, finding out how things work. The following items will help children explore the properties of their world.

GENERAL USE

hand lenses to see small details, microscopes

containers for materials such as basins, jars, cans, cartons, or trays

computers

materials for recording such as notebooks, pencils, tape recorders

materials for reference such as books and posters, magazines, tapes

tools such as trowels, beaters, sieves, measuring cups, scissors, mixing utensils, clippers, pitchers, pumps

NATURAL SCIENCE

aquarium

terrarium

cages and foods for visiting pets, insects, frogs, turtles

bird feeders, bird bath, bird seed, bird charts

binoculars

incubators for hatching eggs

insects nets and boxes

bat house

collection containers for feather, shells, rocks, etc.

plastic bags for temporary viewing of insects, sand, earth, water

ant village

worm garden

plants, seeds, bulbs, ferns, mosses, soil

PHYSICAL SCIENCE

compasses

pendulums

batteries

prisms

magnets and related objects

mirrors

balloons

thermometers

tuning forks

water, basins, basters

hose pieces

bubble pipes

soaps

straws

oil

colorings

powders

rubber bands

gelatins

salt

weather vane

kites

wind funnels

levers, pulleys, ropes

batteries, wires, light bulbs

freezer to make ice

siphons

medicine droppers

TINKERING AND OPENING

hammers and mallets

tweezers

tools for exploring the insides of rocks, seeds, nuts, etc.

tools for taking apart old clocks, radios, machinery and appliances

MEASURING

tapes, rulers, yardsticks

measuring cups, spoons

scales

thermometers

pint, quart, gallon containers

Quiet Games and Manipulative Skills

Many materials promote relaxation, coordination, and social relationships. They may be used by individual children or by small groups.

board games, such as checkers, bingo, chess, lottos

playing cards

paper dolls

materials for pencil and paper, and letter and word games

globes

dollhouses

blackboard games

materials for making homemade games

materials for construction, e.g., table blocks, interlocking cubes, gears

materials for re-construction, e.g., puzzles

model kits

computers and computer games

calculators

jacks, marbles

geoboards

Be sure that games and puzzles are complete and not missing pieces so that goals can be attained. Keep game and puzzle pieces together in plastic bags with zippered seals or bins with lids.

General Furnishings for a Home-Like Atmosphere

Since children are spending an increasing amount of time away from home, the environment should evoke a feeling of welcome, a comfortable atmosphere, and as home-like a setting as possible.

individual storage space for school items such as books, lunch box, papers, etc.

lockers or cubicles for outdoor clothes

storage areas for unfinished projects

display space for "news" items, creations, and art

low open shelves for children's materials and storage containers for supplies

large pillows, bean chairs, mats

appropriately-sized tables and chairs

couches or easy chairs

large cardboard "privacy" cartons, boxes, screening

mirrors (full-length and hand)

shelves for storage of supplies not currently in use

rugs

cleaning supplies: paper towels, soaps, brooms, cleaning cloths, dustpan, bucket, mop, basins, sponges

cooking materials: pots, pans, utensils, slow cooker, oven, electric frying pan, microwave

table cloths

floral arrangements

pictures, posters, photographs

Supplement 4
Play And Other Smart Activities

MORE THAN 1000 EXPERIENCES FOR SCHOOL-AGE CHILDREN

The following activities are suggested as appropriate for school-agers. Some will appeal to younger, some to older, some to everyone. Choice depends on the interests, ages, and developmental levels of the children as well as the available resources. Some activities are for daily choice, others are geared to special times. Staff, families, and the children will add ideas. This text does not detail information on how to proceed with each experience or how to set up, clean up, or gather materials. There are many publications and persons readily available if you need help. Keep the list handy when you need ideas for new staff, children's planning groups, or rainy days.

A

Acrobatics
Advisory council for children and
    youth to meet with staff on a reg-
    ular basis to discuss the program,
    needed supplies, snacks, trips,
    visitors, fund raising, etc
Adopting a city block, family, gar-
    den, grandparent, pet, tree, street,
    stream
Aerobic exercise
Animal care at farms, shelters, zoos
Ant farming
Aquarium
Archery
Archaeological digs
Art and craft activities:
    architectural design
    batik
    ceramics
    chalk
    charcoal
    clay molding
    collage
    colored pencil art
    computer art
    copper-enameling
    crayon art
    cultural art forms

decoupage
doodle-art
dough art
drawing
flower arranging
leatherwork
macramé
marbleized paper
marker art
mirror painting
mobiles
murals
oil painting
paper folding
paper-making
papier maché
photomontage
plasticine
portrait caricatures
print-making
rubbings
screen painting
self-portraits
silk-screening
stained glass art
string art
tie-dyeing
tile painting
tile mosaics
tissue paper sculpture

window painting
Art shows in home or center, side-
    walk shows, at the mall, in muse-
    ums, community buildings
Astronomy
Astrology
Autograph books
Auto racing layouts
Auto Repair

B

Baby care
Backpacking
Backwards day
Backyard camping
Backyard theater
Ball games
Balloon basketball, sculpture, water
    balloons
Basket weaving
Baton twirling
Beadcraft
Berry picking
Bicycle repair, maintenance, riding,
    safety, trips, ramps for jumping
Billiards
Bird feeding
Bird feeder construction
Bird house and bird nest construction
Bird watching and recording
Bird sound recording
Birthday celebrations for children,
    family members, staff, famous
    persons, etc.
Blacksmithing
Block building
Board games
Boating: row boats, paddle boats,
    canoes, sailboats, kayaks, home-
    made boats
Body fitness
Body painting
Book reading, writing, binding,
    browsing, library selections
Boomerangs
Box car construction, racing
Braiding
Bread making
Bubble-making, blowing
Buddy systems
Bulletin board designing

Building with bricks, blocks, boxes,
    logs, styrofoam, rocks, piping,
    scrap wood, cards
Bumper sticker designing
Bowling
Butterfly classification, observation

C

C.B. radio
Cake decorating
Calculator games
Calligraphy
Callisthenics
Camping
Campfire singing
Candlemaking
Car washing
Car painting (washable paint)
Card games
Card making: postcards, occasions,
    holidays, playing cards
Cardboard box carpentry
Carpentry with wood: sculpture, fur-
    niture, lean-tos, playhouses
Cartooning
Cat's cradle string games
Caving
Celebrations for the sun, spring,
    snow, rain, "everybody's birthday
    day," "everybody is wonderful
    day," "everybody is talented
    day," holidays, children's
    achievements, new baby, new
    President, personal hero, best
    news in the paper, the cook's best
    lunch, etc.
Charades
Chemical gardens
Chemistry
Cheerleading
Child care experiences
Child care training
Cloud watching
Clowning
Club house construction
Coaching
Code flagging
Collections:
    arrowheads
    autographs
    bells

bird nests
bottle caps
buttons with messages
coins
comics
decals
dolls
ethnic objects
fingerprints
flags
hourglasses
insects
jokes
keychains
kites
knots
license plates
marbles
magic tricks
maps
match box cars
miniatures
model cars, trains, planes, ships
music boxes
patches
playing cards
puppets
postcards
recordings
rocks
semi-precious stones
shells
stamps
stickers
trading cards
Comic book writing
Communication methods: sign language, braille, Morse code, smoke signaling, signing, hobo signing
Community interviews
Community projects: exhibits, ethnic celebrations, street fairs, sports events
Community service: Big Brothers/Sisters, Boys/Girls Club, Campfire, Y's, community newspapers, gardening, 4-H, friendship clubs, distributing notices, Scouting, errands for the homebound or homeless

Community trips
Community visitors representing a variety of careers, talents, hobbies, ages, cultures
Compost creation
Computers
Computer games
Concert-giving
Concert-going
Cooking: snacks, meals, treats, desserts,
Conflict resolution games
Crabbing
Crocheting
Croquet
Creating equipment: bowling alley, club houses, doll houses and furniture, playground equipment, go-carts, stage, tables and benches, privacy nooks, shelving, tree houses
Cross-generation partnerships with an adult friend, the cook, bus driver, maintenance person, school principal, store keeper, artist, neighbor
Current events discussion

D

Dancing, with and without music: disco, country, modern, ethnic, folk, breakdance, jazz, round, square, tap, social, original choreographies
Darts
Daydreaming
Debating
Decorating committees for parties and special occasions
Designer activities: sports cars, costumes, T-shirts, skateboards, hairstyles, sneakers, etc.
Diary keeping
Do "nothing" together
Doll making
Doll play
Door decorations
Drama: role play with and without scripts, play writing, costuming, make-up, scenery, props, music and song composition, directing,

movement choreography, improvisation

Dramatic Play

Driftwood creatures: collage, mobiles, sculpture, painting

Duck walk in the rain

E

Elections

Electric trains

Electricity experiments

Electronic games

Encyclopedia browsing

Environmental projects: erosion control, insect study and observations, planting, pollution prevention, preservation of animal and bird habitats, recycling

Evenings-out to dinner, theater, shopping malls, fairs

F

Fabric design with batik, crayon, paint, stitchery, tie-dye

Face painting

Fairs: animal, art, hobby, music, dance, food

Family games, parties, picnics, suppers

Fashion design, shows

Farm work

Film and slide shows

Film-making

Financial management: bank accounts, budgeting, investing

Fingerprinting

First-aid, CPR training

Fish dissection

Fish printing

Fishing

Flannel board fantasies

Flooding area to freeze for skating, sliding

Flower arrangement

Flower drying

Flower picking

Flower pressing

Fly-tying

Food preparation

Food tasting parties

Foreign culture and ethnic experiences: celebrations, cookery, discussions, dress, games, languages, literature, plays, movies, radio broadcasts, trips

Forest making

Fortune-telling

Fortune-cookie making

Free play

Frisbee® games

Fruit picking

Fundraising for home, center, community, special persons

Furniture repair, refinishing, designing

G

Games: share ideas, make up new games, make up new rules for old games, try international games

Gardening: finding a spot; growing vegetables, flowers, herbs, trees, mosses, ferns, indoor and outdoor plants; building a greenhouse; lawn care

Genealogy: coats of arms, family trees, treasures, interviews, pictures, meaning of family names, family stories

Gift-making for family, friends, hospital or nursing home patients, homeless shelters, pediatric waiting rooms

Glass melting

Glider and flying toy construction

Golf

Gymnastics

H

Hatching chicken eggs

Ham radio

Hayride

Hiking

Hill-rolling

History: personal, school, neighborhood, particular time period

Holiday celebrations: dances, decorations, costumes, customs, foods, songs

Homework

Hopscotch
Horseback riding
Horseshoe pitching
Housekeeping chores
Hula hoops
Hunts

I

Ice cream making
Ice Play: cracking, painting, snow
   sculpture, ice sculpture, ice cube
   block building, skating, sliding
Inner tube play
Insect observations
Interviewing community residents
   (old and new), shopkeepers, service persons, school   personnel,
   friends, families, young children,
   seniors
Interest Clubs:
   art
   astronomy
   book
   Braille
   card game
   carpentry
   collections
   cooking
   computer
   dance
   discussion
   drama
   ecology
   foreign culture
   game
   garden
   gymnastics
   hiking
   invention
   jokes & riddles
   language
   magic
   math
   media production
   model hobby kits
   mystery
   pet
   photography
   plays
   poetry
   pottery

   prehistoric
   puppets & marionettes
   science
   science fiction
   sewing
   sign language
   sports
   stamp design
   story telling
   travel
   welcome wagon
   writing

J

Jacks
Jewelry making
Job applications: completing forms,
   writing resumés, interviews
Jobs in the community or school-age
   setting: clerical work, answering
   phone, dish washing, housekeeping, cooking, gardening, painting,
   repair work, yard work,
   caring for younger children or
   children who need special care,
   caring for pets, errands for community residents, distributing
   newspapers
Jogging
Joke composition, practical jokes
Journalism: newsletter or newspaper
   for center or community news,
   cover events, conduct interviews, print, distribute, submit
   news items to community media
Judo
Juggling
Jump rope

K

Kaleidoscope construction
Kazoo band
Karate
Kite construction, flying
Knot tying

L

Lawn bowling
Lawn care
Leather work

Leadership training skills

Library use for borrowing, reading, research

Life Skills: reaching own goals, planning for emergencies, handling money, housekeeping, child care, interpersonal relations and communication, self-grooming, health care, abstinence from chemical use and dependencies, self-protection

Lipsynching

Litter clean up

M

Machinery repair, tinkering

Magazine subscriptions

Magic tricks

Map activities: making maps of school, neighborhood, city, routes to favorite places, route of next vacation, of imaginary voyage, of an ideal community; reading maps for finding parks, rivers, highways

Marbles: collect, devise games, make raceways

Marionettes

Marine biological studies

Marsh exploration

Martial arts

Mask making

Mediation skills

Meditation

Mental games

Metal detection

Microscopic work

Mime

Mineralogy

Miniature golf course construction

Mobile making

Model building kits

Model railroad construction

Model rocketry

Money making projects

Moon watching

Mountain climbing

Mudpie cookery, mud sculpture

Mural making

Music experiences:
    music appreciation

band

chamber music

choir

chorus

composition

instrument making

instrument playing (accordion, auto harp, drum, keyboards, percussion, guitar, harmonica, organ, piano, wind instruments, synthesizers)

dance

singing

note reading

rapping

taping

Mystery theater

Mythology

N

Nature trail creation

Neighborhood block party

Neighborhood exploration

Neighborhood improvement plans

O

Obstacle course

Orienteering

Origami paper folding

Outdoor theater

Overnights

P

Pantomime

Paper and pencil games: crosswords, hang-man, scribble, tic-tac-toe, connect the dots

Paper airplanes

Paper dolls

Paper-making

Parades

Parachute play

Parking lot graffiti

Pen pals

Personal improvement: hair styling, hygiene, fitness, manicuring, nutrition, posture, talent and skill development

Pet experiences: books, films, pet shows, grooming, walking, sit-

ting, caring for home or
center pets, studying breeds,
training, consulting with veterinarian
"Pet rock" creations, show
Photography: animation, developing,
still photos, moving pictures,
video, photo art, portraiture
Picnics
Plant care
Plant sitting
Play yard pets: placing bait under
bricks and rocks to see who
comes to live there
Play yard pond: sinking tubs in the
ground to see who comes to live
in the water
Poetry: reading to self, friends,
younger children, hospital
patients, other centers, writing
individual and group composi-
tions, writing to music or in
response to an experience or feelings
Pond and stream exploration
Poster making
Prevention programs: crime, chemical dependency, depression, eating disorders, pregnancy, truancy
Pretzel making
Printing: with clay shapes, gadgets,
natural objects, stamps: etching,
lithograph, silk screen, woodcut,
printing press
Public transportation rides: boat,
bus, metro, sightseeing vehicles,
subways, taxis, trolley
Puddle play: create them, freeze
them, freeze into shapes
Punching bags
Puppetry: constructing puppets, creating stage and scenery, writing
and improvising scripts, giving
shows, using body parts for puppets (painting fingers, feet,
palms, knees)
Puzzles: activity books; creating
original puzzles from paper, cardboard, wood; jigsaw and
crossword puzzles; trick puzzles

Q

Quilt making
Quoits

R

Radio broadcasting using music,
sound effects, tape recordings,
voices
Rap sessions: talking with each other,
staff or visitors about selves,
feelings, or the child care experi-
ence; making plans, sharing
experiences, ideas or wishes;
solving problems, discussing
community happenings and cur-
rent events; sharing funny
stories
Reading and book browsing
Reading to others
Remote control toys
Reproducing machines
Research
Riddle composition
Rock aquarium
Rock climbing
Rock hunting
Rock painting
Rock polishing
Rocketry
Role-play
Room decor
Rope climbing
Rope games
Rope-making
Rope-spinning
Roughhousing
Rug-making

S

Salt gardens
Sand environments: modeling in tray
or basins with damp sand incor-
porating imaginative accessories
(miniature figures, lumber scraps,
fabric pieces, twigs, mirrors,
transportation toys)
Sand Play: at least 8 inches deep for
digging and use of related props
such as water, water pumps,

scoops, trowels or shovels,
   shaped containers, etc.
Sand painting
Scarecrow making
School projects
Scrapbook making
Sculpture:
  clays
  cardboard boxes
  driftwood
  foil
  found objects
  ice
  ice cubes
  metals
  natural materials
  papers
  papier maché
  plaster of Paris
  rocks
  sand
  snow
  soap
  soapstone
  string
  stuffed sculpture
  wire
  wood scraps
  yarn and doweling
Self-affirmation games
Self-defense
Set-designs
Sewing: machine and hand sewing,
   embroidery, needlepoint, mend-
   ing, art objects as well
   as functional items
Shadows: puppetry, tracing, dramatics
Shell art: painting, sculpture, jewelry, cookware
Shopping
Sidewalk art: chalk, tempera paint,
   water, charcoal
Sidewalk café
Sidewalk fund raisers
Sidewalk games
Sign language
Sing-a-longs
Sledding with sleds, boxes, card-
   board slabs, plastic bags
Slingshot making

Snowball targeting
Snow hikes
Snow play
Soda pop making
Solar cooking
Solar greenhouse construction
Space science projects
Spool knitting
Sports:
  archery
  arm wrestling
  badminton
  baseball
  basketball
  billiards
  bobsledding
  boccie
  bowling
  cooperative games
  cricket
  cross country
  cross country skiing
  curling
  dodge ball
  downhill skiing
  field hockey
  golf
  handball
  hockey
  horseshoes
  ice hockey
  ice skating
  jai alai
  kickball
  lacrosse
  paddleball
  ping-pong
  relay races
  roller blading
  rugby
  shuffleboard
  skateboarding
  soccer
  speedball
  squash
  step ball
  street hockey
  tennis
  track and field
  volleyball
  weight-lifting

whiffle ball
wrestling
Special days: foreign country day, local celebrity day, backward day, TV star day, visiting pet day, grandparent or parent day, sisters and brothers day, "Hurray for ourselves" day, "Hurray for our staff" day
Spring cleaning
Sprouting seeds
Spruce tree chewing gum
Squirtgun painting
Stage make-up
Star-gazing
Stilt walking
Stitchery: needlepoint, embroidery, crewel, appliqué, trepunto
Stories: telling by adult or children (try music or painting or an incident to imagine a story), writing (try surprise endings, personal experiences, holiday themes, mood stories)
Stuffed animal zoo
Stunts
Sundial making
Sweep netting for insects and observe in plastic bag with hand lens
Swinging: on swings, from ropes, on tires

T

Table top theaters
Table games
Taffy pulls
Tai-chi
Talent shows
Tape recording
Tee shirt design
Telephone book: make your own
Television: use for discussion, prediction, study of characters, commercial techniques, photographic techniques, current events, historical information and animation
Tent construction
Terrarium, bottle gardens
Tutoring others

Theme ideas: be a cartoon character, fashion model, politician, singing star, super hero, TV personality, etc., or:
carnivals
cultures
environmental disaster
hobbies
holidays
international costumes
interesting toys
jungle environment
magic
prehistoric man
space
sports arena
seashore
wilderness
world's fair
Time capsule creation
Tinkering
Tire construction for climbers, outdoor equipment, privacy areas, for water play containers
Toy lending library
Trail marking for all points of interest in neighborhood or along field or wooded trails
Trampolines
Treasure hunts
Tree houses
Triathalons
Tricks and magic
Trips:
airports
airplane ride
animal breeders
animal shelters
appliance repair shops
aquariums
arboretum
art stores
artist studios (painters, potters, photographers, sculptors, writers)
Audubon society
automobile manufacturer
bakeries
balloon ride
beaches
beauty shops

baseball games
barber school
bird sanctuary
boat rides
boat yards
bottling company
bowling alley
botanical gardens
bus ride
camping
candy factory
candle maker
cereal factory
circus
city hall
city statue hunt
cleaning establishments
clothing manufacturer
college campus
concerts
construction sites
court house
dairies
dance performance
dental office
doctor office
duck ponds
ecology trips
ethnic stores: clothing, groceries,
    gifts
factories
farms: animal, dairy, berry, and
    hatcheries
farmers market
fishery
fishing
football games
forests
government offices
graveyards
greenhouses
hardware stores
hayrides
health clubs
health departments
high schools
high school plays
historical sites
homeless shelters
horseback riding
hospitals

hotels
houses of worship
humane society or SPCA
islands
libraries
limousine ride
mayor's office
movies, movie projection rooms
mountains
museums
music stores
musical instrument repair shop
nursery schools
nursing homes
ocean
orchards
parent's workplace
parks
pet stores
picnics
planetarium
police station
playgrounds
printers
publishers: books, newsletters,
    newspapers, music
puppet shows
radio stations
recording studio
recreation centers
restaurant, restaurant kitchen
rivers
schools: art, dancing, cosmetolgy,
    modeling, music, technology
ships
shoe repair shop
shopping malls
skating rinks
skyscrapers & monuments
sports events
stock exchange
streams
subway rides
swamps
swimming pools
taxi rides
telephone company
television studio
theaters, backstage
theater productions
toy manufacturers

toy stores
train ride
trucking company
veterinarian
watch repair shop
wholesale market
wildlife preserves
zoos
Trust games
Twinning with another program, in
 the community, in another city, or
 in another country
Typing

U

Unicycling

V

Values clarification
Velcro-art
Velcro darts
Ventriloquism
Videotaping
Visits from friends, teachers, guid-
 ance counselors, grandparents
Volcano simulation (vinegar and soda
 in bottle)
Volunteer experiences
Voting experiences

W

Walking: theme walks, errands,
 walking with pedometers, for
 fun, to explore
Washboard band
Water Activities: with hose, sprinklers, pools, water sliding, water
 combined with sand,   earth, toys
 and accessories, washing equipment, dress ups, doll clothes
Water Sports:
 aquaplaning
 body surfing
 canoeing
 diving
 kayaking
 motorboating
 rafting
 raft building
 rowing

sailing
skin diving
snorkeling
surfing
swimming
wading
water polo
water skiing
wind surfing
Weather predicting
Weathervane making
Weaving: strings, wools, feathers,
 reeds, shells, seaweed, fabrics,
 wires and woods
Whale-watching
Wild food collecting, preparing, eating
Wood burning art
Wood carving
Wool spinning
Word games
Worm farming
Wreath making

Y

Yard sale
Yoga
Yo-yos

Z

Zany zoo creations from balloons,
 clays, cardboard boxes, fabric,
 gourds, lumber, papers,
 papier maché, pipe cleaners,
 straws, stuffed animals, wires

Index

academic activities, 26

academic school day, 18, 59

accountable child care, 24

accreditation,   xiii, xiv, 94

activities, 195-199

    1000 experiences, 282-292

    action, 44

    adapting (special needs), 68

    adult-directed, 226

    age-appropriate, 24, 27

    art materials, 277-278

    chart, 198-199

    choice of, 27

    dramatic play materials, 279

    enrichment equipment, 280

    intellectual development, 62

    interest and curiosity, 60

    language development materials, 279-280

    long-range projects, 226

    music and movement materials, 278-279

    planning, 145-148

    quality standards, 268-269

    quiet games materials, 281

    self-development, 57

    self-directed, 226, 230

    self-selection, 94, 95

    sick children, 73

    social, 51

    structured experiences, 168-175

administration quality standards, 270-274

adolescents. See development of, older children; older children

adult-child ratios, 23, 25, 27, 63, 68-69, 73, 95, 119, 185

adult-directed, 194

adventure playgrounds, 29

after-school programs. See school-age care; out-of-school programs

after-school schedule, 224-225

age-appropriate. See activities; equipment; materials; programming

alcohol. See drugs, alcohol, tobacco and

alone. See latchkey; self-care

alone, time, 47, 50, 60, 61, 224

altruism, sense of, 57

American Academy of Pediatrics, 73

Americans with Disabilities Act (ADA), 63

AmeriCorps, xiii

arts, the, 170

Assessing School-Age Child Care Quality (ASQ), 94

assistants,

    adolescents, 127

    college students, 126

    to group leader, 126

    older adults, 127

    supplementary staff, 129

    volunteers, 128

Association for the Care of Children's Health, 72

Attention Deficit Disorder (ADD), 64-65

Attention Deficit Hyperactivity Disorder (ADHD), 64-65

Australia, xiii

babysitting, 18

before school, 18

before-school schedule, 222-223

behavior (of children), 139-176

    abusing or neglectful family, 10

    adolescent parents, 11

    aggressive, 84

    difficult child, 64-65

    families with multiple problems, 10

    feelings, 140-141, 169

    guiding, 143-176

    helping relationship, the, 154-155

    incapacitated family, 11

    parents in school or training, 10

    preventing problems, 145-152

    problems, special needs, 63-65

    psychosomatic illness, 85

    single-parent working family, 9-10

    submissive, 84

    two-parent working family, 9

    why behave as they do, 141-145